here.

Published in the United States
by the Pennsylvania Academy of the Fine Arts
on the occasion of the exhibition

here.

October 22 – December 31, 2011.

Project Director & Curator: Julien Robson
Guest Curators:
Christopher Cook
Mark Harris
Rebecca Ruth Hart
Claire Schneider
Teka Selman

PENNSYLVANIA ACADEMY
OF THE FINE ARTS

PENNSYLVANIA ACADEMY OF THE FINE ARTS
128 North Broad Street
Philadelphia, PA 19102
www.pafa.org

Publication Editor: Julien Robson
Publication Coordinator: Catherine Sirizzotti
Design and Production: Julianne Domm
Printed in the USA by Capital Offset Company

ISBN: 978-0-943836-35-5

WILLIAM PENN
FOUNDATION

Elizabeth Firestone Graham Foundation

PAFA's special exhibitions in 2011-12 are supported by generous contributions from Max N. Berry, Esq, Donald R. Caldwell, and Jonathan L. Cohen.

here.

Essays by
Erika Doss
Christopher Cook
Mark Harris
Rebecca Ruth Hart
Julien Robson
Claire Schneider
Teka Selman

PENNSYLVANIA ACADEMY OF THE FINE ARTS 2011

BUNK NEWS ARTS COLLECTIVE

SUE CHENOWETH

LIZ COHEN

LEWIS COLBURN

PAUL COORS

GUY MICHAEL DAVIS AND KATIE PARKER

ELSEWHERE

TERENCE HAMMONDS

HARRISON HAYNES

SCOTT HOCKING

CHIDO JOHNSON

MICHAEL KRUEGER

JENNIFER LEVONIAN

MEGAWORDS

ERIKA NELSON

ABIGAIL ANNE NEWBOLD

TIM PORTLOCK

POSTCOMMODITY

AARON ROTHMAN

GREGORY SALE

AARON STORCK

STACY LYNN WADDELL

GLENDA WHARTON

WHOOP DEE DOO

contents

6 **director's foreword**
Harry Philbrick

10 Introducing ***here.***
Julien Robson

17 Cultural Globalization and Critical Regionalism in Contemporary American Art
Erika Doss

curator essays

28 Trespassers: A Conversation with Christopher Cook and Hesse McGraw
Christopher Cook

40 A Local Culture: tradition and risk in Cincinnati
Mark Harris

54 ... we hope for better things
Rebecca Ruth Hart

68 Being Here
Julien Robson

80 Greater America
Claire Schneider

96 Carolina At Close Range
Teka Selman

106 **artist pages**

154 **checklist of the exhibition**

157 **contributor biographies**

director's foreword

As the first school and museum of fine arts in the United States, PAFA has, for over 200 years, been continuously engaged in defining the nature of American art both through the training of young artists and the presentation of exhibitions that interpret and contextualize American art. As well as charting this history through the creation of one of the nation's finest collections of paintings, sculptures, and works on paper, PAFA has actively contributed to defining our visual arts heritage through the continued presentation of Annuals, major retrospectives, and landmark thematic exhibitions. Continuing this tradition and refreshing PAFA's commitment to exploring the concept of the American in art, ***here.*** is a project that celebrates the work of twenty-four emerging artists from six different areas of the country.

Exploring the role "place" plays in an artist's work, ***here.*** prompts a discussion about the ways that local and regional insights engage with the broader art discourse. Turning its gaze away from the dominant centers of American art, such as New York, Los Angeles, and Chicago, ***here.*** focuses instead on six "peripheral" regions. Six curators who work and live in these regions have each selected four artists to take part in the project. ***here.*** can be seen as a platform that makes art from the periphery visible to the wider art world. While it is an exhibition that champions the participating artists, ***here.*** raises a vital discussion about the ways in which an artist's experience of place informs his/her work and how an acknowledgement of the importance of "the local" aerates and enriches the global discussion of art.

It is appropriate that ***here.*** has been developed and presented in Philadelphia, a place where the visual arts have a continuous and thriving history since the founding of the nation. While we live in the long shadow cast by New York, Philadelphia is a city with a burgeoning contemporary art scene that is uniquely its own, one that is nurtured by a host of nationally recognized art schools, major museums, commercial galleries, and highly supportive funding agencies. As a part of this ecosystem, PAFA is committed to developing exhibitions that lead important artistic debates and contextualize the regional within a nationally significant framework.

here. is an ambitious project, and there are countless people we wish to thank for their participation, support, and assistance. The artists, first and foremost, deserve our deepest appreciation for their participation and, in many cases, for creating new works in response to the project. Their individual contributions to the catalogue have provided important insights about how the *here* they occupy saturates their work. The curators, who each respectively chose four artists, are due thanks for the time they spent visiting studios and considering the context of their own contributions. Writing about the artists, they have provided keen insights not only into the nature of each artist's practice but also into their own sense of being here where they are. We are also grateful to Erika Doss for contributing her insightful overview of the exhibition that introduces its subject and opens doors to fresh discussions about Regionalism and the importance of the local to artistic practice in a global context.

Julien Robson, Curator of Contemporary Art, conceived of ***here.*** before my arrival at PAFA. It has been my great pleasure to get to know Julien as a colleague; I appreciate his distinct view of the contemporary art scene, a view that informs and animates this exhibition. He has ably directed the development of the exhibition over the past two years, seeing all aspects of this complex project through to fruition. Assisting Mr. Robson, Curatorial Intern Catherine Sirizzotti has provided essential support to museum staff, the guest curators, and the artists.

For the staff of PAFA, who are listed on page 159, this project has created unusual opportunities and responsibilities. In particular, the thoughtful planning of Associate Museum Registrar Robert Harman and special attention of Chief Conservator Aella Diamantopoulos made sure that works were carefully transported from across the country and assembled at PAFA without incident. We are grateful to Chief Preparator Brian Murray for his logistical advice and for helping guide the installation. Murray and Associate Preparator Mark Knobelsdorf—and their team, Michael Gibbons, Jason Kourkounis, and Jeremiah Misfeldt—deserve credit for their keen attention to the needs of the artists and for installing the exhibition beautifully. Special thanks also go to Monica Zimmerman, Assistant Director of Museum Education, for the public programs that accompany ***here.***, and to Executive Vice President of Marketing and Communication Marsha Braverman and Public Relations and Advertising Manager Heike Rass for their sterling work in promoting the project.

The encouragement of the School at PAFA has also been important to the realization of this project, and we are glad to have this opportunity to thank the staff and faculty and, in particular, Executive Vice President of Academic Affairs and Dean of the School of Fine Arts Jeffrey Carr and Dean of Student Affairs Anne Stassen. The exhibition has offered a unique opportunity for students to gain experience working with artists during installation, and gratitude is due to Student Services Coordinator Colette Seidel for organizing these assistantships. Many patrons have equally contributed goodwill to this project, and we offer our sincerest thanks to all of them for making it possible to house the artists and curators involved in the project during their visits to Philadelphia.

We offer a special thanks to those organizations and individuals without whose financial support the project would not have been possible. From the outset, the William Penn Foundation has given full and generous support to this project and, along with the encouragement of Director, Arts & Culture Olive Mosier, has helped us realize a significant exhibition and catalogue. In addition, the Elizabeth Firestone Graham Foundation has supported this publication. We at PAFA are also grateful to the generous patrons who are supporting our program of special exhibitions in 2011 – 12: Max N. Berry, Esq, Donald R. Caldwell, and Jonathan L. Cohen.

Finally, for their careful attention to the many details of this publication and their responsiveness, we appreciate the design and production contributions of Julianne Domm and Chuck Gershwin.

Harry Philbrick
Edna S. Tuttleman Director of the Museum

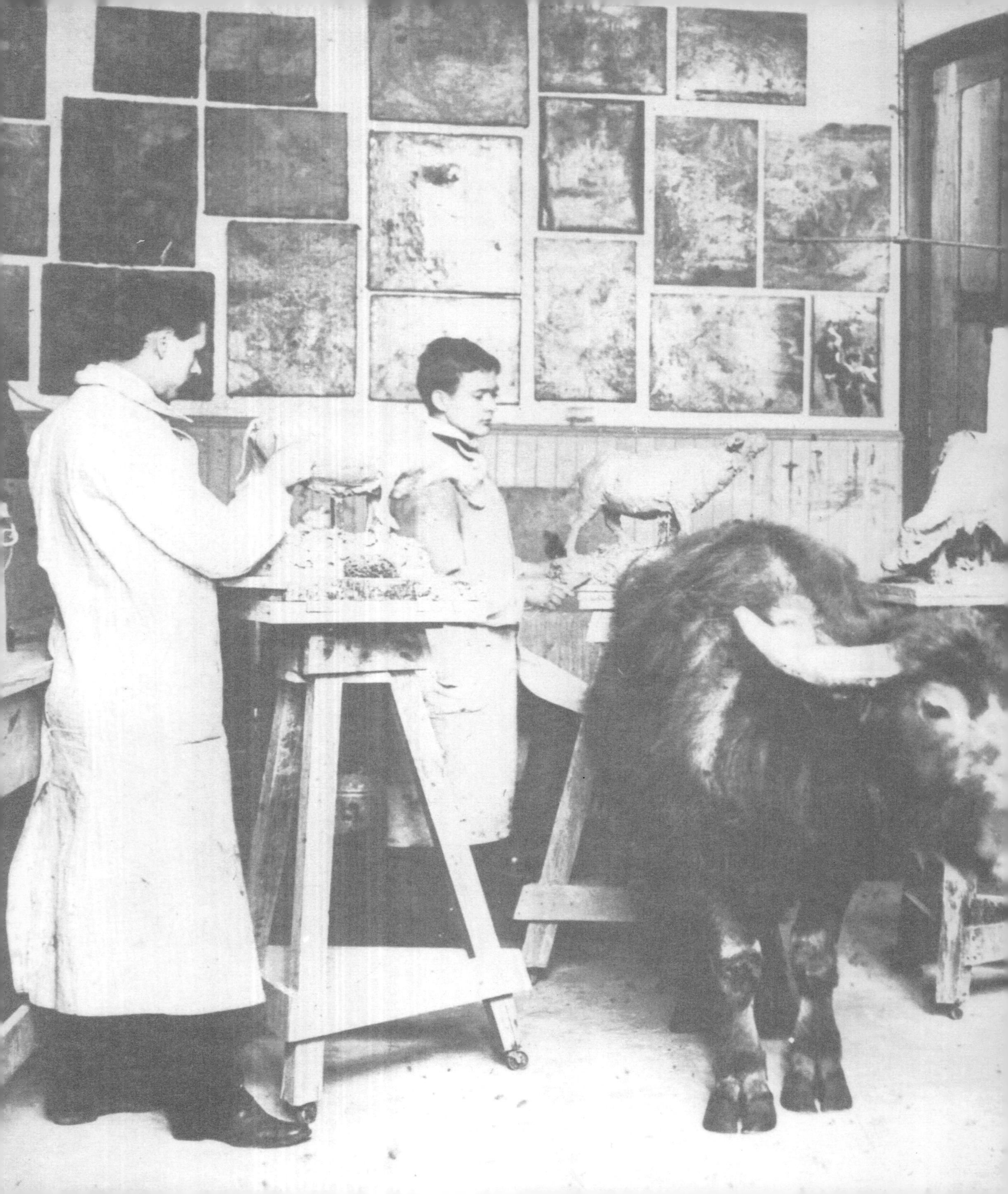

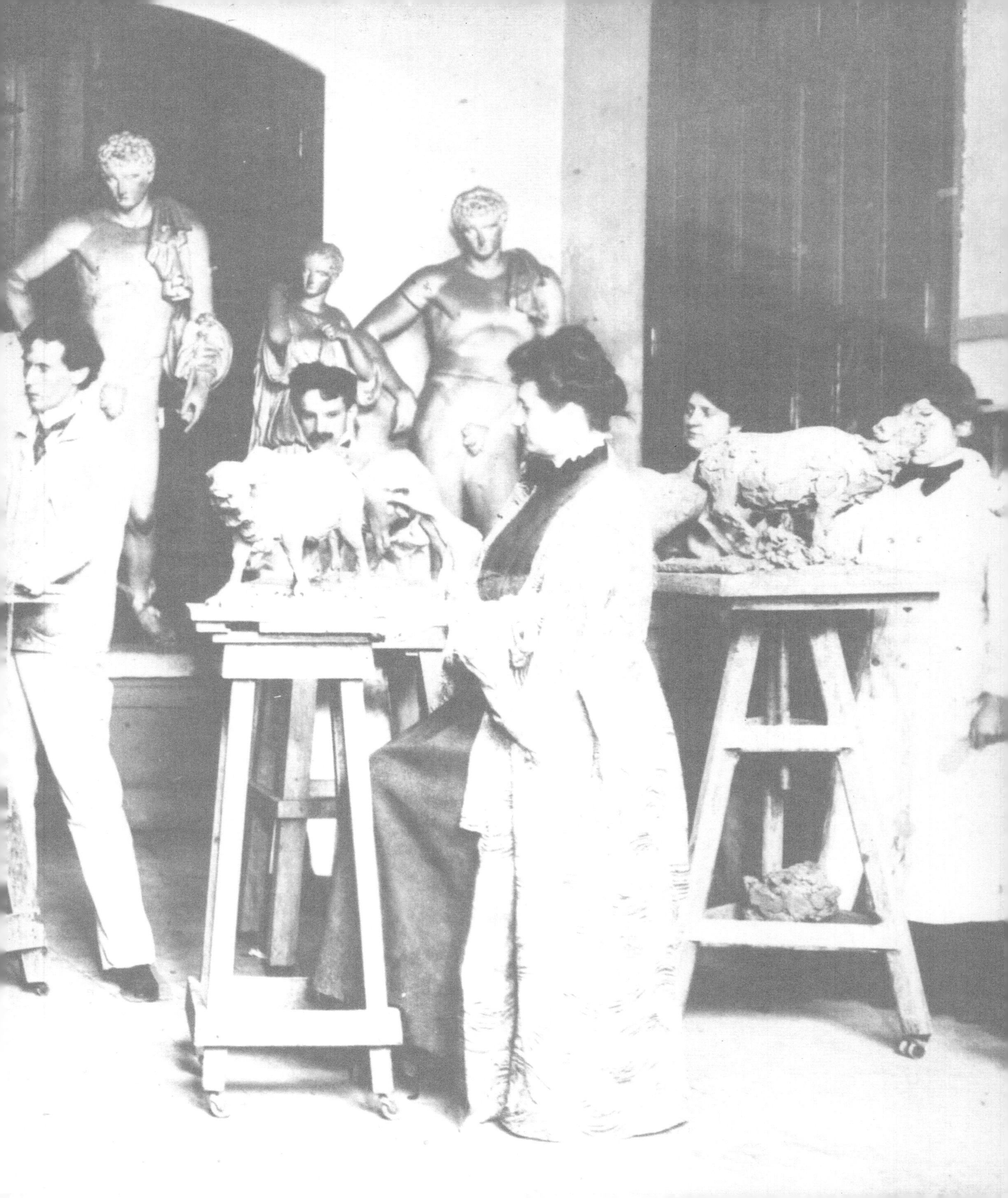

Introducing *here.*

BY JULIEN ROBSON

Previous spread:
Photographer unknown, Academy students modeling a musk ox, ca. 1904
Pennsylvania Academy of the Fine Arts, Philadelphia. Archives

"As much as an artwork is intended to go beyond the actual location of its creation, it is first of all and above all saturated with the artist's experience in this particular concrete place."

ROBERT MENASSE[1]

I remember, it was only a few months after moving to Philadelphia in 2008 that I looked again at a short essay I had written in a brochure for a show called *Nowhere*.[2] It was a small show that I put together in 2005 and exhibited during the Styrian Autumn Festival in Graz, Austria, and it presented five young artists from Louisville, Kentucky, whose works reflected critically, as well as imaginatively, upon the place they lived. Invited to address the festival theme of "City," I saw the exhibition as a perfect platform for a subject that had interested me for some time: namely the tendency of the main centers of art to regard art scenes in the regions as provincial. This was not, however, an excuse for Southern "boosterism" but, rather, an opportunity to engage with the complex, reflexive, and often humorous questions about self-identity that the artists I had selected seemed invested in, where myth, cliché, and mundane everyday reality were employed to play up the tension between internal and external perceptions of this place and its culture. In this context, one aspect of the project focused on a discussion about the relationship of the artistic center to the periphery and how artists from the regions are disadvantaged when it comes to participating in the marketplace. Equally—and more interestingly—though, the exhibition raised a challenge to the reductive narratives that are projected onto the periphery from the artistic center, and the project asked reflexively of both, not only who *we* think we are but also who *others* think we are. Recognizing that artists in the "regions" have access to and freely participate in discourse that has a global reach, the project opened up a discussion of how the work of art, while engaging this discourse, arises out of the local—how it is, in the words of Austrian novelist Robert Menasse, "saturated with the artist's experience in this particular concrete place."[3]

What brought me to think again about *Nowhere* was a chance remark, made to me shortly after my arrival in Philadelphia. In this conversation, after disclosing that I had come to the city following a number of years spent in Louisville, I was surprised at the reaction, which went along the lines that I must be relieved to have gotten away from Kentucky and continued, without pause and with a suggestion of relief, that at least Philadelphia is close to New York City. Having, during the previous nine years, become somewhat numbed to wry comments about Kentucky's presumed lack of cultural sophistication, it amused me in this instance to hear such a speedily issued rejoinder that cast Philadelphia in the same provincializing shadow as Louisville, albeit closer to the presumed summit.

At the time of this conversation, my own perception of Philadelphia was of a city with its own artistic vitality and way of doing things; a city where artists developed their own systems of support, formed collectives, managed alternative spaces, published periodicals and blogs, and built bridges to other art communities. To this newcomer, it appeared to have a rich and healthy array of art institutions, including PAFA, the Philadelphia Museum of Art, the Fabric Workshop and Museum, and the ICA, as well as a group of nationally important art schools. It could also boast two major arts foundations. And, as articles in the press a few years earlier had reported, the city has become a place to migrate to, where "cheap space and a less frantic environment"[4] have made it possible for artists to find studios and actually spend time in them. Meanwhile, in among this infrastructure a group of galleries promote established and emerging artists and strive to create a market for contemporary art in the city and to bring Philadelphia's artists to other places. What drew me here had nothing to do with its proximity to New York but everything to do with an opportunity to work in a new art environment that I conceived of as having qualities and characteristics, as well as challenges, that were distinctly its own. And so my first encounter with Philadelphia's "sixth borough" inferiority complex came as a bit of a surprise.

This drift of the conversation did, however, start me thinking again about how the view from New York still "normalizes" a hegemonic outward gaze, and how artists from the regions generally gain little traction in the New York art world. Encouraging this New York centrism, over the past sixty years the scene in the "Big Apple" has developed into a powerful economic engine of the art world in general and, complemented by the critical appreciation of its internationally distributed art press, it has continued to attract artists from across the globe to live and work there. Of course, artists living and working in other parts of the United States have always been keen, if possible, to get a foothold in this market place but, as Lucy Lippard has noted, "The difference between New York and the "local" art scenes is that other places know what New York is up to but New York remains divinely oblivious to what's happening off the market and reviewing map."[5] Yet, while for decades the city's domination of the art conversation has been supported and maintained by its critical and market infrastructure, nowadays its hold on the center is being eroded by the idea of globalism, where a multi-centered approach acknowledges the import of the regional and the local in a global conversation. Of course, America's "art capital" is not going to disappear, but its hegemonic hold on the art discussion is giving way to an understanding that the New York art world is also a local context of production.

In the new environment of the World Wide Web, artists in the regions have become less and less dependent upon specialist art magazines to direct the artistic discourse. The Internet's global reach and interactive nature has begun to threaten the printed word in all its paper forms, and it now allows artists to freely gather information and imagery to the places where they are situated. Liberating the art discussion, this new connectivity allows artists to engage directly with a plethora of diverse artistic conversations across the globe. Here, in the world of blogs, on-line magazines and newspapers, videos, and institutional and artist websites, the hierarchical structure of the art world starts to flatten and, as Philadelphia artist Jeremiah Misfeldt has put it, "notions of hegemony have a curious way of fading from view when confronted by easily accessible, equally-viable alternatives."[6] As this process occurs, the binary opposition of center and periphery is being replaced by a divergent multi-centered network that starts with everyone and goes everywhere, a structure that not only furnishes artists with information but allows them an equal role in the development of global art discourse. In this context, the local takes on a new significance and, just as the experience of place saturates the artist's work, so the work itself permeates global discussion with the particularities of the local. Here, place—with its familiar histories and memories—energizes the global, aerating it with local concerns and interests and promising a refreshed critical engagement with regionalism.

Addressing this interest in a refreshed critical engagement with regionalism, ***here.*** is a project that, emerging from *Nowhere*, presents the work of twenty four artists and artist collectives that live and work in areas of the country that lie away from the internationally visible centers of American art. Chosen by six curators who live and work in the regions, it is an exhibition that, on the one hand, explores the ways that the experience of place saturates the work of the artist and, on the other, seeks to acknowledge and make transparent the subjectivities that permeate curatorial choices.

Focusing on regions around Philadelphia, Cincinnati, Detroit, Raleigh-Durham, Phoenix, and Kansas City, my ambition as the project director was not so much to create a survey as to bring together an array of curatorial perspectives, where considerations of the artists' engagement with questions of the local would be focused through the lenses of curators who are invested in their respective art communities. While the project turns its gaze away from those centers that dominate the art market in America, these six places were chosen to some degree because they constitute centers at the periphery; places that can boast strong communities of artists and infrastructures that include art schools, museums, alternative spaces, and in some cases, strongly supportive arts foundations.

Responding to the exhibition brief, from the beginning of the project, each curator was given complete independence to select four artists and, in this sense, the project differs from many examinations of work from the regions by focusing from the interior rather than from some distant place, from the point of view of the visited rather than the visitor, so to speak. It is a multi-centered curatorial approach that also allows the curators' contributions to the catalogue to engage with their own sense of where they are and for them to address the role of "this concrete place" in their selections. It also allows for works by artists from differing parts of the country to find their own connectivities in an undetermined way, revealing how shared concerns emerge across a spectrum of art communities and how they differ in their particularities because of their relationship to place and local circumstance.

The regions can come to life as myth and cliché in the outsider's imagination but, for artists who live in the regions, "place" is the juice of lived experience that infiltrates their artwork whether expressed directly in the freedoms their environment affords, the subject matter it provides, or the material and conceptual needs that it satisfies. Recognizing how place influences and infiltrates each artist's work in unique and complex ways, ***here.*** highlights the many different reasons why these twenty four artists find themselves situated "here" and uses these stories as a means of exploring their various approaches and responses to place. It develops a discussion about how "the artist's experience in this particular concrete place" saturates what he or she creates, and by elaborating ideas about history, engagement with location, desire for community, displacement, the economics of the periphery, support, and the freedom afforded artists living in the regions, reconsiders what the regional and the local mean to an artist's practice while contributing to the ongoing conversation about what constitutes art in America today. As Lucy Lippard has so succinctly put it, "Everybody comes from someplace, and the places we come from—cherished or rejected—inevitably affect our work."[7]

[1] Robert Menasse, "A Plea For Centers At The Periphery" in LKW: *Dinge Zwischen Leben, Kunst & Werk / Things Between Life, Kunst (Art) & Work (Lebenskunstwerke)* (Linz: O.K. Centrum für Gegenwartskunst Oberösterreich, 1990), 228.

[2] The exhibition was commissioned by Galerie Eugen Lendl in Graz and was organized by the Speed Art Museum in Louisville. After showing in Graz, it was presented at the New Center for Contemporary Art, Louisville.

[3] Menasse, "A Plea For Centers At The Periphery," 228.

[4] Steven Stern, "Liberal Arts in Philadelphia," *The New York Times*, November 19, 2006, http://travel.nytimes.com/2006/11/19/travel/tmagazine/19liberal.html.

[5] Lucy Lippard, *The Lure of the Local: Senses of Place in a Multicentered Society* (New York: The New Press, 1997), 36.

[6] Jeremiah Misfeldt, "Philadelphia: The Kids Are Alright," *Pew Fellowships in the Arts Newsletter*, no. 5 (2005): 1.

[7] Lippard, *The Lure of the Local: Senses of Place in a Multicentered Society*, 36.

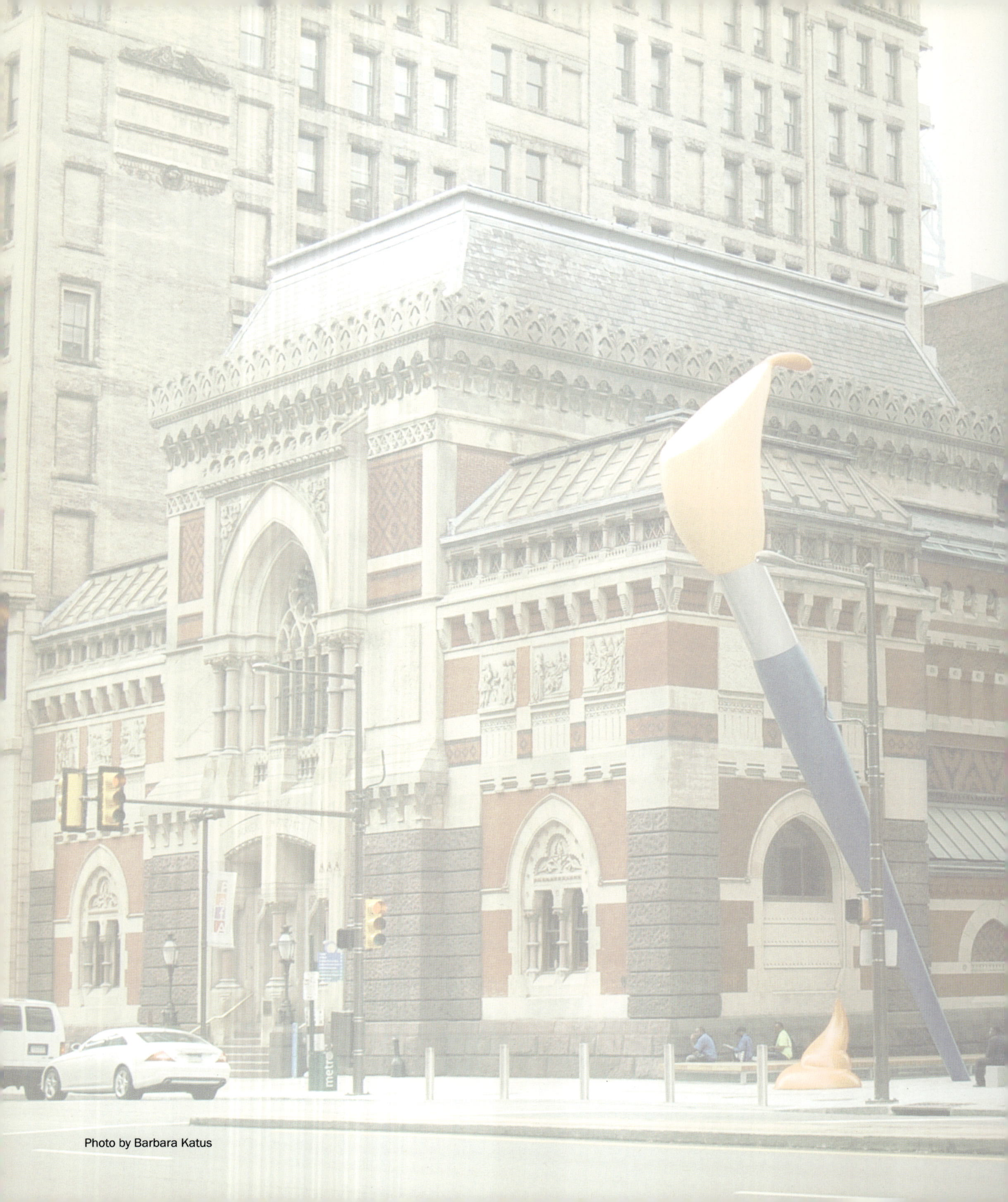

Photo by Barbara Katus

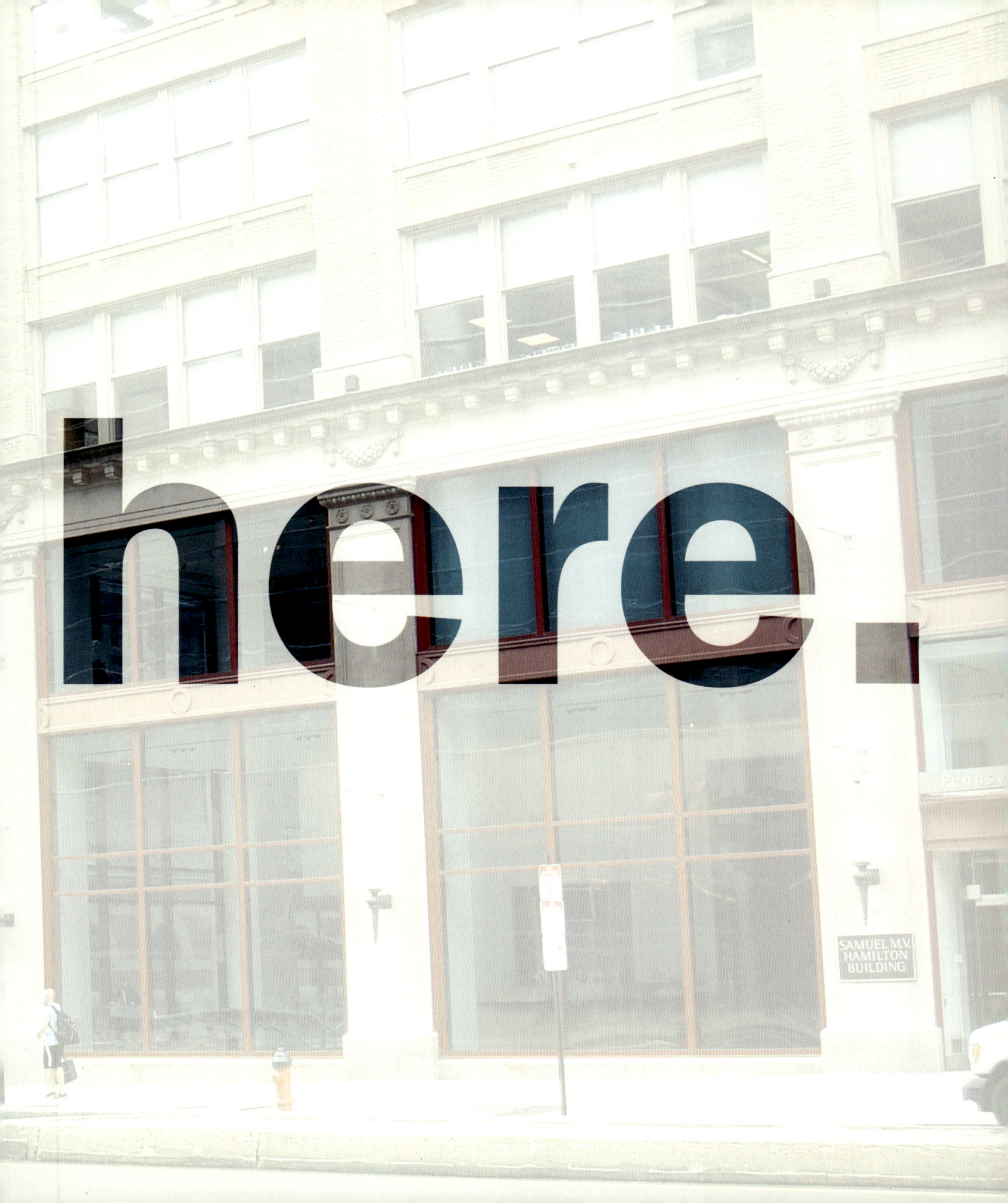
here.
SAMUEL M.V. HAMILTON BUILDING

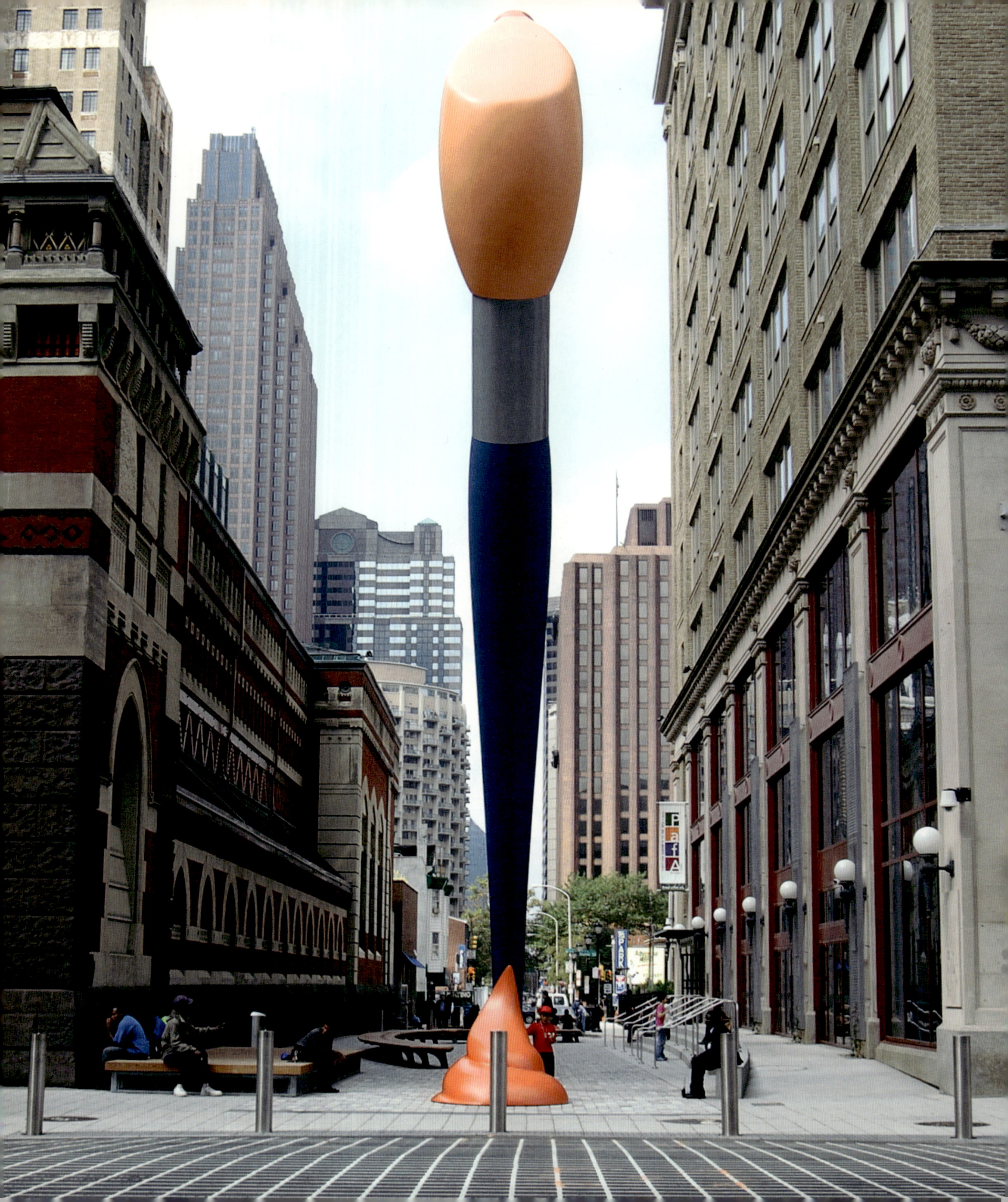
PafA
PARK

Cultural Globalization and Critical Regionalism in Contemporary American Art

BY ERIKA DOSS

Opposite:
Pennsylvania Academy of the Fine Arts
Lenfest Plaza
Photo by Barbara Katus

Over the past several decades, the contemporary art world has been increasingly enthralled by the practices and promises of cultural globalization. International art fairs, biennials, and triennials—not just those long held in Basel, Kassel, New York, São Paulo, and Venice but recent upstarts in Beijing, Cairo, Dubai, Havana, Mexico City, Miami, Mozambique, New Delhi, Santa Fe, Shanghai, Singapore, and elsewhere—along with internationally networked museums, galleries, dealers, auction houses, collectors—and artists, of course—have all helped define and direct this phenomenon, and the impact has been tremendous. French writer Nicolas Bourriaud argues that contemporary globalization has generated a new kind of artistic modernity, an "altermodernity" that discards limiting or restrictive notions of "nationalism and identity-tagging" in favor of more ambiguous and synthetic aesthetic approaches.[1] Chrissie Iles and Philippe Vergne, curators of the 2006 Biennial at the Whitney Museum of American Art, similarly suggest that globalism has accelerated and revised standard assumptions about both the nation-state and the art world:

> The definition of what constitutes "American" is in dramatic flux. Artists, and curators, are moving round the world with an ever-greater fluidity, often living or working between countries, traveling back and forth from New York, Los Angeles, Puerto Rico, and Chicago to Istanbul, Thailand, Zurich, Berlin, Milan, and London. This fluidity has created a complicated network of communication and artistic exchange that refuses to be contained by geographical borders and that creates arcs which traverse vast distances.[2]

Whether or not today's cultural globalization is simply an updated version of cultural colonialism, a rather blatant sign of neoliberalism's rapacious global reach, or a more authentic indication of cultural expansiveness predicated on genuine interests in global artistic diversity, is open to debate.[3] So are questions about the continuing dominance of certain metropolitan art capitals in today's global era. While some say cultural globalization has loosened New York's century-old hold on that claim (and Berlin, for example, has become the twenty-first century's new art capital), others disagree. Likewise, globalism is often seen as a reductive process of cultural homogenization, raising questions about its sweeping tendencies toward a standardized, universal Ikea-esque aesthetic.

Globalism especially upsets conventional assumptions about local, regional, and national art styles or expectations about the links between certain places and certain kinds of art. That is: while the cultural and social dynamics of globalization have certainly helped "de-territorialize" much of the planet, has this also made issues of place irrelevant, or insignificant, for contemporary artists? If today's artists are constantly in motion, moving "round the world with an ever-greater fluidity," what does "place" ultimately mean in terms of their work? What role does attachment to place play in terms of their creative vision? What does the local mean in today's globalized art world? Is regionalism a useful concept when we think about contemporary American art?

These are the sorts of issues that connect the artists in ***here.***, an exhibit that pools the work of some two-dozen contemporary artists who live and work in six different regions of the United States: Cincinnati, Detroit, Kansas City, Philadelphia, Phoenix/Scottsdale, and Raleigh/Durham. There may not be a particularly "regional" art style that marks these places today, an identifiable "Cincinnati" or "Philadelphia" aesthetic that is shared by the artists in these cities and spaces. Still, notions of place saturate contemporary art in diverse ways.

For some artists, place is literally referenced in images of distinctive local and regional landscapes, such as in Tim Portlock's inkjet prints of Philadelphia buildings, Aaron Rothman's photographs of flowering weeds near Phoenix's airport, Michael Krueger's colored pencil drawings of the Great Plains, and Stacy Lynn Waddell's scorched paper watercolors of slave ports and slave ships in Mississippi and other Southern states. For other artists, place is remembered in performances that transpose traditional tribal rituals onto the spaces of 21st century tourism, which is the subject of *Na'nízhoozhí da' nijahigi na' a'ahi (Gallup Motel Butchering)* (2011), a four-channel video produced by Postcommodity, an American Indian arts collective based in Phoenix and Albuquerque.

For other artists, including Whoop Dee Doo, an improvisational collective based in Kansas City that aims for what it calls "creative progression," and Gregory Sale, a multidisciplinary artist who now works in Phoenix, place is defined in terms of relational art practices that engage specific local publics on social and political terms. For his 2011 installation *It's not just black and white*, Sale partnered with inmates and officers in Arizona's criminal justice system. An extension of the project for ***here.*** will be similarly focused in Philadelphia. As Sale observes:

> Black-and-white-striped uniforms, pink underwear for male inmates, chain gangs for men, women and juveniles, and a Tent City jail in the desert have become commonplace. This local vernacular weaves its way throughout the artwork's multiple dialogues that serve as jumping off points for questions of how a country that prioritizes freedom and democracy could be the world leader in incarceration and how this could be the first generation to spend more on incarceration than education.[4]

And for still other artists, place helps to re-vivify regional history and memory. Cincinnati native Terence Hammonds, a printmaker who grew up in the mostly African American neighborhood of Over-the-Rhine, draws on locally specific cultural resources such as newspaper clippings, record album covers, and political buttons to narrate the struggles for civil rights in the 1960s and 1970s in that segregated city. Animator Jennifer Levonian, who grew up in West Virginia, Iowa, Virginia, and Florida and now lives in Philadelphia, relies on place as a backdrop to personal memories, yet the places she references—from suburban lawns and superhighways to upscale grocery stores, Starbucks, McDonald's, and mega-churches—are places familiar to many Americans today. Her video for ***here.***, which is accompanied by Rachel Mason's song "Oven Sky" (2010), references the recent gentrification of Philadelphia's Kensington neighborhood, where Levonian lives.

Erika Nelson's truck full of T*he World's Largest Collection of the World's Smallest Versions of the World's Largest Things Sideshow Extravaganza* (2001 – present) re-animates just a few of the many places she and her family visited every summer, year after year, on long road trips when she was growing up. As she observes:

> The roadside vernacular architecture making up the bulk of my explorations has a dual identity, dual purpose, dual viewpoint. The towns and communities erecting these identity markers are creating cultural icons, symbols, and representations of who they are. Visitors and explorers coming to these monuments see these iconic structures as items built for them, tourist attractions designed to entice the traveler and make them stop for a moment. ... My practice examines these perspectives, exploring the transient yet rooted stories that intersect at points on the atlas.

In other words, despite contemporary globalism's profound reconfiguration of cultural, economic, and social exchange, the specifics of place—geographic, civic, political, historical, remembered—remain resonant for many of today's artists.

On the other hand, while cultural globalization has certainly helped connect the world, it has simultaneously helped undermine notions of a central, or singular art capital: a monolithic or "most important" place where artists must live and work if they are going to be taken seriously. Of course, loss of faith in "the center" is not just a cultural phenomenon in contemporary America: consider the nation's fractured political condition today and the growth of grassroots groups such as the Tea Party, whose members denounce "Washington" and "big government" and rally instead over bills and legal measures that assert states' rights and aim to nullify federal authority. Whether political or cultural, backlash against central authority, or those who seemingly represent such authority, is rampant in America today. While New York still claims to be the art capital of the world, and perfunctory coverage of mega-million dollar annual art sales at Sotheby's and Christie's helps it maintain such status, the emergence of "second city" art capitals like Chicago, Los Angeles, Miami, Minneapolis, Santa Fe, and Seattle suggests the art world's de-centralization—at least in the United States. Yet each of these "second-tier" capitals has its own corresponding mix of galleries, markets, and museums.[5]

No matter: for many contemporary artists, blue-chip art markets, whether in New York or anywhere else in America, hardly constitute what art is or means today. However significant, cultural globalization's impact on the economics of art obscures more compelling accounts of cultural practices in today's mobile era, and what place and region mean to today's generation of artists. In *The Lure of the Local: Senses of Place in a Multicentered Society* (1997), Lucy Lippard argues that "place is latitudinal and longitudinal within the map of a person's life. It is temporal and spatial, personal and political. A layered location replete with human histories and memories, place has width as well as depth. It is about connections, what surrounds it, what formed it, what happened there, what will happen there."[6] As a synthesis of space and memory, place is an expansive terrain for artistic exploration. It is especially meaningful, Lippard suggests, when artists critically examine their place in, and relationship to, particular places—especially those in which they may be newcomers, or outsiders. And for many Americans, that may be often. While the nationwide slump in jobs has certainly slowed American patterns of mobility in recent years, statistics suggest that the average American moves from one place to the next about once every five years, sometimes just across town, sometimes across the country.

Lippard, who now lives and works in Galisteo, New Mexico, readily admits her preference for slower, smaller, non-urban places. "In some ways," she argues, "I am advocating an updated "regionalism." The movement for cultural democracy springs from the concern that the homogeneity of corporate culture ... is melting down the multiracial, multicultural differences that are this country's greatest strength."[7] She notes, however, that today "the term *regionalism* ... [is] used pejoratively, to mean corny backwater art flowing from the tributaries that might eventually reach the mainstream but is currently stagnating out there in the boondocks."[8]

Regionalism was one of the leading movements of modern American art during the 1930s.[9] In the wake of World War I, with Europe's art capitals in ruins and the United States experiencing unprecedented prosperity, many believed America's time for Western cultural ascendency had arrived. "We have been sponging on Europe for direction instead of developing our own," complained critic Paul Rosenfeld in the mid-1920s, exhorting American artists to establish their own independent, individual, and place-based aesthetic identities.[10] Writing in 1939, Peyton Boswell, editor of the popular magazine Art Digest, reflected on how the American artist had, over the past decade, "returned to the soil for his subject material":

> He stepped down from his ivory tower and out into the fields, the streets and the factories. ... He fared forth on the highways and byways of America or he returned to his boyhood habitat and painted the subjects that had subconsciously thrilled his heart. A fascinating panorama unfolded. America is a vast physical area with not one but a thousand aspects. It is a variegated, mosaiclike picture in which the parts add up to the sum of the whole.[11]

If writing from the unenlightened assumption that all American artists were male (Georgia O'Keeffe? Isabel Bishop?), Boswell's overall point was clear: in the 1930s, American art was especially focused on specific American places and represented by a style called Regionalism.

A narrative, anecdotal style of painting, Regionalism is often identified with a "triumvirate" of American artists, each associated with a particular Midwestern region: Thomas Hart Benton of Missouri, John Steuart Curry of Kansas, and Grant Wood of Iowa. From Benton's murals of self-resilient Midwestern workers to Wood's pictures of stern and stoic farmers—like those depicted in his classic painting *American Gothic* (1930)—and vast fields of corn and wheat, the Regionalists explored the ethnology of the local with particular ideological purpose: to provide an aesthetic counterpoint to an American art they felt was overly dominated by New York, to celebrate the distinctiveness of vernacular Americana, and—somewhat ironically given its art historical label—to generate a national style of American art.

If Regionalism was branded provincial and anti-modernist, Benton, Curry, and Wood were actually fluent in multiple strains of avant-garde art: each studied modern art in Europe and Benton, for one, wrote an erudite series of articles on the mechanics of pictorial composition.[12] Each consciously developed a contemporary art style that embodied modernist forms and American Scene subjects and paralleled the liberal, reformist politics of the era. As Benton later recalled, the paintings he produced during the 1930s were "very largely affirmative of the social explorations of American society and resultant democratic impulses on which President Roosevelt's New Deal was based."[13] There were other Regionalist artists, too, such as the Dallas Nine, a group of painters based in Texas and Oklahoma, and the Mystic Painters of the Northwest, four artists (including Morris Graves and Mark Tobey) who combined their interests in the landscapes of the Pacific coast with their adherence to Asian religions.[14] Regionalism's lure of the local was used as the currency of cultural nationalism: if focused on specific places, Regionalism corresponded to the New Deal's larger cultural and political project of blending America's multiple regions (and publics) into a national picture of unity, an especially crucial endeavor during the economic and political exigencies of the Great Depression.

In the 1940s, however, Regionalism was eclipsed by new strains of American art, especially abstract art, much as New Deal political cultures were subdued by the postwar era's anxious fixation on Cold War strategies of anticommunism and consensus.[15] Artists' interests in American place, region, and social reform shifted to personal expression and formalist experimentation, and attention to "the local" or to subjects of distinction and difference was often viewed with suspicion in an age that prized conformity. Regionalism, in fact, was now denounced as parochial and even politically dangerous. In 1946, for example, art historian H. W. Janson wrote that while Regionalism's intense popularity had faded, it was still "dangerous" because it had been supported "by some of the fundamental ills of our society—the same ills that, in more virulent form, produced Nationalist Socialism in Germany" during the 1930s.[16] As Clement Greenberg, Harold Rosenberg, and other critics advised, the most appropriate form of modern art for post-World War II America was the nonobjective and seemingly non-political art of Abstract Expressionism. Ironically, regional themes did not exactly disappear: Abstract Expressionism was also called the "New York School" because many of its artists lived and worked in New York City. And many abstractionists alluded to the specifics of place—consider the references to American Western landscapes in Clyfford Still's epic paintings.

But it was not until later in the twentieth-century, with the emergence of the environmental movement and eco-consciousness, with the expansion of a multifaceted approach toward local American landscapes and geographies called the "New Regionalism," and the development of a theoretical vocabulary (derived chiefly from architectural studies) called "Critical Regionalism," that issues of place and "the local" were revitalized in contemporary American art.[17] Today's regionalism is remarkably diverse, less a shared aesthetic with a particular political agenda like much of the Regionalism of the 1930s than a variety of creative responses that consider how the local, however disrupted, denigrated, or displaced, persists in the new age of globalism.

Many of today's place-centered artists follow the directives offered in Kenneth Frampton's influential 1983 essay, "Toward a Critical Regionalism"—namely, to make art that recognizes the links between the local and the global, and negotiates their distinctions. Today's regionalist artists understand how American places are invented, used, abandoned, and, in some cases, rediscovered and re-purposed; they see how places are mutable, how they are always susceptible to ever-shifting American needs and expectations. As the artists who developed Elsewhere, a thrift-store turned living museum in downtown Greensboro, North Carolina, observe:

> Elsewhere is both here and there, a place and presence. It is a site where formations are emerging. It is an idea that everything is re-forming all at once. Elsewhere, everything seems close and distant, ordinary and extraordinary, historical and contemporary, remembered and forgotten. Here, inventions are arranged and discovered from facts and fictions. We find ourselves beside ourselves. ... Our aim is to unfold cultural commons where the environment speaks, listens. By repurposing cultural remnants as creative elements, we activate new stories, tales, and echoes from our material past. From these spaces, we create playgrounds for experiencing concepts.

Over the past few years, museums and galleries have organized more regionally focused exhibits including *Nowhere* (New Center for Contemporary Art, Louisville, 2005), *The Old Weird America: Folk Themes in Contemporary Art* (Contemporary Arts Museum, Houston, 2008), *Heartland* (Smart Museum of Art, University of Chicago, 2009), and *American Story* (John Michael Kohler Art Center, Sheboygan, 2009).[18]

here., at the Pennsylvania Academy of the Fine Arts, is similarly engaged with assumptions of a particular art world "center," and thereby of various regional (read: marginal) art scene peripheries, as opposed to the non-hierarchical premises of Critical Regionalism, with its more nomadic and territorially unbounded ideas about place. Places, of course, are real: physical, geographic, historical, and tangible; they are natural, cultural, and industrial. Today's critically engaged regionalist artists explore both dimensions of place: its rootedness and its fluidity.

Artists, like all of us, obviously live where they live for lots of reasons. Jobs are big lures, and at least one-third of the artists featured in ***here.*** teach at colleges and universities in their respective regions. Certain regions have outstanding cultural support structures, including galleries interested in showing the work of local artists, percent-for-art programs, grant-giving bodies and foundations, and critical engaged media networks. Some places are less expensive, others are more amenable; some artists move to certain places for big spaces and big studios, others for big sky. Others seek places where they can make art, live affordably, and sustain relationships: the aspirational "triple play," as one of ***here.***'s artist's told me. Self-proclaimed "trash wizard" Aaron Storck, takes full advantage of the vast, if cluttered, spaces of America's heartland in projects that critique aesthetic purpose. Born and raised on the upper west side of Manhattan, Storck left New York to study at the University of Kansas in the late 1990s and continues to live in Lawrence where, he remarks, "there are plenty of hip liberals and hard-core conservatives" and he feels "connected to the enigma that this country *is*."

Some artists move to certain places for their distinctive technologies. As Katie Parker and Guy Michael Davis explain, Cincinnati provides "access to a variety of industrial processes, situated on either end of the technological spectrum. There is an abundance of overlooked materials, leftovers and detritus from a booming river town. Cincinnati has a rich history in the production of fine things: silver, furniture, print, and ceramics to list a few. We can comb through junk shops and antique malls, estate sales and flea markets, searching for subjects that fit within our aesthetic." Likewise, Liz Cohen specifically moved to Detroit to learn how cars are made for a decade-long photography, installation, and performance project titled *BODYWORK* that contrasts the manufacturing (and selling) of sex-trade workers and automobiles in the United States, Europe, and Central America.

Other artists live and work where they were born and raised, responding to the familiarity of the local on different, personal terms. As Harrison Haynes, a drummer and a painter in Durham, relates, "Living in the same area of North Carolina where I grew up has afforded me a dependable stream of autobiographical content. At one time I accepted bits of this material as ready-made subject matter for visual art. More recently, though, I've come to regard my practice's relationship to my locality as a resist, as a layer of impermeability that challenges the absorption of intuitive gestures, and thereby generates a counterpoint within the work." In contrast, Scott Hocking, a photographer in Detroit, observes: "I'm still here, and still inspired. I've experienced the Motor City on foot, found solace within the empty factories and overgrown lots, and discovered beauty in the decay and transformations. This is my home base. It has taken time, but I love the clarity that comes with that time."

The indigenous members of Postcommodity—Raven Chacon, Cristóbal Martínez, Kade L. Twist, and Nathan Young—originate from, and live in, the Southwest (Arizona, California, New Mexico, and Oklahoma), inhabiting both traditional tribal homelands and the mega-city of Phoenix, the sixth largest city in the United States. Today, while a majority of American Indians live and work in urban America, tribal affiliations remain strong, often because of place-based associations. As the members of Postcommodity state: "Everything that defines us, as Indigenous people, and our relationships—worldview, culture, spirituality, memory, context, meaning, etc.—goes back to the land. Locality is not just a particular place that relates to a particular art practice; it is the source from which all things emerge, are experienced, accounted for, and remembered."

However broadly it is defined and understood, and however diverse their aesthetic approaches, place is clearly meaningful for many contemporary American artists. However frequently they move from one place to the next, memories of the local travel with them and filter into their creative work, often through practices that engage the tenets of Critical Regionalism. Despite a dominant "cultural turn" toward globalization, issues of place and region are embraced and cultivated and, as the art in ***here.*** suggests, they flourish.

[1] Nicolas Bourriaud, "Altermodern," *Altermodern*, exh. cat. (London: Tate Publishing, 2009), 12.

[2] Chrissie Iles and Philippe Vergne, "Preface and Acknowledgments," *Whitney Biennial 2006: Day for Night* (New York: Whitney Museum for American Art, 2006), 19.

[3] See the essays that explore these and other issues in *Globalization and Contemporary Art*, ed. Jonathan Harris (London: Wiley-Blackwell, 2011).

[4] Gregory Sale, statement for ***here.*** (2011). Unless otherwise noted, all quotes from ***here.*** artists stem from the statements they provided for the 2011 exhibition.

[5] Georg Schöllhammer, "Art in the Era of Globalization," in Oliver Ressler, ed., *The Global 500* (Vienna: Edition Selene, 1999), at: http://eipcp.net/transversal/0303/schoellhammer/en (accessed June 22, 2011).

[6] Lucy Lippard, *The Lure of the Local: Senses of Place in a Multicentered Society* (New York: The New Press, 1997), 7.

[7] Ibid., 282.

[8] Ibid., 36.

[9] The term actually originated in the 1920s among a group of writers called the Southern Agrarians; see Twelve Southerners, *I'll Take My Stand: The South and the Agrarian Tradition* (Baton Rouge: Louisiana State University Press, 2006). It should be noted that this book was originally published in 1930.

[10] Paul Rosenfeld, *Port of New York: Essays on Fourteen American Moderns* (New York: Harcourt Brace and Company, 1924), 281-295.

[11] Peyton Boswell, Jr., *Modern American Painting* (Garden City: Garden City Publishing Company, Inc., 1939), 58-59.

[12] Thomas Hart Benton, "Mechanics of Form Organization in Painting," *The Arts*, vol. 10, no. 5 (November 1926): 285-289; vol. 10, no. 6 (December 1926): 340-342; vol. 11, no. 1 (January 1927): 43-44; vol. 11, no. 2 (February 1927): 95-96); and vol. 11, no. 3 (March 1927): 145-148.

[13] Thomas Hart Benton, *An American in Art: A Professional and Technical Autobiography* (Lawrence: The University Press of Kansas, 1969), 192.

[14] The group was so-named by *Life* magazine; see "Mystic Painters of the Northwest," *Life* (September 28, 1953): 84-88.

[15] Erika Doss, *Benton, Pollock, and the Politics of Modernism: From Regionalism to Abstract Expressionism* (Chicago: University of Chicago Press, 1991).

[16] H.W. Janson, "Benton and Wood, Champions of Regionalism," *Magazine of Art*, 39 (May 1946): 184-186.

[17] See Charles Reagan Wilson, ed., *The New Regionalism: Essays and Commentaries* (Oxford: The University of Mississippi Press, 1998), and Kenneth Frampton, "Towards a Critical Regionalism: Six Points for an Architecture of Resistance," in Hal Foster, ed., *The Anti-Aesthetic: Essays on Postmodern Culture* (Seattle: Bay Press, 1983), 16-30; on the use of the term in cultural studies see Douglas Reichert Powell, *Critical Regionalism: Connecting Politics and Culture in the American Landscape* (Chapel Hill: University of North Carolina Press, 2007). The term "Critical Regionalism" was coined in the early 1980s by architectural theorists Liane Lefaivre and Alexander Tzonis, who traced the concept to critics Lewis Mumford and J. B. Jackson, both of whom wrote profusely on vernacular architecture, landscape, and design.

[18] It should be noted that although shown at New Center for Contemporary Art, the *Nowhere* exhibition was curated and organized by the Speed Art Museum, Louisville, Kentucky. Also, the *Heartland* exhibition was produced in collaboration with the Van Abbemuseum in Eindhoven, Holland.

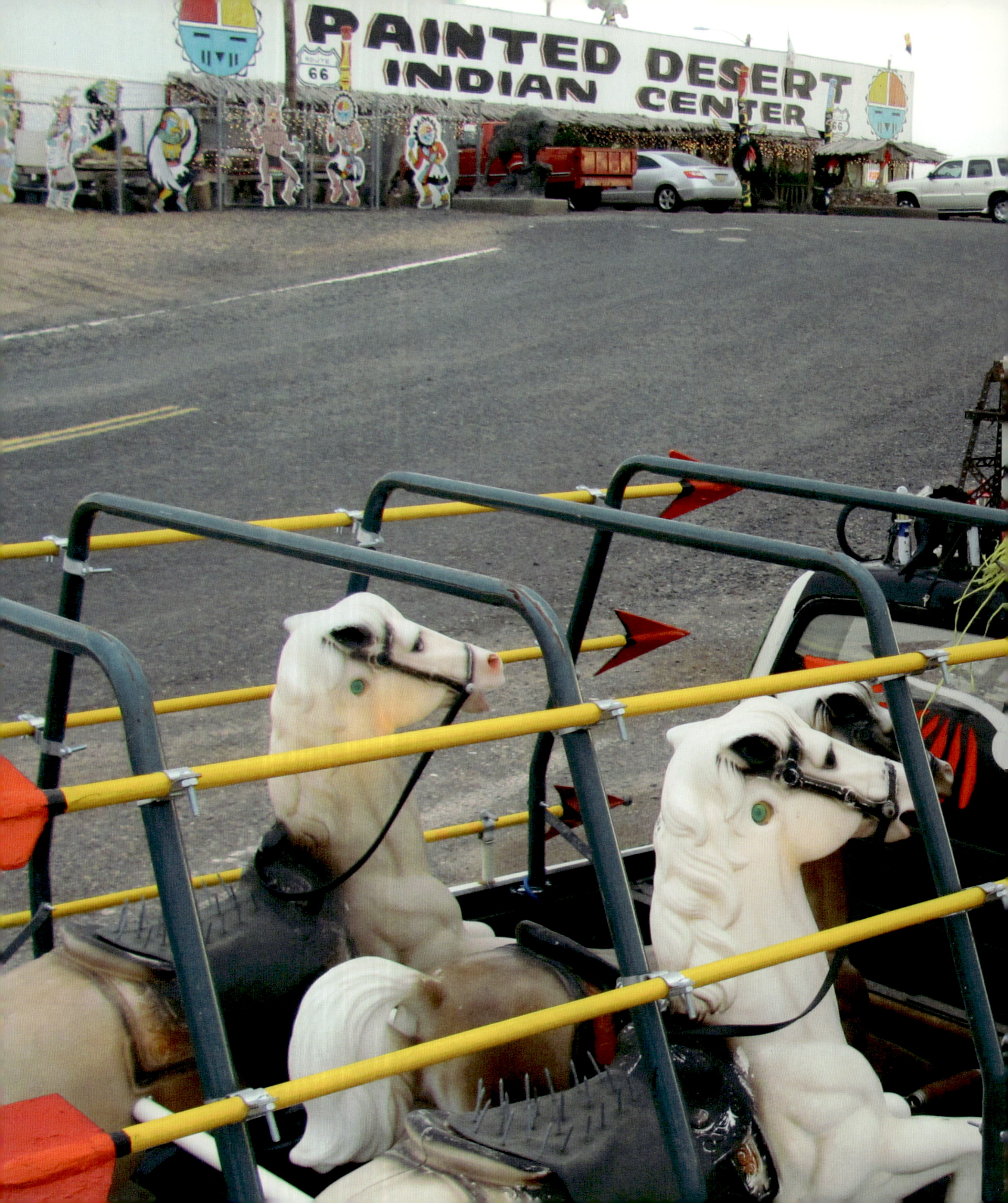
PAINTED DESERT
INDIAN CENTER
ROUTE 66

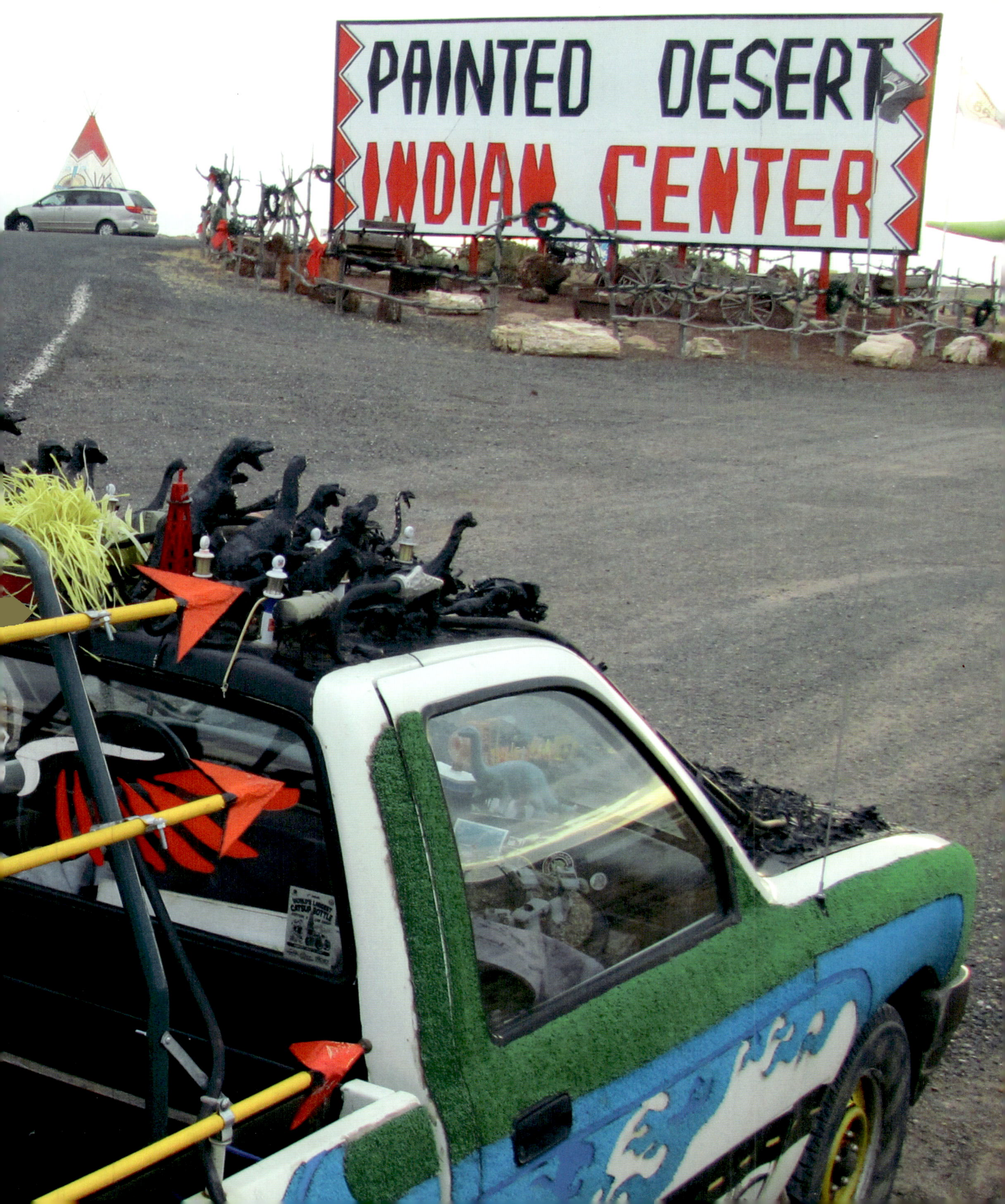
PAINTED DESERT
INDIAN CENTER

Trespassers:

A CONVERSATION WITH CHRISTOPHER COOK AND HESSE MCGRAW

Previous spread:
Erika Nelson
Daily Driver Art Car "Scout" at Painted Desert, Arizona
Image: 2010, Art Car: 2003 – 2010
Mixed media on 1995 Toyota Pickup
80" x 70" x 200"
Photo courtesy of the artist

Christopher Cook: Hesse, I would like to start with the title of the exhibition, and ask you: what does *here* connote for you?

Hesse McGraw: *You know I always hope there is a* here, *that picks up on the question 'is there a there, there?', but I think more important is the sense of there being a* here, *no matter where you're at. With respect to artists working in certain places, I think I'm always wondering, what impact they are having on that place, rather than wondering what impact is the place having on them? I'm always interested in the trail the artist leaves behind, the sort of imprint he or she imparts on the place. I think that interest extends beyond the idea of artists as place-makers and bleeds into the idea of artists as markers of place.*

CC: Do you feel that is a legitimate role for contemporary artists today? To leave a mark, so to speak, to influence their place?

HM: *I think they do so, perhaps without intending. For artists that have a social practice or a spatial practice or an expanded practice that occurs beyond the studio or beyond the gallery, that may be a goal. Although, is it a role or a characteristic that is intrinsically embedded in the act of making work in a given place? Thinking about Kansas City specifically, I've always been incredibly floored by the impact Kansas City artists have had on the city across many fields. So when you start to trace back virtually anything interesting in that city—whether it's a neighborhood or a developer or a small business—all of these things came out of the artist community. There's a legacy of a way of thinking about the world that the artists possess. They're actively making work in the studio or being entrepreneurs or working in some capacity to make the world they want to live in; artists impact places in ways that other folks don't.*

CC: From the Kansas City area, and let's think of this within broad terms—so Kansas and Missouri—I've selected four artists/artist groups to be in the exhibition. The artist group Whoop Dee Doo (see page 152) primarily lives and works in Kansas City proper and has a socially-based practice, involving performance, installation, and viewer participation, and requires a number of hands to make very outrageous and ambitious projects. How do you see this group impacting its immediate community?

HM: *Yeah, it's a great question. I feel like Whoop Dee Doo has raised the bar of what's possible for an artist collective. So much of their work hinges on this extremely adventurous outlook on the everyday. Whether they're doing a performance in Kansas City, Missouri, or Omaha, Nebraska, Portland, Oregon, or Malmö, Sweden, they're interested in figuring out the extreme vernacular of that place. This might be a drag queen or a body builder, a punk club or six-year-old beauty pageant. In bringing those things together in one space, they start to outline some underlying rhythms of that place. Or, they start to ask: "What are the margins of community in the city?" I think as a viewer of their work you start to wonder about the margins of your own cultural perspective. What might you as a viewer consider to be culture? Is a punk club culture? Is a beauty pageant for six-year-olds culture? I think that's a provocation. But it's a provocation based on an extreme joy that's most immediately felt by children. So as an adult in that* *situation, you start to ask yourself, "What are the boundaries of culture as I define them in the city, and why are they so narrow? Could they use a bit of expanding? Could my personal culture become more eclectic? And, is there a way in which I can expand the routines of my experiential relationship with this place?"*

CC: I think one impact that is quite profound is their ability to push participants to ask the quite valid questions: "This exists in Kansas City? These people live in my community? How is that possible? Why don't I know of them?" And so beyond offering a mirror to a place, they give it a more comprehensive illustration. They start to sketch in the negative places in a landscape so you start to see a fuller picture of a community and all of the disparate elements that are essential to making it vibrant. I think many of the artists that make up the artist community in the Kansas City area do that in their own unique ways, whether it's their prime mission or an afterthought.

HM: *I think that's an incredibly utilitarian stance, but it's also doing a couple of things. It asserts and provides evidence that, as a member of contemporary culture, your perspective of culture in your place is very narrow and also very hierarchical, so ultimately that realigns any notion of here as it relates to a cultural community or a cultural sphere. Walking out of a Whoop Dee Doo performance, I find my understanding of place totally exploded. It's about possibility, and it's a challenge to break apart your routine, to drive out of the way, to trespass. It makes you see that any idea of place is contingent on the routines that you have related to that place. Once you start to trespass a little bit and, in a sense, go somewhere you're not welcome, your experience of a place expands and your perception of that place expands too. I think that's the ride Whoop Dee Doo takes people on—this sort of willful and ecstatic trespassing.*

CC: I want to use some of that language—the driving, the trespassing, the going a route that is unfamiliar—to segue to Erika Nelson's ongoing project, *World's Largest Collection of the World's Smallest Versions of the World's Largest Things Sideshow Extravaganza* (2001 – present) (see page 134). Nelson drives to tourist attractions in Kansas, Missouri, the greater Midwest, and throughout the country in order to photograph the outrageous phenomena—the world's largest this or that—on which communities really pride themselves and pin their identity: "We're a small town and can really only offer so much. But you know what? We have the biggest ball of twine. Please come by and check it out." Throughout the project, Erika travels to these places and photo-documents these typically large-scale, human-made works and then crafts miniatures of them and displays those miniatures in a mobile museum next to photos of the real objects. I think it calls forth our human desires to understand and grasp a sense of place and, therefore, have a better sense of identity and purpose in the world. But the project also drives home the fact that a lot of these towns have dwindling resources and their last resort for economic viability is to create this artifice that will somehow generate tourist dollars.

HM: *I love this. Kansas is home to many huge things, and these pitiable epic attractions were for years the greatest tourist destinations in Kansas. So the ball of twine, Big Brutus, the electric steam shovel, these are the attractions you would visit on a Kansas road trip. That changed, at least the rankings changed, in 2003 with the development of Cabela's outdoor sporting shop and Nebraska Furniture*

Mart, the Speedway, and the Village West shopping development twenty miles west of Kansas City. Within a year, these conglomerate destinations became seven of the top ten tourist destinations in Kansas—usurping Big Brutus, the ball of twine, and other vernacular sites. Ultimately, that shift in ranking was about, to my mind, operating within a sphere of artifice but ramped up and amplifed to the highest power. All of those developments—Nebraska Furniture Mart, Cabela's, the Chateau Avalon Hotel—are these phenomenal abstractions that are three times removed from any specific place. These are sites at which space and time are extremely compressed, like a themed hotel where you can stay in the Egyptian room or the New York room or the Paris room and it's all made of fiberglass and you go there with a whole bunch of Viagra. This is the way that we live in the world! We've been taught that our own lives are insufficient, and so we attempt to create a more fantastic existence. This is something I've written about in the past, this idea of the mega-life, which is a life bigger than what you actually deserve. I think it gets really interesting when you start to think about the ways in which these grabs at "bigger and better" are often propelled by debt.

CC: I think one of the most obvious contrasts between the place-making ability of Nebraska Furniture Mart or Cabela's and somewhere like the Garden of Eden in Lucas, Kansas, is that the Garden of Eden tells a story about a place while Cabela's does not. It's the same store wherever you find it and it has no narrative.

HM: *I would disagree. I think Cabela's does tell a story about a place, but it's very carefully constructed. Maybe the same way that Garden of Eden is. It's just constructed towards the ends of the corporation, towards making money. It's saying: go back to nature, but take a bunch of stuff with you.*

CC: Including guns.

HM: *Yeah, don't go anywhere without your gun. You might not turn out OK.*

CC: But what specific qualities does Cabela's reveal about the city that it exists in—other than rampant consumerism and a very specific perspective on our relationship with nature?

HM: *I think it says that authenticity is very difficult. How do you maintain some sense of authenticity to a place in the midst of rampant artifice? A good example of this is Arthur Bryant's BBQ, which many people consider the most authentic place in Kansas City. Of course the restaurant opened up a satellite Arthur Bryant's BBQ in the middle of Village West, next to the Speedway, next to Nebraska Furniture Mart. They did this because of a demand, but it's not the same experience. So it's more or less the same food, but I think what one would characterize as the authenticity of Arthur Bryant's BBQ is the experience of going to the restaurant on Brooklyn Street, which Calvin Trillin called "the best damned restaurant in the world" in 1974. I don't think he would say that about the Arthur Bryant's next to the Speedway. His original statement was never disproven, by the way.*

CC: I think it's quite challenging to recreate an authentic experience. I think the Garden of Eden is the end result of someone being terribly authentic to himself and his family and his life values. It's a sort of beacon of authenticity and that's why many people see it as a holy place.

HM: *But it's also a product of a pure mania. It's driven by this obsession. He's compelled to build this place. And he's compelled to leave his body behind in a Plexiglas-encased tomb.*

CC: How is that not authentic? What's wrong with that? Most of the world's greatest creations are based on obsession.

HM: *It is. I absolutely don't want to say that it's inauthentic, but I guess what I want to try to understand is: Are the compulsions in building the Garden of Eden any different from going to Cabela's and buying into the myths that they're selling?*

CC: Belief in mythology is a primary area of interest for Aaron Storck (see page 146). He's focused on the mythology of the artist and the object, and on the demystification of both, but he's also concerned with authenticity in terms of the artist's role in society.

HM: *It's a set of ideas I try to think about a lot—the simultaneous hyper-authenticity and hyper-artifice that Aaron cultivates in his work when he says, as almost a kind of a rant, "I am a Kansas artist!" How do you take that? It's a direct statement but with multiple layers that may or may not be a complete piss-take on the idea of having a regional practice. In a singular way, Aaron is someone who is extremely genuine while being a trickster. His work can be confusing through its directness. And he's doing so many things at once. He's poking fun at the mythical figure of the artist while completely staking out his agency in the spirited act of being an artist. What I really like about that double agenda—and how I see it aligning with the cultural, social, and political histories of Kansas—is that it delves into this culture of contradiction. So Thomas Frank's book* What's the Matter with Kansas *was, I think, an attempt to parse out the seeming contradictions between certain economic and social value systems. But I think what he missed was how that's actually par for the course in a state whose founding and whose early historical moments were all rooted in really intense contradiction and conflict between opposing ideologies.*

CC: And these are literally played out in many of his videos where he's running around through the Kansas prairie with a shotgun and a magician's hat and shooting live rounds up into the sky... or ranting in front of a video camera next to a campfire. The layers that he's pushing forth are really interesting and complex and they point to the true contradictions of Kansas. When I first started talking to him about this project, he made a very explicit point of how this work was only possible because he lives in Kansas. He had moved to New York and then moved back to Kansas because he needed the space. And I think needing that space is much more than a literal "Hey, I can afford a certain size studio space." It's, "I need a space that is less top down and more horizontal." Because there is so much going on in Kansas—politically, culturally, historically—on a single level. And his take on how to approach this is really compelling. And in many of his videos he takes this preacher, almost...

HM: *He's a charismatic evangelist...*

CC: Soothsayer,

HM: *Crossed with a hyper-intense car salesman and a circus showman.*

CC: But what he's selling you, what he's trying to convince you of is completely unclear. And that ambiguity flies in the face of much of politics today. "I really don't know what this talking head is selling me."

HM: *There's no clarity there whatsoever. I'm interested in the idea of the radical normality of artists. So when you think about a political sphere, it becomes a place where really useless ideological oppositions, switchbacks, filibusters, and shirking the question are all part of the game. Somehow you get to a point where all of that is so extreme but so marginal, so far flung from any rational perspective on actual social or economic or cultural realities. Who's actually asking real substantive questions about the world? I believe it is contemporary artists. Maybe it takes some intentional mystery to arrive at a point of clarity.*

CC: Aaron Storck is currently based in Lawrence, Kansas, which is where you went to undergraduate school and it's also the home base for another exhibiting artist, Michael Krueger (see page 128). Michael primarily creates prints and colored pencil drawings that look into the political and social histories of Lawrence and the city in which he was raised, Sioux Falls, South Dakota. Lawrence, for decades, has been a hotbed for liberal thinking and lifestyles in Kansas and at times runs counter to the rest of the state's identity. Michael's work deals a lot with this tension and this history, and it tries to figure out how a community and a state, and the people of that state, think about this conflict and work through its complexities. Having lived in Lawrence yourself, how have you personally experienced and interacted with that sometimes "muddy water"?

HM: *I think in Kansas, Lawrence is almost a mirage, a place that only exists in the imagination unless you're in the middle of it. It's a perfectly livable city but then also extremely transitional, just due to the fact of the University of Kansas being based there and a large percentage of the population being students. I think an interesting thing about Lawrence is that it has so many really creative people—artists and musicians—who pass through but often don't remain there. Because of that turnover, there's never really been a footing for a permanent arts community. It seems like that's beginning to change, particularly with the direction of the Spencer Museum of Art at the university. But there have always been marginal, community-based art centers that didn't receive a lot of interest or have a lot of connections with the larger contemporary art community. It's always interesting when you find artists with a broader connection to the contemporary art world huddled down in Lawrence. It seems that Aaron and Michael have both found a way of doing that while continuing to build their careers and expand connections.*

CC: And due to the fact that Kansas City is a 45-minute drive east of Lawrence, a lot of the artists that might have attended the university in Lawrence immediately migrate there. It has a larger community of practicing artists and there are more funding mechanisms in place that directly support them. So it seems like a more vibrant community. And I think Lawrence has that rather typical transitory nature because it is a college town and, if you're not intimately connected with the university, it's tough to have an identity in the community to feel like you're a part of something larger than yourself. Michael's work includes both general and specific markers of historic political topics—certain rallies in the community or on campus and public debates around social/political issues. I think his work is a great example of what we were talking about earlier in terms of the many paradoxes of the state of Kansas and the multifarious nature of all of the competing ideologies and values that constantly collide in the state and, oftentimes, bleed over into the neighboring states—Nebraska, Missouri, Oklahoma, etc. I'm wondering—since you work in Nebraska but have lived in Kansas—if you see a lot of that bleed over, if you see cultural similarities among these Midwestern states.

HM: *The states of the Midwest are retaining individual identities because of their citizens' will to do so. For a Missourian, it's like 'God forbid' you are confused for a Kansan. It's similar with Kansas and Nebraska. These rivalries are alive and they flare up and they have obvious sports implications, but I think also political and social implications. So I think it's more interesting to try to understand what the cultural strains are that connect artists working in the broader Midwest. What are the necessary conditions for an artist to sustain his or her practice largely outside of the market? There are the rare artists who are able to find a market for their work beyond the Midwest, who have representation in New York or Los Angeles or wherever. And, there are artists who teach and sustain their practice that way. Something that has always been interesting to me is the brand of ingenuity that springs up among artists who are neither teaching nor actively selling their work. How are they making a living? How are they maintaining a studio practice? I feel like the difficulty of doing that comes out in a visible way in the rigor of the work.*

CC: One concrete example is the practice of Whoop Dee Doo. In a commercial sense, the group does not make marketable work and they are not represented by a commercial gallery. All its members have their own ways of paying the bills, but their practice is very rigorous and their work is well-known nationally and internationally. And they have developed a resilience to the demands and pressures that most artists feel, oftentimes rightly so, to move to a coast where there is a stronger marketplace for their work.

HM: *At the same time, I think their resilience is cobbled together; it's a month-to-month resilience. "How long can I stretch this out, what do I have to do next month to pay the bills? What do I have to do next month to keep my volunteers energized?" I think the questions that these artists are asking are not always strategically planned; they're kind of feeling it out as they go. I think this kind of condition has huge implications for the ways that art schools should be functioning and the ways that non-profits that support artists should be functioning. I actually don't think we've reached a point where—within academia or within non-profit artist support models—we're able to adequately recognize the unique market pressures or "lack-of-market" pressures that exist for artists living in the Midwest.*

CC: I think what you're referring to is a new phenomenon for artists. It's quite typical for an institution to be lagging behind in knowing and implementing effective tools to properly support artists because the institution is, in many ways, responding to the current situation of artists. So I agree. We're not there yet. But in many ways both of our institutions recognize that fact and hold direct support for artists at their mission's core. And there are more institutions—small, scrappy non-profits in the Midwest—that are working in this way and have identified this because there is a larger artist community that is less market-driven than on the coasts.

HM: *And I think it's incumbent upon us to recognize the range of opportunities through which we can effectively support artists. Of course, that happens through exhibitions and residencies and community engagement projects, but also employment, contract labor...*

CC: Invitations to dinner parties...

HM: *Invitations to dinner parties! One thing that I'm particularly excited about is having recently been able to commission James Woodfill to do a large sequence of infrastructure commissions at the Bemis Center for Contemporary Arts. Jim redesigned our library; he's redesigning our staff offices, and he's designed and fabricated a hundred-foot-long guardrail, handrails, exterior lighting, and interior signage. So this is now a pretty extensive project. But something that we're asking is: "Regardless of what the project or initiative is, how can an artist be at the center of that project or process?"*

Whoop Dee Doo has been to Omaha twice. It was remarkable to me how—on an extremely compressed budget—they were able to put so much energy into their performances. Aaron Storck is about to start a residency at Bemis. He was also in the exhibition Hopey Changey Things *last year. These relationships build over time and they become richer and the possibilities become larger. I think it's important for organizations operating in the Midwest to think about two things: their role within a global context of presenting and producing contemporary art, but also their role in supporting and growing the process and presentation of artists who are living in the Midwest. I think often the debate that happens from an arts organization perspective is: "Who are we here to support, and who are we here to present? Are we supporting contemporary art in a global way and presenting it to a local audience? What is the scope of our support and audience?" So those questions and that kind of geographic elasticity as it relates to one's mission are important things to consider. It's not ultimately about importing and exporting, it's about allowing things to exist side by side. And it's about creating a platform where that existence seems seamless, where it's not anointed as a local artist institution or a national/global artist institution—those types of programs need to operate within the same organization.*

CC: With all of that in mind, I think it would be relevant to ask about the idea of a new American Regionalism. What is that really? What could it look like? Is it viable? Is it useful? Is it something that would actually benefit artists in terms of how they think about their work and how they present it to the public?

HM: *Yeah... I think it's impossible to tidy up those questions. They will probably remain questions. It's going to sound like a Chamber of Commerce idea, but I think the retention of artists in a given place is incredibly important. As attrition happens, as artists move from Kansas City to New York or from Omaha to Portland or Seattle or wherever, the stability of the cultural identity of that place dissolves or becomes* *transitional. Dave Hickey talked about this maybe 10 years ago—this idea of losing a region's cultural identity. His example was that 20 to 30 years ago, if you went to Seattle and you went to the Seattle Art Museum, you saw the best painter in Seattle. Now, everywhere you go you see the newest Anish Kapoor piece. The implication is that this extreme globalization strategy ultimately serves to homogenize culture. It becomes this even, flat, predictable space in which, regardless of where you're at, you're going to see the same things, which is what the Biennale trend is doing. It feels both dangerous and extremely exciting, and so how do you expand those parameters, how do you begin to contextualize Anish Kapoor's work alongside the most interesting painter in Seattle? I think that's a curatorial question, not a question for the artist. I think the question for the artist is, what do you need to make your practice work in the city that you're living in? I had a conversation with Whoop Dee Doo recently where the group suggested that it's somehow considering leaving Kansas City, which seems heart-wrenching. I think there's something so interesting about this practice that is rooted in a place but is elastic enough to move around the world—and when they land in a new city, whether it's Portland or somewhere in Sweden, the work is about that place, but it's also about Kansas City. And it's about the specific cultural energy and camaraderie and spirit that lives in that city and within that artist community. That's a camaraderie that I've never witnessed anywhere else.*

CC: The Kansas—and Missouri—based artists in this exhibition are all seriously thinking about, and incorporating and reflecting on, their immediate contexts—the people and places that make up their everyday experiences. Whether it's the present or events that took place during the 1960s, I think that one of the points to be made is that these artists are engaged in their environments, but they do need to make those environments, like you said, work for them. No matter where those artists were to move to next, they would immediately dig into their communities and flesh out what interests them. It's not about this place versus that place; it's more about finding the unique qualities of every place. Whether or not that discovery plays into the larger conversation of this burgeoning category of Regionalism, I'm not sure.

HM: *There's something about the Kansas City region that makes the possibility of Regionalism particularly potent. It's about the place itself. There's this idea that there's no more perfectly American place than the 75-mile radius surrounding where the Kaw River meets the Missouri River, which is Kansas City. There's also this idea that Kansas City is the northern-most Southern city, the eastern-most Western city, the western-most Eastern city, the southern-most Northern city. It's the vortex where the cultural Venn diagram of our country meets. On the other hand, it's the place where nothing meets up, and it's this kind of weird void that's constantly receiving pressure from every side. And, within that void and the negotiation of various pressures, the uncanny emerges. For me, that's the thing that binds the work of these four artists, something about the uncanny within the mundane. The idea of the* unheimlich*—it's a sense of being thrown off balance from the place that seems like it should be the most balanced. This is Middle America, and it's completely out of equilibrium.*

CC: I wonder if this is specific to *here* or if it is happening everywhere. Perhaps that's what the other artists in the exhibition will illustrate.

HM: *I hope to learn.*

CC: What's your learning style?

HM: *It used to be spatial, now it's kinesthetic. I have to touch things.*

CC: Have fun touching.

Hesse McGraw is Chief Curator at the Bemis Center for Contemporary Arts in Omaha, Nebraska. At the Bemis Center, he has presented projects with Aaron Storck and Whoop Dee Doo. He was the founding director of Paragraph in Kansas City and the former associate director of Max Protetch Gallery in New York City.

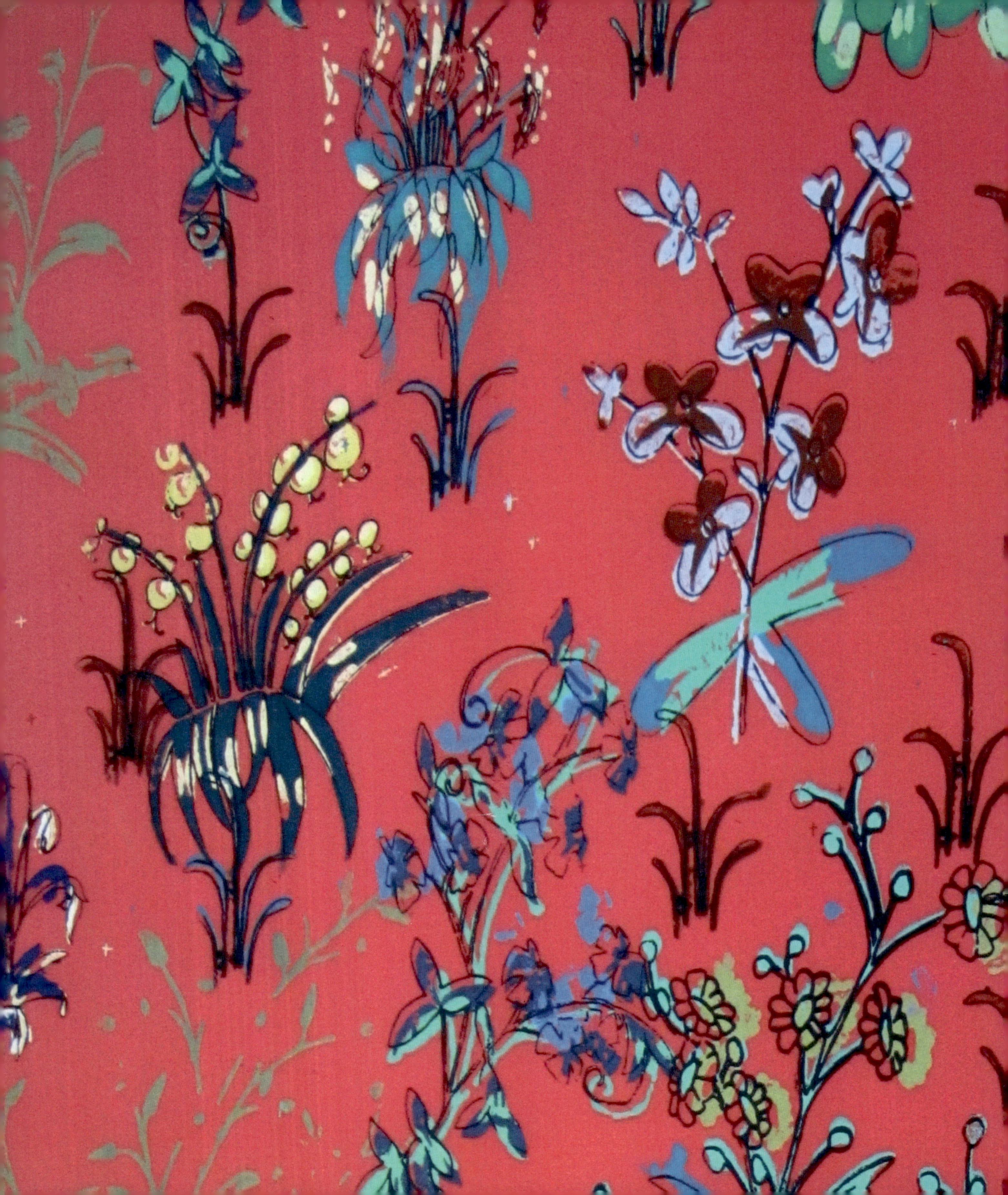

A Local Culture: tradition and risk in Cincinnati

BY MARK HARRIS

Previous spread:
Guy Michael Davis and Katie Parker
Wallpaper detail from
Hy-que Monkey in Captivity, 2011
See exhibition checklist
Photo courtesy of the artists

daydreaming of success
of enhancing culture, of collaboration
bringing this city up with all of our brilliance
bringing this city to life with all of our passion
filling this city up with our art, with our sounds
with our faces and ideas

Excerpted from "Rubble of The Mind" by Jim Swill,
Caustic Nostalgia: selected works 2007–2010, self-published chapbook

Here is Cincinnati, a medium-sized city in the southwest corner of Ohio, across from Kentucky's smaller riverside towns of Newport and Covington and only an hour and a half's drive from Indianapolis, Louisville, or Lexington; close enough, therefore, to form one center of a tri-state cultural area whose art networks sporadically intersect. Though Cincinnati may be the more cohesive and prosperous art center in the region this is not by much of a margin. All these cities suffer from a low ebb of economic activity and dwindling state support which undermines their institutions' abilities to prosper in ways that would enable them to secure an important role for contemporary art in the region. There is never enough local support and investment in art to initiate the kind of urban engagement with contemporary visual practices that could attract the migration of new businesses and raise a city's confidence in its creative identity. In that sense Cincinnati is quite dissimilar to Vancouver, Chicago, or Philadelphia, all cities with strong art institutions and dependable public and private support.

It is, however, remarkable that Cincinnati's underfunded and understaffed institutions, such as the Weston Art Gallery and Contemporary Art Center, are able to pull off such impressive shows of local and national artists. With a steady supporting hubbub of background activity led by artist-run spaces, university and art academy galleries, and some commercial spaces of national reach, there is always good, new art visible. The artists selected from Cincinnati for ***here.*** represent a cross-section of the kinds of engagement enabled by this bare-bones but functional gallery system. Ranging from a university faculty member, the founder of a former artist-run space, a member of a DIY music and art collective, and an artist without commercial representation and unaffiliated with any group or institution, you have a selection that displays the extent of economies in which local artists are embedded.

Because Cincinnati is very affordable,[1] and offers many options for live-work spaces, the students of the city's art programs frequently stay after graduation. For the enterprising there are unusual opportunities for rental and purchase and, although the business livelihoods are precarious, these affordable areas are far from being urban wastelands. Northside, Brighton, and Over-the-Rhine retain much of their 19th century Italianate architecture and possess strong neighborhood identities. Though the drug problems in Over-the-Rhine are little changed from their depiction in Steven Soderbergh's film *Traffic*,[2] that neighborhood has restaurants, bakeries, cafés, and galleries and is only a five-minute walk from the downtown business and entertainment district. Brighton neighborhood artists have benefited from a single benevolent property owner, Fred Lane,[3] who has welcomed many into the area with his low rent live-work industrial spaces. Northside's now thriving alternative businesses include unconventional bars and restaurants alongside galleries, vintage clothing, furniture, and vinyl record stores.

Along with art handling and front desk jobs in museums, galleries, and libraries, these businesses provide a survival wage and flexible hours for many artists. Non-profits, such as ArtWorks, Happen Inc., and Prairie,[4] involve young artists in public art projects or urban educational initiatives and engage key local businesses in sponsorship roles. Importantly, since these neighborhoods are close to one another and their architectural fabric is intact, they further the perception of a contained and lively visual arts community whose gallery programs nevertheless develop independently of one another. The alternative galleries in Cincinnati have been an essential feature of the emergence of local artists and the introduction of artwork from outside the city, and two of the artists in ***here.*** have played key roles in this narrative.[5]

The significant history of print in the city has indirectly impacted all the artists selected from Cincinnati.[6] The city's print shops were engaged with the beginnings of lithographic processes. Being the largest city on the westward migration route along the Ohio River,[7] German and Italian artist immigrants brought the stone lithography trade with them to Cincinnati, establishing some of the first commercial printing companies here and later influencing the development of curricula and facilities at local art schools. For example, from the mid-1800s, the Strobridge Lithographing Company was based in the center of Cincinnati, producing the first large-scale advertising for local concern Procter and Gamble before specializing in circus and movie posters. A large collection of these circus posters is held by the Cincinnati Art Museum where, during the 1940s and 50s, WPA graphics coordinator Gustave von Groschwitz worked as Curator of Prints. In the 1950s, the five Biennials of Color Lithography that von Groschwitz curated had an enormous influence on local artists, among them Jim Dine, who was taking classes at the Art Academy during this period.

Extending the city's engagement with printmaking into a series of print and exhibition projects with local and international artists, Mark Patsfall's Clay Street Press has been influential on many fronts in Cincinnati art life, helping to set up other local presses and designing and fabricating Nam June Paik video sculptures in the 1980s and 90s.[8] Patsfall's contacts in Germany and Korea have enabled him to bring international artists to Cincinnati and initiate projects like the *Fluxfax Portfolio*[9] he produced in 1994. He has provided a halfway house for students of the university and academy as they figure out how to move into professional life. In the early 1980s, Patsfall's donation of an old etching press to the School for Creative and Performing Arts (SCPA) initiated frequent art class study visits to Clay Street.[10] As a student at SCPA, Terence Hammonds interned with Patsfall, later becoming an assistant printer and installing his own exhibition, *Quiet Riot*, at Clay Street Press in 2006.[11]

Paul Coors' artist-run space, Publico, was next door to Clay Street Press. Publico's founding artists comprised of graduates from Art Academy and University of Cincinnati programs who sometimes worked with Patsfall to complete the graphics for their own gallery. With a strong emphasis on painting, sculpture, and print practices, Publico featured many local artists and brought in work from further afield, including projects by Ryan McGinness, David Ellis, Detroit's Object Orange, and Philadelphia's Vox Populi. And although not the only Publico artist-designer, Coors' designs for the gallery announcements sustained a run of a hundred or so smartly conceived posters, invitations, and magazines that left an unrivalled paper trail. Ceramics was one other industrial craft flourishing in 19th century Cincinnati,[12] although its success came late and was due to very different factors than those stimulating print production. Cincinnati ceramics studios, of which the most famous was Maria Longworth Nichols' Rookwood Pottery, grew from women's society initiatives promoting the development of Cincinnati manufacturing.[13] In the late 1880s, such advocacy led to the foundation of the Art Academy of Cincinnati and the Cincinnati Art Museum, where an emphasis was placed on building a historical collection of ceramics for study purposes. These Cincinnati women's advocacy groups were successful because they anchored their appeals for support to improvements in regional industrial design and the education of local communities. To some extent, the productive relationship that the University of Cincinnati's current industrial and graphic design programs have to regional businesses, like Proctor and Gamble and General Motors, is a legacy of those 19th century objectives.[14] Rookwood has recently relaunched in Cincinnati developing new ceramic product lines that reference original moulds and decoration.[15]

Skilled mould-makers themselves, Guy Michael Davis and Katie Parker are artists whose work is inspired by historical European examples, such as 17th century Meissen ceramics,[16] as well as 20th century assemblage practices, and the contemporary aesthetics of kitsch.[17] They scour flea markets and antique malls for overlooked decorative arts residue that can be modeled or scanned as 3D images, rescaled, output as rapid prototypes, converted into moulds, and variably decorated with decals and painted glazes. They apply technology to unconventional ends, like their recourse to rapid prototypes to emphasize the imperfections of found objects by their enlargement, or of letterpress to generate die-cut paper for use in assemblages.

The promiscuity of their scavenging and its transformation is a striking feature of their studio. On a shelf, there is a stuffed garfish waiting in reserve for a project. Along one wall is a series of lamps made from porcelain casts of a squirrel (that originated from an animal carcass Davis had taxidermied) shown slumped over a branch. Overhead is a chandelier made of crouching clay rats that were enlarged from a smaller toy prototype. On a table at the back of the studio, Davis has disassembled a plastic lobster so that he can make separate moulds of the legs, while on the wall hang two garishly colored crustacean decorations made for the resort restaurant trade. Another table is covered in pink letterpress covers for a sound art project collaboration with New York-based artist Ken Montgomery. To one side, Parker's die-cut paper work forms polychrome topiary models in the shape of a fir tree and a dog's body, and elsewhere lies a roll of wallpaper silkscreened in floral motifs derived from a medieval tapestry. In most cases, these are subversive decorative objects that question historical models, revealing continuity of image treatment but at the same time a dislocation from original contexts. Davis and Parker's accumulations bring together disparate sources to form indeterminate image conundrums in refined porcelain finishes that deliberately court kitsch. The aggregate structure of these works seems to condense the pandemonium of their heterogeneous studio stuff. Surprisingly, from that workroom wunderkammer emerge these refined porcelain conglomerates of meticulous surface finish and painted detail.

Davis and Parker's recent exhibition, *Still[ed] Life* (2011) at the Taft Museum, consisted of a group of scaled down clay replicas of Hiram Powers' portrait bust of William Taft's father, partially covered in decorative motifs and patterns sourced from the furnishings and artifacts of the museum itself (see page 116). The pieces became inventories of overlooked details of the building's furnishings. The busts were set on porcelain sconces installed around the room's perimeter. Adding to the sense of a museum simulacrum gone awry were several porcelain clusters of oddly matched still life objects (moles clambering through fruit, forexample), piled up in monochrome accumulations whose whiteness suggested ossified relics. The intricate and finely painted polychrome patterns on the busts sometimes ignored physiognomy, covering eyes or petering out halfway across a form. Part of this work's interest derived from appearing both industrially replicated and handmade, with the sleek surface quality of commercially produced statuettes and the nuanced irregularities of handpainted patterns.

In terms of fabrication techniques, Davis and Parker's connection with these Cincinnati artisanal traditions is as resourceful modernizers who arrive at traditionally finished porcelain mutations through contemporary modeling processes. Recalling earlier Cincinnati pottery traditions, they sustain a workshop/factory practice, effectively a cottage industry for the production of multiples. Their serial works are anti-individualistic and anti-expressive, celebrating the anonymity of production where their use of mould-making and rapid-prototype techniques further remove evidence of the hand. Their treatment of clay,[18] surface color, and firing is exact; the result of years of practice-based research. They develop a glass-like finish to the porcelain, embellished with the sharp detail of line-drawn decals they frequently use or the precise coloring of the Taft work.

As opposed to these rigorous technical procedures for handling clay, their appropriation of images is done more freely. Their sourced objects often originate in Cincinnati but most are of indeterminate origin. The clockwork toy monkey, whose replicas comprise *Hy-que Monkey in Captivity* (2011) and is one of their installations for ***here.***, was found in a local antique mall but was most likely manufactured abroad (see page 116). Intending the porcelain finish of their figurines to evoke the Meissen monkey musicians that were first produced in 1730, Davis and Parker mash up histories by positioning their sculptures in front of two different oval-shaped examples of wallpaper, hand-printed with motifs from the Cluny Museum's *Lady and the Unicorn* tapestries.[20] Davis and Parker are as curious about the taxidermy forms of animal bodies as they are in how these bodies have been rendered in historical craft and modern commercial replicas. They see these as divergent ways in which the natural world has been interpreted, and note how those representations have themselves become models for further replication and distortion through global industrialization.

This obscuring of boundaries between the natural and the manufactured acquires other inflections in the work of Terence Hammonds, where images drawn from popular culture and civil rights history are embedded in acanthus leaf motifs. For the *Quiet Riot* show that he made at Clay Street Press, Terence Hammonds, like Davis and Parker, produced wallpaper that incorporated a specific decorative motif. He first made this work as an undergraduate senior at the School of the Museum of Fine Arts in Boston after noticing a particular wallpaper vignette in the background of a music video for *Shake It Fast* (2000) by Louisiana rapper Mystikal, who had used the mansion from the movie *Gone With The Wind* (1939) as a set location. Hammonds screenprinted this vignette as the repeating motif of his wallpaper. In the center of each, he incorporated images from a popular book on breakdancing,[21] and included portraits of the first two-hundred-and-fifty rap music performers selected from *Ego trip's book of rap lists*[22] and other sources, arranged randomly across the repeated pattern. Standing against the wallpaper, a dining room cabinet contained tableware with screened news images of protests from black history during the 1960s. When this work was reinstalled at Clay Street Press, Hammonds replaced the generic dishware with mid-century Russel Wright tableware, so as to be more specific to Cincinnati,[23] and he propped up the cabinet on secondhand beat culture books like those by LeRoi Jones and Normal Mailer's *The White Negro*,[24] collected by Hammonds in the course of a search for origins of the concept of "cool."

These procedures, developed early in his career, of inserting images of protest and pleasure into the domestic fabric have remained central to Hammonds' practice. For his recent exhibition at Cincinnati's Aisle Gallery, he covered most of a long wall with a work called *Stand Up! Organize!* (2010), a set of conjoined, framed silkscreen prints in which he had embedded Civil Rights imagery amongst vignettes of red and yellow flames (see page 120). The collection of images used in that work included photos of draft card burning and of Timothy Leary, amongst representations of demonstrations and portraits of Black Liberation

Movement leaders. Hammonds explains: "With that piece I was trying to get away from the work just being about Civil Rights...there was a whole social upheaval happening that was really more at the point of what I was trying to get at...I'd hope for it to be more universal. There's something about using black bodies in my art that I want to do, but I don't want it to necessarily be just about the African American experience. So I think they're American stories, not just African American stories."[25] Here the representation of Civil Rights activism as an incendiary history was tempered by the attractive overall patterning that lured in the unsuspecting viewer.[26]

Hammonds feels close to these news images because they were part of the stories his mother would tell him growing up, while musicians like James Brown that he includes in the work stand for the music his mother would listen to.[27] That these representations emerge from the background city clamor and domestic sanctuary of his childhood, and are not solely a protest against a history of oppressive state actions, would make Hammonds' use of décor and furnishings a setting for his own family's life at the center of wider struggles, even if the photographs are only occasionally of Cincinnati. For example, the 2001 riots that occurred in Cincinnati[28] suddenly brought Civil Rights history into the present day for Hammonds, who at the time was living in Boston. Watching CNN, he saw a brick thrown through a window of his mother's building, and these events remain a powerful source of new imagery. Recently, Hammonds has been photographing the architectural details of a house on Dayton Street, just behind the Brighton location where he lives, finding himself fascinated by the details in wood carving, wallpaper, and glazed tile work that are the residue of the achievements of 19th century Cincinnati craftsmen.[29]

In a group of works quite distinct from his silkscreen prints, Hammonds makes austere graphite drawings that greatly enlarge Civil Rights era buttons. Isolated in the center of the paper, these summarily sketched circular images resemble lithographic prints, an association Hammonds cultivates. In one image, two palms meet in an interracial handshake as they are framed by the words "UNITED WE SHALL OVERCOME"; in another is the single word "GROW" in a condensed sans-serif white font against a black background. Two other images depict buttons of The Congress of Racial Equality, one saying "FREEDOM NOW CORE" and the other, "SUPPORT CORE SIT-INS." The text is always uppercase and the graphics economical and direct. One thing that interests Hammonds in these works is the equivalency of visual thresholds for effective communication in artwork and mass culture. The buttons are the most reductive form for communicating an affiliation to the highly complex history, mission, and structure of an organization like CORE, whose shift from a racially balanced, peaceful protest group in the 1940s to militant Black Power advocacy in the 1960s charts key changes in international protest movements of the time.

Hammonds' work shows a complex perspective on protest movements with contrasting photographs of Civil Rights turbulence that might juxtapose iconic portraits of Angela Davis, a reflective Nina Simone, naked men embracing, or a photograph of a white woman injured in riots, this last being an image that was used as anti-black propaganda by George Wallace.[30] Hammonds is not only using the most conspicuous Civil Rights imagery, but he is also interested in overlooked pictures that may reveal more of the complexity of that time. In a very different way to Hammonds, Paul Coors has also used print to reference histories, albeit ones with an indeterminate or rootless location in the past. In developing a trademark Publico design look, Coors arrived at a retro-frontier graphic where old-style poster typefaces and a hand drawn approach conveyed a down-to-earth feel, while enacting a semantic detour of playfully misleading signs that introduced deviations in communication. In Publico's program and Coors' work, inventiveness of idea and image was relished above all. In the 2005 one-person show titled *Them*, that Coors held at Publico, some eight mixed-media works used sharp-witted visual jokes and graphic elements to set up a play on language and concept. The painted paper work *Some of Them* showed twenty versions of the word "Them" hovering over a blue background, in the style of sensationalist typefaces found on the posters for 1950's Hammer Studios horror movies.

Publico closed its doors in January 2008 and, in celebration of its achievements, an intense month-long series of exhibitions and events incorporating interests of the previous five years were held. Film screenings, music performances, poetry readings, photography, painting and kinetic sculpture exhibitions, food art displays, and parties followed one another in rapid succession. Before the end of that year, Publico was given an end-of-career retrospective by the Weston Art Gallery.[31]

For a year or two after, Paul Coors worked on less declamatory material, including two local partnership projects using text and sound. In the first of these, Coors' design for the vinyl LP foldout sleeve for *Receiver* included eight images (several of which modified Velvet Underground album imagery) to provide local musician Spencer Yeh with an unconventional score to make the music for the record contained within. The second project, called *I Want This Forever*, was a book of four tipped-in postcards and a two-sided print, all designed by Coors as oracular images for which poet Dana Ward's luminous writing provided empathic commentary in the form of a poem, satirical play, short story, and movie review, all focusing on Cincinnati.

Since then, Coors' tactic of intersecting handmade with digital processes has confounded distinctions between the two and, at times, incorporated error as a design feature. In the 2010 cover design for the 7-inch Flaherty/Corsano/Yeh and Oren Ambarchi & Matt Skitz Sanders record, what looks like digitally-rendered, thickly-matted hair in fact derives from a straightforward ballpoint drawing. Other record covers apply print misregistration, indecipherable transparent images, and an exaggerated halftone screen effect to interfere with legibility. In the production of several other pieces, like the poster for the band In Tall Buildings and the cover for musician Epstein's[32] *Seeless See* cover (both 2011), Coors manipulates a sheet of text as a photocopy, generating a distorted original that can later be digitally reworked. As it develops, Coors' work is characterized by a passion for realigning signifiers. Coors has said, "I'm interested in the imagery of advertising (and design in general) because it's perhaps the most commonplace aesthetic language; however, it's problematic in that it often provides simplistic answers and asks very few (if any) questions."[33]

This manual interference with electronic processes was also used by Coors in his 2010 exhibition at Clay Street Press, which suggests the technique preceded its application to design projects. In that show, Coors worked again with Ward to produce a mural-sized vinyl text work titled *Tell me what else you need from me (That's what C-3PO said)*, where each word underwent extensive photocopier stretching and fragmentation before digital finishing, the incoherence of the text accentuated by its distortion. As has been the pattern in other shows, very few pieces of work shared a resemblance to one another. Two postcard installations (both 2009) used circular and diagonal arrangements of pushpins to secure to the wall hundreds of images of the costume that Michael Jackson, had he lived, intended to wear on his world tour. Two smaller works, *Thisa Way, Thata Way* and *Paper*, used geometric arrangements of numerous colored pushpins stuck into framed prints on which the faintest halftone image of a folded sheet of paper had been silkscreened. Also in the show were a series of strange monoprints titled *Living Room*, made from impressions of poured wax.

These coiling shapes, resembling images of explosions, bore no comparison to Coors' earlier work other than by their shared disparity.

Over the last four years, there have been several projects that explicitly intersect Coors' design and art practices. The *Collapsible Kiosk* (2008)—made for the live acts and film screening marking Publico's last appearance at the Weston Art Gallery—resembles nothing so much as a Gustave Klutsis agitprop kiosk from the 1920s.[34] With its retractable screen, enclosed sound system with suspended speakers, drawers for print material, and festooned with banners and flags, it poses as the mothership for all the publicity material Publico generated down the years. Included in ***here.*** are Coors' fake offset litho movie posters that crash together disparate sources to produce image labyrinths (see page 114). Of these Coors explains: "I feel it's important to consistently reevaluate the present, and its cultural artifacts, in order to give way to an unexpected (and hopefully better) future. Movie posters seemed like an appropriate vehicle for this idea, considering that a poster's function is to be a stand-in representation/advertisement for a much larger, more complex idea."[35] In these intricate and cryptic symbolic representations, we arrive at a contemporary version of baroque allegory, legible only to those whose childhood and contemporary milieu share the cultural references. Cumulatively, the posters offer perspectives on a world distorted by mass culture mediation. As if lacking a space to think that is not polluted by advertising, they cannily resort to deploying his childhood movie icons in an enquiry into the meanings of adolescent and adult experiences. The viewer's pleasure is in decipherment; in the unscrambling and then re-entanglement of photographer William Eggleston and *The Wizard of Oz*'s Dorothy, of rapper Lil' Wayne and the film *E.T.*, of media personality Paris Hilton and actress Zooey Deschanel, and politician Dick Cheney and the animated show *Looney Tunes*. Oversized and glaring, they leave the handmade far behind for a cleaner mass-produced look, for Coors has said he would like them to be printed industrially, and to have no hand in their production.[36]

Coors' delight in the play of indifference and engagement afforded in confronting mass culture imagery would have no traction in Bunk's aesthetic, whose posters revive early 20th century critical montage practices and suggest a prelapsarian aesthetic position—one still optimistic for the impact of radical initiatives. With a scathing attitude toward mass culture and no more than a passing interest in local art circles, Bunk News has worked hard to maintain a position of independence and integrity, based as much on avoiding contamination from external influences as on sustaining a set of raw practices that are as direct as possible in their communication. There is no postmodern irony or mediated enquiry here.

Like that of all radical groups, Bunk News' position as cultural outsiders is complicated by experimental and retrenched artistic strategies (see page 106). With echoes of 19th century settlers moving westward and relying on their own wits to survive, Bunk has enacted a retreat into the urban interior, away from conventional institutions and networks. One of Bunk's frequent partners, Mavis Concave of Realicide,[37] explains, "You don't pay for school; you might drop a little money on some equipment, like a $200 laptop on Craig's List; download a cracked version of Photoshop, and get to work... Yeah, it's partially illegal, but we're not rich. DIY's also like an act of social defiance, proving you can do it. You don't have to rely on what they tell you to rely on."[38] Here, resourcefulness and cultural integrity matter most.

Emerging from local DIY music and art circles, Cincinnati residents Graham Nelson, Chris Liedtke, Davy Howard, Ben Brown, and Steve Adkins founded Bunk News in 2005 as a means of coordinating art parties in various apartments where murals, paintings, and video projections could be made and bands could perform. Before starting work with John Rich and Jon Lorenz of Cincinnati experimental noise and sound art space Art Damage, local musician Chris Adams worked with Brown to secure the lease on the Findlay Street ground-floor warehouse space that, for most of that year, served as their optimal venue, a place that allowed their experimental programming full scope with an expanded team of participants. Brown then worked as a liaison for Evolve performers Jim Swill and Colin Murray, and for musicians Robert Inhuman, Kevin Bruce, and others to book touring bands at this new space, then called Bunk Spot.

Cincinnati's ready supply of empty buildings and storefronts has helped many artists' spaces get established. In local artist-run history, most of these galleries have been concentrated in Over-the-Rhine, the large area of densely clustered residential buildings, where it might have been difficult to find a remote warehouse space to stage the noisy events that Bunk was planning. At $500 a month, their rent on the Findlay Street space was manageable, and the remote location meant the sound was not a problem for neighbors. The attraction for Bunk, if only by some unspoken consensus, was this unusual opportunity to generate an innovative, energized collective of art and music.[39] In this way, it became a kind of regional magnet, pulling participants back to Cincinnati from other locations once they recognized the potential of the new space. For example, Swill returned to Cincinnati from St. Louis, and Concave returned from Boston.

Surrounding a raw industrial space that was infinitely adaptable and durable, Bunk's hallways were regularly tagged and filled with improvisatory installations like skateboard ramps made out of recycled signs and scrap wood. None of the spaces Swill and Concave performed in around the country were like Bunk Spot, with its flexibility allowing for a build of energy and experimentation. The attraction for many of the participants was the open, non-exclusivity of the events. The venue was remote enough in a sufficiently deserted part of town to put off all but the most committed. However, this was changed by a front page article in the local alternative newspaper *City Beat*,[40] which stimulated sudden interest from people well outside Bunk's circle of acquaintances. Attendance increased dramatically to a peak of over 600 visitors on the night of one exhibition and concert. Since the pay-what-you-like policy was only loosely adhered to, the potential for raising money to invest in programming went by the wayside.

For the launch of Evolve's LP in late 2009, Bunk Spot staged several distinct events. Coordinated by local artist Allie Elrod, a multimedia installation, running the full length of the eastern wall of the large main space, was conceived as a reaction to Evolve's music. Amongst the many artists involved in its production were Adkins, Alexandria Dupont, Iza McIlvain, Ava Roberts, and Tim Larson, students from both the Art Academy and University of Cincinnati. Tucked into the northwest corner of Bunk Spot were several tables on which a wide range of food, including vegetable stews and fruit pies (all salvaged from Trader Joe's dumpsters), was being served. Towards the center of the room, bunches of flowers were for the taking; like the food, rescued from local trash. A high-energy gig by Realicide occurred early on, with Concave and Swill participating alongside other singers. Swill and Murray, as Evolve, were the last to play; Murray wearing his typical stage outfit of a dress and wig, and Swill out front singing, declaring, rapping with great intensity. After pausing for a change of set and costume, Swill led five other performers, parodically dressed as a degenerate Procter and Gamble board of directors in suits and diapers, in a sketch criticizing the ruthless promotion of commodities and their excessive consumption. Across the course of the evening's events, building towards an apotheosis of collective ideals, Bunk News succeeded in enabling a set of new experiences to be felt.

Of the Cincinnati artists in ***here.***, Bunk News' considerable paper trail is exceptional for current artist-run spaces, although they have none of the regard for curating it that Coors' Publico demonstrated. According to Swill,[41] whose solo and group performances (with Realicide or Evolve) have been at the center of Bunk's activities, his interest in the posters lasts only until the show they publicize is underway. After that, he is focused on the next event. Swill's posters and poetry chapbooks are sometimes anarchically humorous montages of hand drawn text and image. For the 2009 Bunk show *Last Supper*,[42] he substituted Disney cartoon heads for the disciples in Leonardo da Vinci's painting and placed corporate logos across the front of the tablecloth. In another work, the images of an enlarged ant and hand appear to float over a background of a star-filled galaxy. Many of Bunk News' 11 x 17 inch posters are in the tradition of photocopied fliers for band performances enduring since the 1970s. Local designer Brian Uhl's posters, for example, are a compelling accumulation of line-drawn horror vacui compositions combining humorous with apocalyptic imagery. Brown's posters show an interest in montages of saturated color and skillful contrasts of scale, where cinematic panoramas suggestive of science fiction wastelands are juxtaposed with retro images from 1960s lifestyle magazines and incorporate a wide array of typefaces.

The last show at Bunk Spot was in November 2009, after which the organization moved their events to the Mockbee in Brighton.[43] As a shared space, this hasn't allowed them the same freedom as Findlay Street. While providing continuity, the temporary status of the Mockbee venue has afforded the many participants and organizers of Bunk News the opportunity to review their roles and the future of the collective.

This fondness for bricolage and a resourcefulness with different print and fabrication techniques, both improvised and carefully practiced, is an approach that Bunk shares in common with other Cincinnati artists and performers. The comparison, however, is one of degree, for while Bunk News' dumpster-salvaged catering and self-published music and poetry may lie at the furthest extremity of DIY culture, Hammonds' sampling of civil rights imagery and black music icons screened on wallpaper and on found ceramics lies somewhere towards the center alongside Davis and Parker's hybrid and historically-savvy constructions. By contrast, Coors' self-financed silkscreen, book, and record collaborations follow a studio model but hover liminally at the threshold of different art, music, and poetry economies, engaged as he is with self-published records and books as well as commissioned design work.

Although the verse by Swill, that opens this essay, directs an ambition towards an entire city, in practice the posters and chapbooks circulating around Bunk News take the artisan's approach underground towards extreme low budget and lo-fi productions tailored for a tightly defined audience of sympathetic artists and musicians, whose responses are the primary benchmark with which Bunk measures their own success. Engaged as they are with disparate local audiences and institutions, for each of the other artists "local" has a very particular complexion. Given his working partnerships with confidants, Coors sustains a close inner circle as a legacy of his time with Publico. The devices used by his work convert public images into private hieroglyphs that double as a supposedly legible common language of abstract motifs connected to other contemporary art practices. It is this subterfuge and deflection of interpretation that gives Coors' work its allegorical dimension. Hammonds achieves something similar by embedding personal history in the visual evidence of Civil Rights struggles whose massively circulated documentation beguiles us into assuming this to be a common inheritance of agreed upon meaning. Yet, by adding to this legacy his own interests in punk and rap music and in Cincinnati decorative arts, Hammonds shows how faceted local history becomes in a process of nuanced reflection independent from more totalizing national narratives. Like Hammonds, Davis and Parker have been engaged in extensively reworking local craft techniques, although their modeling and decorating zeal may surpass the traditional skills of their predecessors and thus underline their prodigal appropriations of source material with new irony. Their pleasure in surrendering to exacting traditional methods, while maximizing the license that contemporary art strategies have granted to the conflation of aberrant imagery, has certainly been facilitated by the opportunity for invention and risk afforded by an enthusiastic local audience.

To a large extent, the audience for Cincinnati's artists is always going to be homegrown and somewhat narrowly circumscribed. The absence of institutional mechanisms and visionary curators, gallerists, or collectors that might propel local art to national attention prompts a curious art community to a high level of attainment and mutual encouragement on home base. What enables good art to be produced in Cincinnati are rich local histories, on which to draw for material and content and the space and time to bring forward new ideas and to work through aesthetic innovations without much distraction. Paradoxically, the circumstances that prevent this art from circulating at a national level are the same that enable it to gain its distinctive local color and depth.

[1] Writing for Forbes.com in January 2011, Morgan Brennan listed Cincinnati as fifth in the nation for affordability in a comparison that included cost of living index factors. http://www.forbes.com/2011/01/06/bargain-cities-affordable-real-estate-personal-finance.html.

[2] Released in 2000, Soderburgh's *Traffic* was a commercial cinema narrative of the North American drug trade economies and their impact on individual lives. The family of the federal drug tsar, played by Michael Douglas, was depicted living in Indian Hill, the most prosperous Cincinnati suburb, with his daughter scoring her drugs in Over-the-Rhine.

[3] Looking for ways to stabilize a neglected neighborhood, Lane has been buying and then leasing studio and gallery spaces in Brighton to artists, architects, and performers at low rents since the mid-90s.

[4] ArtWorks is located in Over-the-Rhine, and Prairie and Happen, Inc. in Northside.

[5] Paul Coors led the collective of artists and poets in directing Publico during its five years of exhibitions, readings, and concerts in Over-the-Rhine, while Ben Brown worked with other artists and musicians to set up Bunk News which has, over the years, migrated from one space to another.

[6] I am indebted to local printmakers Don Kelley, Jim Williams, and Mark Patsfall for information about the development of lithography in Cincinnati. 19th-century German lithographers brought their expertise (and Bavarian litho stones) for hand drawn illustrations in local print media, stimulating the early establishment of printmaking classes at the Art Academy, and later at the University of Cincinnati.

[7] Between 1803 (when Ohio achieved statehood) and 1840, the immigrant population of Ohio increased thirty-fold. Such growth was facilitated by the ready passage offered along the Ohio River, which had not been safely navigable until the defeat of the Native American Western Confederacy at the end of the 18th century.

[8] Working with Nam June Paik and Carl Solway Gallery during the 1980s and 90s, Patsfall constructed and installed some 300 Paik works as public commissions and gallery pieces. This process was outlined in detail by Solway in the Paik Round Table discussions held at the University of Cincinnati in 2010. http://www.daapspace.daap.uc.edu/art/eart/paik/tabletopics.html.

[9] This project, published by Paik and Patsfall, involved thirty-five Fluxus artists in producing a portfolio of lithographs and screenprints where the artwork and print instructions were faxed in to Clay Street Press. http://www.patsfallgraphics.com/pages/fluxfax.html.

[10] Patsfall, correspondence with the author.

[11] Hammonds, conversation with the author.

[12] Comparisons drawn between domestic and international ceramics seen at the 1876 Philadelphia Centennial led to an understanding that American work was inferior to European and Chinese examples. The strong engagement of women in American cultural organizations, including Cincinnati, and their presence as exhibitors in the Women's Pavilion in the Philadelphia Centennial, enabled a concerted redress of this perceived inferiority. Exhibiting at the Centennial were Cincinnati ceramicists Mary Louise McLaughlin, who ran the women's Pottery Club that produced work and raised funds for the Centennial, and Maria Longworth Nichols, who later established Rookwood Pottery and by the late 1880s gained international recognition for her work. (In conversation with Amy Dehan, Curator of Decorative Arts at the Cincinnati Art Museum. See also Millard F. Rogers Jr., Kenneth R. Trapp, Betty L. Zimmerman, and Carole W. Schwartz, *Cincinnati Art Museum: Art Palace of the West–A Centennial Tribute, 1881-1981* (Cincinnati: Cincinnati Art Museum, 1981).

[13]Directed by philanthropist Elizabeth Perry, The Women's Art Museum Association of Cincinnati was an early arts and manufacturing advocacy organization lasting from 1877-86. It grew out of an earlier group that successfully fundraised towards the construction of the Women's Pavilion at the Philadelphia Centennial. Without The Association's diligent planning and fundraising to set up educational and museum facilities, it is unlikely that the Cincinnati Art Museum would have been inaugurated as early as 1881 nor benefited at the outset from an enduringly stable financial base.

[14]Confirmed in communication with Robert Probst, Dean of the College of Design, Architecture, Art, and Planning at the University of Cincinnati.

[15]Rookwood still owns some 4,000 moulds from the 1880s through the 1930s but can no longer use original glaze recipes that once incorporated lead and uranium. (In conversation with Terence Hammonds who works at the pottery studio and with Chip DeMois, President and CEO of Rookwood.)

[16]Both Davis and Parker have completed artist residencies at a ceramics factory in Dresden not far from where Meissen ceramics continue to be manufactured.

[17]See Gillo Dofles, *Kitsch: The world of bad taste* (New York: Universe Books, 1970). Generally impatient with the contemporary proliferation of kitsch, Dorfles nevertheless admits that "some of the most ghastly objects can be transformed into artistically positive elements, if not masterpieces, which aim to create a sophisticated atmosphere through the devaluation/revaluation of those objects..." (22).

[18]They use kaolin clay without impurities, adding silica and a melting agent to achieve a specific limpid finish.

[19]The Nymphenburg porcelain wolf's head they recently replicated probably ended up in Cincinnati through German immigration.

[20]In conversation with the artists.

[21]Hammons explains that the book was *Breakdancing: Mr. Fresh and the Supreme Rockers show you how to do it!* (New York: Avon Books, 1984).

[22]Sacha Jenkins et al., *Ego trip's book of rap lists* (New York: ego trip Publications, Inc., 1999).

[23]Wright's early art training, while still in high school, was under Frank Duvenek at the Art Academy of Cincinnati.

[24]Poet and political activist LeRoi Jones, later Amiri Baraka, published his first book of poetry, *Preface to a Twenty Volume Suicide Note*, in 1961. Normal Mailer's *The White Negro* was published in 1957 by Lawrence Ferlinghetti's City Lights Press after first appearing as an article in the magazine *Dissent*.

[25]In conversation with the artist.

[26]The implication that the furnishings of our domestic lives reveal the violence underlying our prosperity, as if by negation, is familiar from Walter Benjamin's writing on the masking effect of bourgeois plush furnishings in the 19th century.

[27]In conversation with the artist.

[28]The riots followed the police shooting of Timothy Thomas in Over-the-Rhine. Thomas had been unarmed.

[29]The 1960s construction of Interstate 75, that split the Western part of the city in two and displaced tens of thousands of residents, most of them African American, accelerated the decline of so much of the area, including the historical section of Dayton Street. That many of the displaced families were relocated to Over-the-Rhine further entwines Hammonds' family history with that of the city.

[30]The white politician George Wallace moved opportunistically from liberal leanings to a pro-segregationist stance, playing on race fears to secure the Governorship of Alabama in 1962.

[31]The Weston Art Gallery exhibition featured most of Publico's publicity material and ephemera as well as new work by the remaining members, including a commissioned series of posters. A series of live poetry, film, and music events completed the retrospective.

[32]Epstein is one performing name for Roberto Carlos Lange.

[33]In communication with the artist.

[34]Gustave Klutsis was a revolutionary Russian artist, eventually executed on Stalin's orders, whose work included designs for propaganda kiosks, newsstands, and radio loudspeader structures.

[35]In communication with the artist.

[36]In conversation with the artist.

[37]Realicide (whose most enduring members were Jim Swill and brothers Mavis Concave and Robert Inhuman) and Evolve (Jim Swill and Colin Murray) have been the two Cincinnati bands whose working relationship with Ben Brown and other Bunk artist organizers made them de facto collaborators. Realicide stopped performing after a demanding European tour in 2010. The two bands have shared members and production and distribution practices.

[38]In conversation with the artist.

[39]In conversations with Ben Brown, Jim Swill, Mavis Concave, and Cincinnati artist Allie Elrod.

[40]This Adam Severing article was published in *City Beat* on May 13, 2009.

[41]In conversation with the artist.

[42]Leonardo da Vinci's *Last Supper* is a late 15th century painting on the end wall of the refectory of Santa Maria delle Grazie in Milan.

[43]In conversations, Brown has explained that since the Mockbee is not Bunk's own venue, they categorize their schedule events as Bunk @ Mockbee.

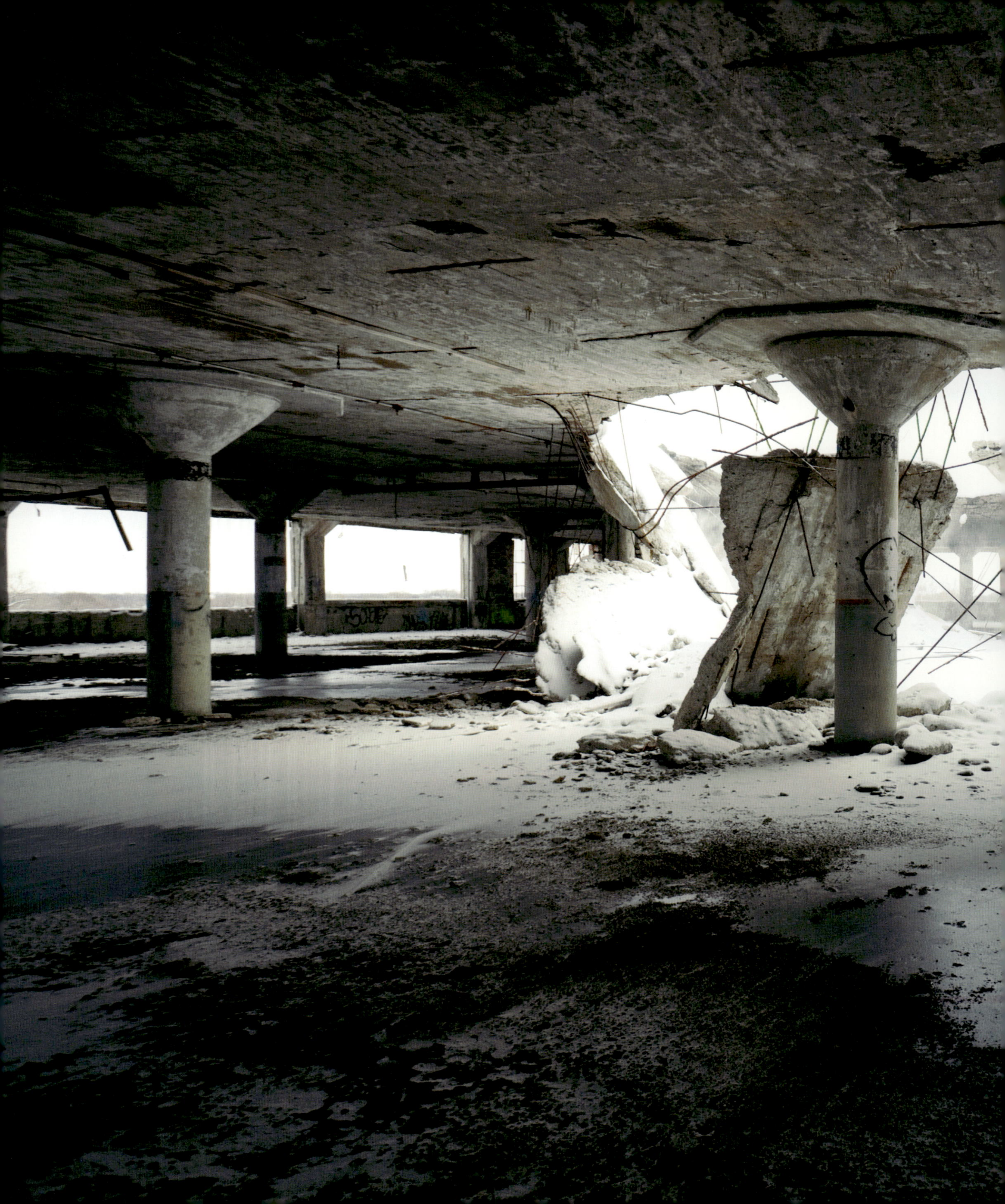

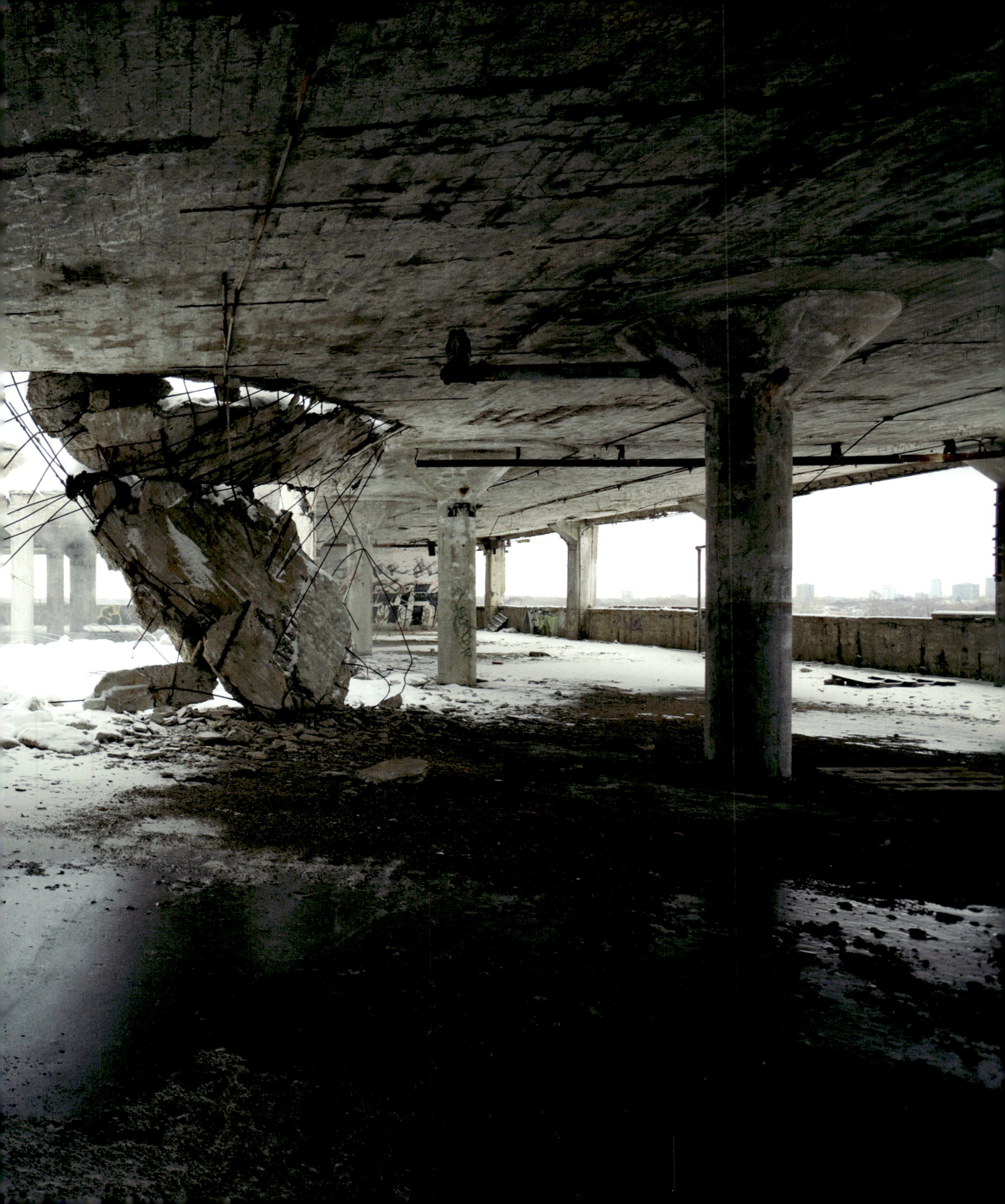

... we hope for better things

BY REBECCA RUTH HART

Previous spread:
Scott Hocking
Zeus Whirlwind – from the series:
Garden of the Gods, 2009 – 2010, 2010
Archival pigment print / Mixed media installation
Print: 33" x 49.5" / Installation: Dimensions variable
Photo courtesy of the artist and Susanne Hilberry Gallery

Detroit's first claim on the European imagination was as part of the uncharted New World upper country: the *there* of an unknown water route far into the wilderness; a legendary place that peeked the curiosity of Samuel de Champlain beckoning him to explore the far-away *there* of Michigan's water wonderland, which he navigated in 1615 passing through the straits (now known as the Detroit River) on his voyage to Lake Huron. Early on this region was a land of imagination and strife, of subsistence living while battling the northern climate, holding the potential for fortune or doom, a region that fostered solitude and self-sufficiency far removed from established settlements. The city was founded by French settlers in 1701 on the banks of the river that connected Lake Erie to Lake Huron. It was this proximity that gave Detroit a name: *le détroit du Lac Érie*, derived from French meaning the strait of Lake Erie. It grew from a settlement to a town on the frontier of Canada and the Great Lakes wilderness.[1]

Ethnic identity and race have been defining characteristics of the city for more than three centuries. Ottawa Indian Chief Pontiac contested jurisdiction of the nascent village in the Siege of Fort Detroit (1763) when he attempted to displace the British settlers. During the raid, his followers carefully targeted British soldiers while leaving French colonists and troops alone. The attack on the British was vicious, torturing and mutilating the soldiers, one of whom was ritually cannibalized as was the custom among some Great Lakes Indian cultures. Eventually, Pontiac's attacks were quelled; he withdrew his forces, ending the siege. Again the hegemony of these groups was challenged when Shawnee leader Tecumseh successfully made an alliance with the British and together they captured Fort Detroit during the War of 1812. By the war's end in 1815, however, the city was returned to the American territorial governor who restored control of local affairs to the people of Detroit with the election of a board of trustees and enactment of a charter for the city.

Not twenty years later, this city served as a haven for runaway slaves when the First Congregational and Second Baptist churches became stations on the Underground Railroad. In the basements of these buildings, freedom seekers rested in safety before crossing the Detroit River into Canada—the only sure way to shake off the U.S. Federal Marshals and bounty hunters. Ironically, however, Detroit—a city that had welcomed and harbored blacks—was bloodied by a race riot during the Civil War in 1863.

The city absorbed tremendously large numbers of blacks immigrating from the south seeking better employment opportunities between 1905 and the Great Depression. Jobs for blacks in the auto industry were plentiful but housing was not, as they had arrived in a polyglot metropolis that had already incorporated French, English, German, Polish, Irish, Italian, Syrian, and Greek immigrants. Mixing people of diverse prides and cultural heritage sometimes led to conflict, outbursts of violence, and culturally segregated districts. The city's 200,000 black residents were relegated to a cramped, eastside ghetto that was ironically called Paradise Valley, while white citizens diligently, sometimes militantly, guarded their segregated neighborhoods. A stronghold of the Ku Klux Klan, and that organization's commitment to white supremacy, intensified black-white tension. It's no wonder that a race riot erupted on a summer's evening in 1943 when a sailor's girlfriend was insulted by a member of another race and rumors, about white men attacking black women circulating almost as quickly as tales of black men attacking white women, ignited an already volatile population and tensions over employment opportunities in the factories exploded into violence.[2]

A quarter century later, the racial conflagration begun on July 23, 1967—obviated by a history of strife, distrust, and conflict—was among the worst to be witnessed in America during that fateful summer. And to this day, some believe that Detroit will never recover from this deep and still-healing wound.

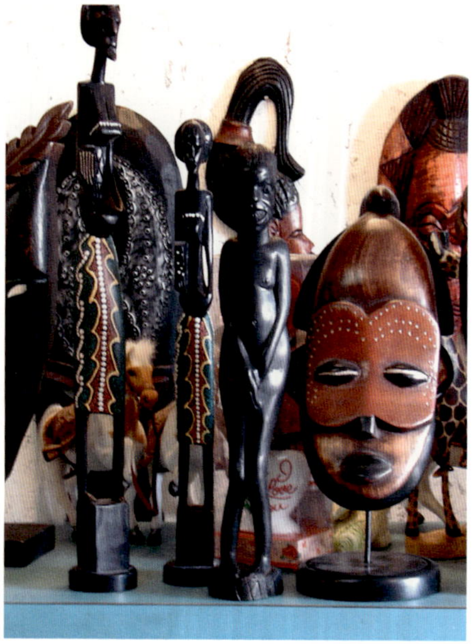

In a city like Detroit, race is almost always conjoined to issues of identity. Here, the painful legacies associated with racism fostered a culture that notices skin color before considering an individual's talents, skills, or virtues. Chido Johnson, who was born in Rhodesia and raised in Zambia and Zimbabwe, found refuge in Detroit because it looked and felt like his homeland. He is a white Zimbabwean, the child of a medical missionary and her artist husband, who led an unusual life for someone of white American descent: attending the village schools in rural Africa, speaking Shona as his native tongue, and making his first white friend at age 17 when he left home for college. (By contrast, other Americans and Europeans in Rhodesia attended elite schools, never learned an African language, and made friends among other colonials.) Johnson feels like he fits in Detroit as a white African; for him making a home in a place where the racial mix is 82% Black and 10% Caucasian allows the artist to live in a demographic region similar to that of his origins. This depopulated city, with the highest proportion of black residents in the nation, is a place of Beaux Arts and Art Deco buildings in close proximity to open land and shanty buildings that more closely resemble certain African settlements than average American neighborhoods.[3] Its built environment invites contingent use: an empty corner is a proposition for art performance or a griot, a cleared block invites a farming co-op, and unused factories are being converted into studios, farms, and living spaces.

Identity and the narratives that construct it are primary occupations for Johnson (see page 126). His most enduring identity is that of an African. His work is conditioned by the experience of realizing he was the "other" in his native Zimbabwe just as here, in Detroit, he is the "other" marked by race and national origin. He works in interstitial spaces that exist between cultures and looks for the congruence and disjunction between histories to establish a theoretical platform for his work. "I want to bring ideas into the conversation, for what inspires me to make art are the uncertainties, the grey areas."[4] These conditions inform work like *me me me* (2008) (Fig. 1), where the artist purchased an African figurine made for the tourist trade or, in the artist's own words, "airport art." Unlike its traditional counterpart, the commercial figure was un-inscribed because it had not been venerated or used in rituals, nor had it been intended for use in such rites. Johnson understood this and transformed the figure by giving it a unique identity; he re-carved the head,

Figure 1. Chido Johnson, *me me me* (installation in an African tourist store, Detroit), 2008, Carved from an existing tourist artifact, 11" x 2" x 1.7", Photo by George Rahme

fashioning his self-portrait using somewhat Africanized features in place of the generalized face of the commercial object. This once anonymous *tchotchke* was imbued with a unique and specific identity that is part African and part American. It shows the stylistic characteristics of an African trade object and reveals the artist's layered likeness also. This re-envisioning of "airport art" is Johnson's way of declaring that African attributes are an integral part of who he is while equally acknowledging his American ancestry. With *me me me*, the figure is part African, part American, but not conventionally African-American. The uneasy tension of exemption, allowing the viewer to know what the work is not, challenges us to rethink assumptions about race and ethnicity. With this ambiguity, Johnson draws the circle of inclusion wide enough that the viewer is caught and implicated in cultural and personal conflicts about race and identity. This conundrum brings us to a very personal place, not to the African there or, from an African perspective, an American there, but to the specific here of our inherited ancestry, predispositions, prejudices, and values. As Detroit is the most densely black-populated city in the United States, how could Chido Johnson's work have such cultural valence in another American city? Where else would Johnson's socio-psychological dramas be so vivid?

■ ■ ■

In Michigan, we live to the rhythms of the auto industry: twice a year schools and many businesses close for a "retooling" holiday, which reflects the periodic need to adjust the assembly line; in manufacturing areas, traffic patterns mirror the shift changes at plants; communities flourish during times of high commerce and wither as commercial demands for autos decline; buildings are used and then deserted; manufacturing, commerce, collapse. This practice is not new. The automotive industry gave union workers steady employment for decades, and later, the union-guaranteed work rules included provisions for retraining, layoffs, strikes, buy-outs, and relocation offers.

Auto manufacturers constructed, used, reused, and abandoned purpose-built structures over the past century. All along, in good times and bad, cars were bought and sold. The car industry convinced consumers that the pleasures of comfort and assurances of safety were reason enough to purchase another or different vehicle; even if one already had adequate transportation. Although this is not unique to Detroit, this manufacturing practice has a fanatical feel to it because such a high proportion of the population is involved in automotive industries. In the early part of the twentieth century, citizens working in the factories had to purchase a car as a condition of their continued employment. The large numbers of skilled workers bought and, to this day, continue to buy cars that identify them with specific manufacturers. They also apply their mechanical know-how to maintaining and customizing their treasures. Each summer more than a million and a half enthusiasts converge on the city for "Dream Cruise," a day long drive up and down Woodward, the main street (and first paved highway in America) connecting cities from Detroit to Pontiac. During the cruise, lovingly restored vintage cars share the road with souped-up roadsters and low-riders of all description. Detroit's car culture is unlike any other in America.

This phenomenon bid conceptual artist Liz Cohen and her *BODYWORK* project to Detroit. Searching for a tangible metaphor for radical physical transformation, she began the series nearly a decade ago as an outgrowth of another series titled *CANAL* (2000), which was completed in Panama. While in the isthmus, the artist was intrigued by trans-gendered sex workers, a marginal population that radically altered their bodies and identity, and she began to explore the boundaries of membership in groups where she didn't

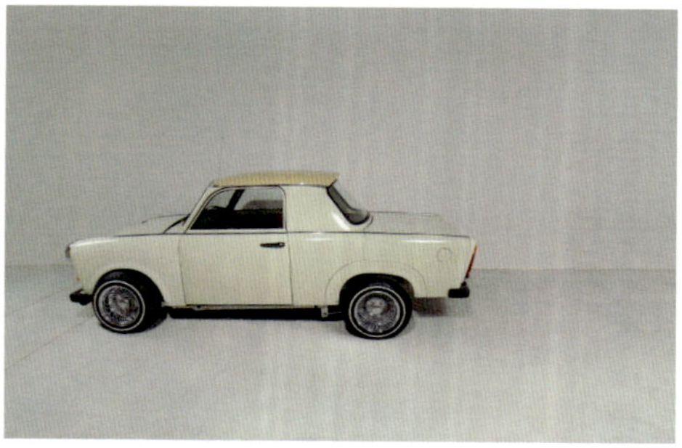

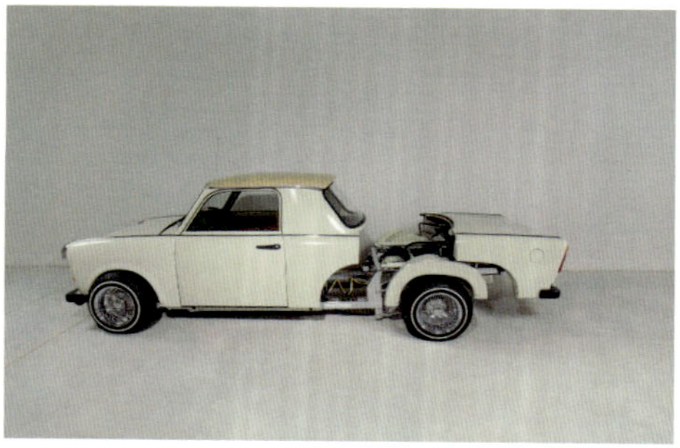

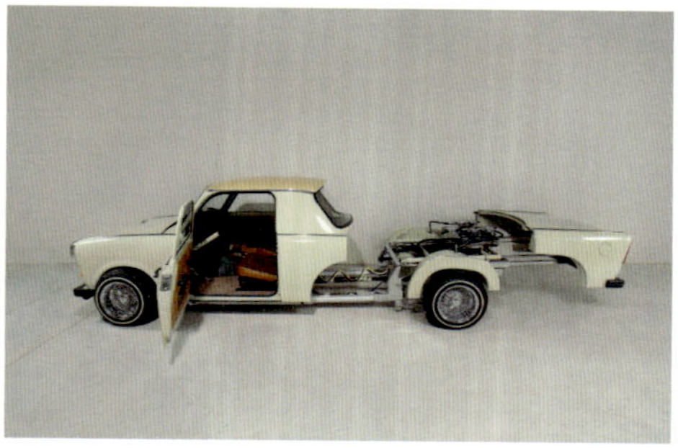

Figures 2-4. Liz Cohen, *Trabantimino*, 2002 - 2010, Mixed media, 112" x 66" x 56" (collapsed) / 226" x 66" x 64" (expanded), Photos courtesy of the artist and David Klein Gallery

belong. Car fanatics and pinup girls were the two she adopted, and in the resulting series *BODYWORK*, Cohen explores two parallel types of conversions: the production of a custom car and the development of a sexualized body and persona. During a trip to Berlin in 2002, she purchased an East German Trabant as her "starter" car. While it was a measly Soviet era attempt to provide personal transportation to the proletariat, over a thirty years period, thirty thousand people were employed in Zwickau where they produced three million two-stroke engines for these cars that, for their myriad inefficiencies, were emblematic of the foibles brought on by centralized planning. What could be more radical than to fabricate a hybrid car that shared attributes of the Trabant and an American muscle car, the El Camino? As improbable as this sounds, over the next eight years Cohen doggedly mastered automotive mechanics; first among the low-rider culture of California before working with master mechanic Bill Cherry in Scottsdale, Arizona, and eventually trailering her monster car to Detroit. The hybrid car, *Trabantimino* (Fig. 2, 3 and 4), retains the shell of a Trabant while low-rider hydraulic technology allows it to expand to the perimeter dimensions of an El Camino. During this project, Cohen mastered auto mechanics and became a legend for her innovative low-rider technology.

As odd as her mechanic persona may seem, Cohen performed an equally outlandish role as a bikini clad model posing with the car in various stages of transformation. For *Zwickau Routine* (2010) (see page 110), she struck poses reminiscent of the Romanian gymnast Nadia Comăneci while holding a sickle and hammer. Cohen's performance in the abandoned Trabant factory, and its documentation, could easily be mistaken for scenes in Detroit and as remarkable as this comparison might seem, the parallel is actually coincidental. While the "Trabbi" was undergoing its metamorphosis, the artist also did her own personal bodywork. During a residency at Färgfabriken, in Stockholm, Sweden, she divided her day between ripping the car apart and body building with a personal trainer. She records both processes in *Bodywork Trainer* (2006) (Fig. 5) appearing as a buff pin-up model, legs spread, atop a workout ball flexing her bicep under the burden of a chrome free-weight. The image is completed by a well-maintained male body and the Trabant "in process." Cohen is tom-boy mechanic and a sexualized calendar girl both, two extremes along the continuum of female identity extending from plain Jane to Marilyn Monroe.

The searing humor of *Trabantimino* and the *BODYWORKS* series is a poignant reminder of the hubris in Detroit, a metropolis that for a century bought into the allure of the automobiles manufactured here. The industry was predicated on planned obsolescence yet its titans held tightly to outmoded ideals, losing their competitive edge and eventually succumbing to more innovative competition from elsewhere. Cohen's project—though international in conception, scope, and execution—is what American mythologist and writer Joseph Campbell might have called a myth for this region.[5] Her performance embodies male and female attributes and takes an obsolete manufactured object from a derelict state into a new condition of serious but innovative reality. If given the chance to look back and relive the past three years, I bet that the top brass at the "Big Three" would have preferred Cohen's ride to their recent trip through bankruptcy and government oversight.

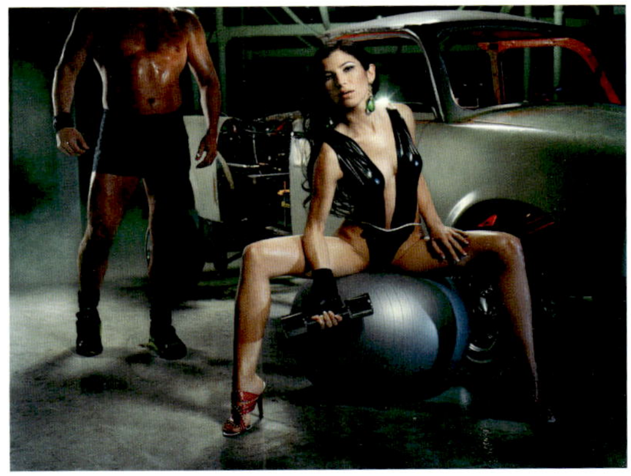

Figure 5. Liz Cohen, *Bodywork Trainer*, 2006, C print, 50" x 60 ¼", Photo courtesy of the artist and David Klein Gallery

For nearly ten years I awoke shortly after 2:00 a.m. I wondered why my sleep was fitful: why it was always 2:12 – 2:14 when I checked the clock; why I was awake despite few worries. Why not 2:15 or 3:00 a.m.? Why would I waken if I didn't need to use the bathroom or cough? Why, if I was not too hot or cold? Why, if others in the house did not stir? Something somewhere broke the nocturnal stillness of my sleep and wrestled me into consciousness. One Michigan evening our windows were open to the sweet coolness outside. The din of Woodward Avenue, America's first paved highway, could be heard a half block away—on weekends, cars and hotrods race or cruise up and down this road until midnight. Then silence falls. One night I slept uninterrupted at 2:12, and the night after, and the next. Since fall last year I've had sound sleep. I was given back those few minutes to sleep and somehow managed to stay asleep all night.

Months later something clicked in my head: the parts train rumbling north, supplying the Pontiac GM truck plant, woke me so predictably for a decade. Idled in September 2010 by the restructuring of the auto industry, the train no longer made deliveries in Pontiac; it no longer stopped traffic several times each day as it switched onto sidings off-loading chassis and coupling-on containers filled with newly assembled Chevrolet Silverados and GMC Sierra pickup trucks; it no longer roared and clattered me awake at 2:12 a.m. as it rushed to Pontiac. The schedule has changed; the plant has been shuttered. The plant is weathering, its machinery removed and reused or sold elsewhere, its vast parking lots grow high weeds, its supply roads have gone to gravel in eleven short months, half empty coal cars have become mammoth planters for ghetto palms and other trash trees, and its 1,100 employees are moving elsewhere in search of work.

The story behind my wakefulness and the inherent rhythms of capitalism highlight the tangible histories that undergird Scott Hocking's studio practice. He works in buildings, now silent, that once were vibrant manufacturing hubs.

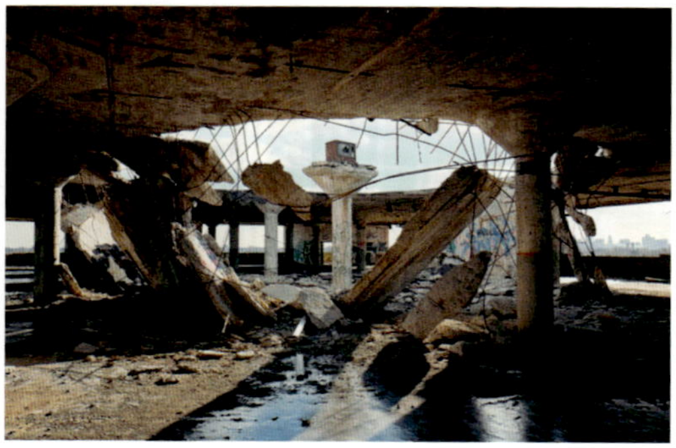

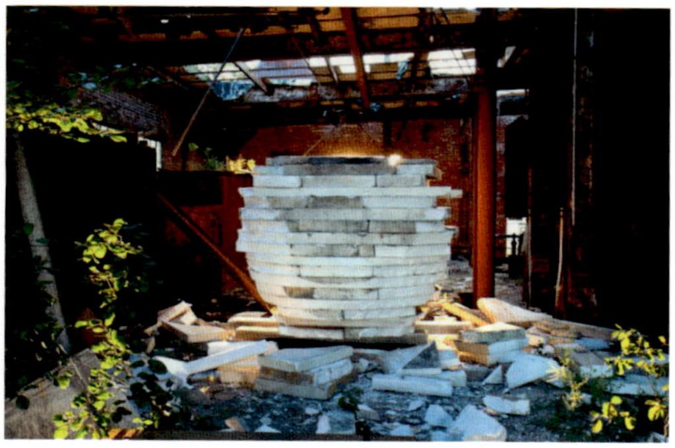

His actions interface with the process of abandonment and the progress of ruin. He enters shuttered buildings to explore and categorize the remaining materials, to map the geography of these vast structures (the Pontiac plant covered 3.4 million square feet), to reuse the fabric of the structure, and to create new mythologies that celebrate the past and consecrate these structures in ruin. Working with these vast spaces and structures, the romantic eloquence of decay is always operative. In Hocking's practice, though, simple sculptures are built, materials ordered, and patterns observed. His constructions, made on site in decaying and sometimes collapsed areas of these buildings, are subject to the elements and physical forces that promote ruin. This work is presented in the artist's exquisite photography and in installations made from materials removed from post-industrial sites. In Detroit, many early auto assembly plants were designed by Albert Kahn and are made of reinforced concrete. The architect pioneered this type of construction at the Packard Motor Car Company plant in 1903 - 05, which closed in 1958 when the last Studebaker rolled off the line. These long-vista buildings are among Hocking's favorite worksites. For fifteen years he's surveyed the terrain of the decaying plants; sharing the space with graffiti writers, squatters, and scrappers; working among equipment simply abandoned the day the plant closed; walking through interiors now exposed to the elements through structural failures.

It's more than a scavenger's eye that guides the artist. Hocking traverses abandoned plants scanning the remains—looking for typologies—which he assesses and inventories with the precision of a librarian. Then he gathers a single type of material—wooden flooring, old work gloves, bricks or other construction materials, old cathode ray tube televisions—and crafts simple, direct forms and installations. For his best-known series, *Ziggurat and FB21* (2007 - 09), made in the Fisher Body Plant #21, Hocking used 6,201 wooden floor tiles to build a stepped pyramid (see page 124). His labor to make a structure with religious connotations honors the labor and enterprise of the thousands of people who once populated and toiled in the plant. Recalling the venerated architecture of ancient cultures with its stepped form, Hocking's work inscribes a nearby locality with universal meaning. He links local history to global narratives.

An image from the *Ziggurat* series was published in *Time* magazine and spread word widely of Hocking's practice. He has since been invited to work in industrial sites in St. Louis and Utica, New York, the scrub-jungle of Florida, the Australian bush, neighborhoods of Shanghai, and the landscape of Iceland. For these residencies, the artist made installations sensitively tuned to the history of a particular place. In Saint Louis, for example, he conflated the

Figure 6. Scott Hocking, *Zeus, Ice (from the installation project and photo series Garden of the Gods, 2009 - 2010)*, 2010, Archival pigment print / Mixed media installation, Print: 33" x 49.5" / Installation: dimensions variable, Photo courtesy of the artist and Susanne Hilberry Gallery

Figure 7. Scott Hocking, *Sisyphus and the Egg of Rejection (from the installation project and photo series Sisyphus and the Voice of Space, 2010)*, 2010, Archival pigment print / Mixed media installation, Print: 33" x 49.5" / Installation: dimensions variable, Photo courtesy of the artist and Susanne Hilberry Gallery

history of the Mound Builders, once native to the shores of the Mississippi River, with the legacy of manufacturing, assembling a mound of rubber work gloves on the site of a former toxic waste transfer facility for a project entitled *New Mound City*.

As the work evolved, Hocking incorporated the language of mythology, not only in the titles but also in the work's scale and ambition. For a work that is part of the *Garden of the Gods* series (Fig. 6), the artist collected televisions from a ground floor room in the Packard Plant and positioned them atop structural columns on the top floor. The roof had collapsed at his worksite, exposing the giant mushroom shaped supports to the sky. Titanic in scale against the Detroit skyline, they mock the ambition of industrial capitalism, its demise most strikingly embodied in the abandoned plants.

This work recalls the past but looks to the future also. Unlike the elegiac incorporation of ruins in nineteenth century romantic painting, which attempts to recall a static moment in classical history, Hocking's installations are subject to the vagaries of time and the elements. The artist acknowledges that his installations are transitory and are preserved only in photographic documentation of the projects. His actions result in temporary structures that give mythic honor to local histories. Rather than creating romanticized views, he presents post-industrial spaces, no longer pristine but posed to become neo-Arcadias, reinscripted by the layering of their past with other histories.

This summer Scott Hocking's work has taken an interesting turn. He is working in the Michigan Central Depot, the decaying train station that has been a singular icon among the ruins of Detroit. This building, however, is undergoing restoration. The artist is racing against time as workmen clean, seal, abate, and re-glaze the station. About his project he writes, "[it] will be built with broken pieces of the sheet marble that used to line the walls and will take the form of an egg. A symbol that spans all cultures since ancient times, the egg represents the unborn potential yet to be hatched; the new beginning; the gestating idea; the primordial matter; creation." (Fig. 7)

In 1805, fire destroyed much of the settlement of Detroit, then the capital of the Territory of Michigan. The city's motto, *Speramus meliora; resurget cineribus* ("We hope for better things, it will rise from the ashes") embodies the fortitude of those who experienced this event. From the devastation, a vision for a grand city emerged, built with a radial plan and a largess of vision not previously imagined. The expansive spirit encouraged the entrepreneurial determination that propelled Detroit on for two centuries and, since the late 1960s, the motto is incanted each time that the city attempts to renew itself. Hocking hopes for better things and with shamanistic intent he notices, orders, builds, conflates, empowers, documents, and reflects realities explored by him alone. Detroit as neo-Arcadia is his proposition—that this place embraces its legacies as it moves from a platform for industry to that of a terrain that welcomes invention and meaningful action.

■ ■ ■

Large tracts of land are open within the hundred and forty-two square miles of the City of Detroit. Because the economy was based around a single product, as consumer demand changed, jobs opportunities waned causing the city to shed half of its population over the past forty years. When architect Dan Hoffman was

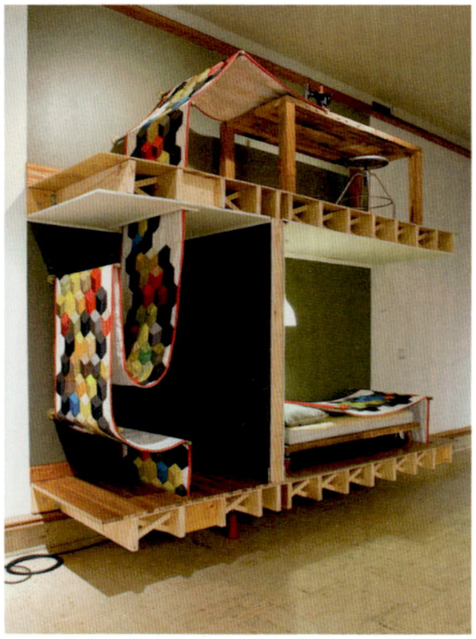

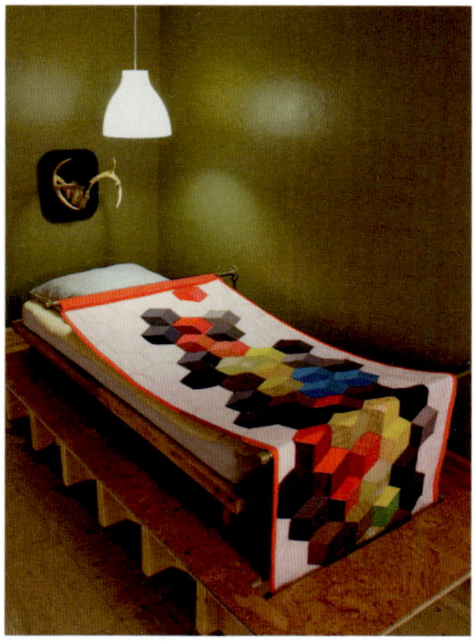

Figures 8-9. Abigail Anne Newbold, *Making Home*, 2007, Mixed media installation, Dimensions variable, Photos by Corine Vermeulen

Artist-in-residence at Cranbrook, he began to document the disintegration of city neighborhoods and infrastructure in a project called *Erasing Detroit: September – October 1991*.[6] By comparing aerial photography taken at different intervals, he documented the abandonment of the city and the destruction of the built environment. As a graduate student at Cranbrook, sitting in a studio in Bloomfield Hills and listening to Hoffman quantify Detroit in this way, I thought about the city only as a *there*. His message in the schematic plan was stunning but more shocking is the experience now of driving or walking through vast spaces that have no structures remaining or only a few remaining buildings—a Detroit *here*. Today a handful of vibrant communities tentatively cling to major transit arteries within the city limits. Elsewhere, one sees a single house or two on multiple empty blocks. Such decrepit buildings inspire nostalgic attachments to the city's past that frequently are recorded by photographers. More interesting though are those artists who see new life in the open fields, who purchase rundown buildings and return them to the tax rolls and building stock, who are creating a culture of ferment that invites new investment.

Peripatetic and curious by nature, Abigail Anne Newbold sees the urban landscape as an invitation to be ready: to make a place for comfort, to make a *here* that she calls home. She assembles groups of consumer goods and repurposed materials and displays them as a set or kit. This array is the artist's way of telling stories through implied narratives derived from material culture. Newbold's collections or kits are carefully edited sets; objects are included because they have a function ranging from essential comforts—food, shelter, warmth—to mnemonic objects, like her father's shirt that triggers memories of childhood, to work gear, like her Epson flatbed printer that she uses to document her practice.

The unaltered retail materials seem like such common items. However, when viewed in the context of other objects that are either made or altered by the artist, the ensemble is given voice. The yards-long quilt, traversing a two-story elevation in *Making Home* (2007) (Figs. 8 and 9), is not only beautiful but shown from the point of manufacture to the place of use. The textile, luxuriously long, cascades from the worktable where it is being made onto a display rod, before it passes beneath the flooring and then emerges suspended above a rudimentary bed. Its traditional "Tumbling Blocks" quilt pattern emphasizes the spatial course of the covering while suggesting also a beehive pattern, a symbol of industry and cooperation. We are amazed at the scale of the covering, perplexed by the absurdity of its length, and all the while wanting to lie beneath its warmth. Its sheer size speaks to the long hours needed to make such beautiful but utilitarian textiles.

Newbold's more recent efforts, like *home maker 2* (2011), are infused with narrative valence as objects are displayed in proximity to others: a nylon-covered bicycle-powered wagon and charred logs stacked like a campfire may suggest overland travel or the "wagons ho" spirit of a pioneer (see page 136). A corset hangs as part of the kit; its inclusion reveals the user as female, furthers the reference to frontier life, and in the incongruity of its presence among camping equipment comments on the artist herself. She infuses the installation with an air of humor based on the scale of the tent stakes in relationship with the light weight take-it-anywhere engineering of other objects in the kit. By conceiving of her installations as kits, Newbold suggests that anyone might use, consume, or rearrange the tools, necessities, and luxuries on display. Interactivity is implied; what if we accepted and, with a DIY know-how, changed the installation on view? Could we use a kit to make a pop-up settlement anywhere within the urban setting? What about backyard camping in the suburbs? Can't we pack it all up and use it in an overland trip? Will you accept Newbold's invitation to be part of a new way of living: something contingent, comfortable, portable, and brave?

■ ■ ■

Throughout this discussion, when I make reference to Detroit I am referring to the incorporated city. Although abandonment and change is occurring throughout the area, it is most extreme within the city limits. Talent and resources available in the larger metropolitan area are being focused within the urban bounds. Detroiters speak of the economic tsunami or hurricane that struck here. We experience the effects of this phenomenon viscerally: seeing empty streets and buildings, having to plan to shop for food outside the city or at farmers markets, going to the suburbs for many services, wondering when we'll come upon an open business when driving, feeling our hearts beating a little faster when we pause to see change in our midst.

And indeed the engagements of these four artists—Chido Johnson, Liz Cohen, Scott Hocking, and Abigail Anne Newbold—highlight some of the city's ills. Johnson creates work that conflates, and thereby confuses, traditional cultural boundaries so that we are lead to think more about a national ethos than race. His cultural miscegenation leads the viewer to rethink how identity is constructed.

Liz Cohen is a builder who assumes three identities: she is the maker, the owner, and the person who performs with her mutant car, *Trabantimino*. She participates in Detroit's love affair with the automobile and is an example of mission-driven design. Her hydraulic inventions are the envy of low-rider culture. She conjoined two cars, an East German Trabant with an American El Camino; two types of cars that when they were being manufactured during the Cold War would never have had influence on the design of the other. Yet through this example we learn that anything is possible, even incorporating ideas that formerly were heretical within the American auto industry. Moreover, Cohen certainly gives us a new persona for the traditional pin-up girl (or low-rider car owner): stiletto shod and bikini clad as one might expect but armed with tools suggestive of a dominatrix. Her sexualization of the car, by modeling as the owner pin-up girl, changes the dialogue about who, stereotypically, is a consumer of cars. Doubling her role—the owner and scantily clad model who sells it—Cohen empowers female enthusiasts while challenging misogynist advertising and, through her example, offers a different paradigm for auto manufacturing.

Scott Hocking finds beauty among the remains of the city. His photography and installations confer mythic dimensions to the landscape. The artist overlays his work with titles that recall Greek gods to imbue his structures with mighty and generative power. In contrast, other artists working in Detroit record the same sites as melancholy places, locations that show the process of decay and ruin unlike the open narratives that Hocking proposes.

Abigail Anne Newbold takes the depopulated city as inspiration to forge a new way of living within the American urban landscape. She bases her practice in commercially available commodities combined with artist modified and handmade craft objects. These combinations invite others to recombine her kits, to make them personal. In a DIY community, they remind Detroiters that we were once a maker culture, a people deeply involved in all aspects of the auto industry; that hands-on work is part of innovation, that the time given to making something can insure its quality, and that re-thinking how we use objects may lead to better understanding their utility as re-purposed commodities.

In Detroit now, incubators for diverse industries are growing, filling to capacity. Neighborhoods targeted for growth are beginning to thrive. Businesses are offering home mortgage incentives to lure employees to move back into the city. Artists are re-envisioning their practice, using the city as raw material and attracting others here to join them. Detroit was the city that was synonymous with the American auto industry and popular music of the 1960s and 70s. The maker/inventor, make-what-you-will attitudes that sustained it are thriving and showing new options. The artists included in ***here.***, through their studio practice, posit their own solutions to some of this region's ills. Creative and entrepreneurial ingenuity once made Detroit a thriving city. Why not take the examples of Johnson, Cohen, Hocking, and Newbold as viable options for the future? *Speramus meliora; resurget cineribus.* We hope for better things. We hope that that the city resizes, rethinks, reinvents what urban life is in a shrinking city. For in that re-creation, Detroit is a lived here, a place in the momentary present looking to an enduring future.

[1] There are two fascinating histories of the exploration and settlement of Detroit. For a historical record, see John T. Blois, *Gazetteer of the state of Michigan, in three parts ... with a succinct history of the state, from the earliest period to the present time ...* (Detroit: L. S. Rood and Company, 1839) part 1 and 3; and Philip Marchand in *Ghost Empire: how the French almost conquered North America* (Westport: Praeger Publishers, 2007) is a good overview of the French and British struggles in the Great Lakes region and Canada.

[2] For detailed histories, see Walter F. White and Thurgood Marshall, *What caused the Detroit riot? : an analysis* (New York: National Association for the Advancement of Colored People, 1943) and Dominic J. Capeci and Martha F. Wilkerson in *Layered Violence: The Detroit Rioters of 1943* (Jackson: University of Mississippi, 1991).

[3] Assefa Mehretu has written about the similarities between southeast Michigan and Africa. See Assefa Mehretu and Lawrence M. Sommers, "Towards an analysis of microspatial marginality in the Detroit region," in *Technology, landscape, and arrested development: essays on the geography of marginality: papers from the 1995 PIMA Conference*, ed. Vincent P. Miller and Daniel Leininger (Indiana: Indiana University of Pennsylvania, Department of Geography and Regional Planning, 1997), no. 1.

[4] Chido Johnson, quoted in *domestified angst: second recording projects by Chido Johnson*, ed. Dick Goody (Rochester: Oakland University Press, 2008), 9.

[5] In *The Hero with a Thousand Faces*, American mythologist and writer Joseph Campbell introduced the concept of a *monomyth*, the idea that there is a single foundational myth or story that is held in common within a community, defining the cultural structure and beliefs of a group or region. In Detroit during the twentieth century, the *monomyth* might have been interpreted as "Detroit and the Big Three dominate auto manufacturing; its industries make products that are in demand world–wide, therefore the products and business practices of the Big Three are strong as they are and don't need to change." With the restructuring of the auto industry in 2008-2010, it became apparent that the Detroit *monomyth* needed to be amended. Today perhaps our *monomyth* is: Detroit's auto products compete in a global market that rewards innovation and economy; the Big Three are incorporating work practices that allow the industry to have nimble response to competition and insure that their products fulfill customer demand worldwide. For an explanation of monomyth, see Joseph Campbell, *The Hero with a Thousand Faces* (Princeton: Princeton University Press, 2004), 1-42.

[6] See Dan Hoffman, *Architecture Studio: Cranbrook Academy of Art 1986-1993* (New York: Rizzoli, 1994), 28-29, and Siemon Allan, Rebecca Hart, and Kinsey Katchka, *Julie Mehretu: city sitings* (Detroit: Detroit Institute of Arts, 2007), 58.

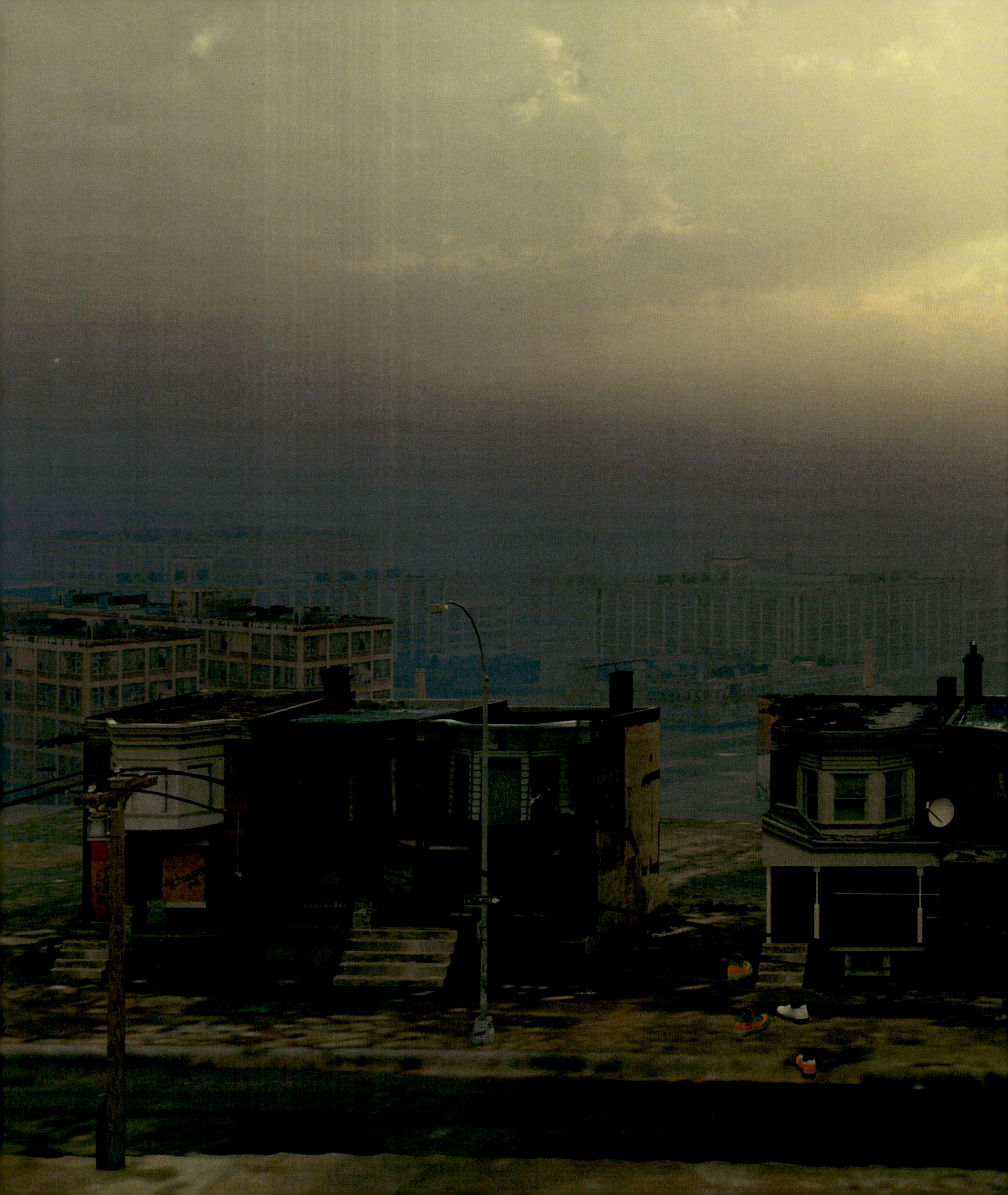

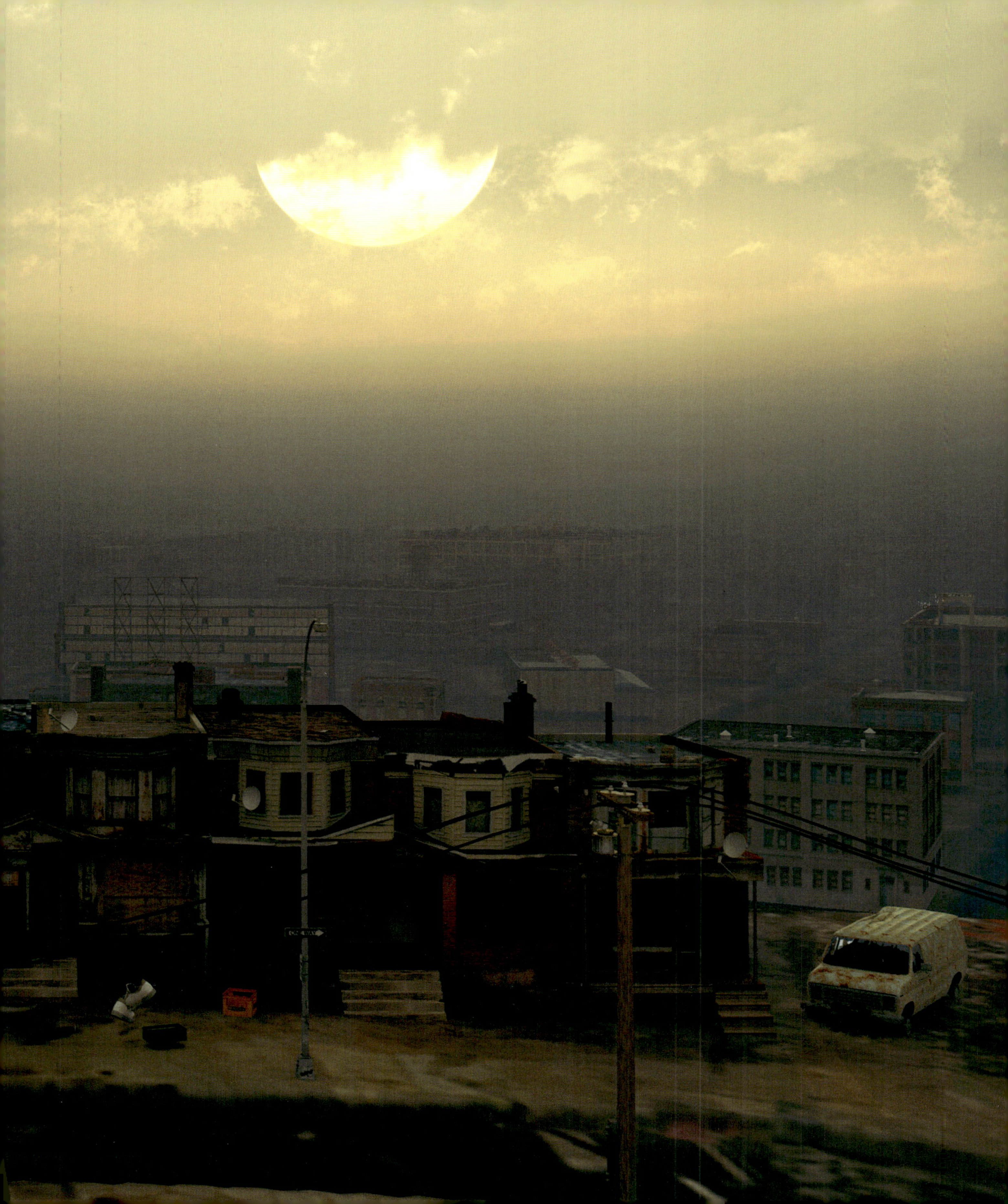

Being Here

BY JULIEN ROBSON

Previous spread:
Tim Portlock
Sunrise, 2011 (detail)
Ink jet print
54" x 72"
Image courtesy of the artist

"Even in Philadelphia, with its 40,000 vacant properties and a quarter of its population living below the poverty line, the Kensington neighborhood still shocks. On a frigid afternoon, a prostitute lingers in the shadow of the elevated train tracks, waiting restlessly for customers. Husks of long closed factories stand amid thigh-high winter wheat. Streams of garbage flow down the streets, as if both the people and the city government had agreed to forsake the effort of propriety."

DIANA LIND[1]

Each morning I set off from home to travel on the Market-Frankford line to my office at PAFA. At this end, it's a short walk to the station and then an easy ride to the center of the city; a journey that usually takes around twenty five minutes, door to door. The area I live in is known as Fishtown, a name first given to this part of the old Kensington District of Philadelphia in the early 1800s because of the many fishermen's families who lived here.[2] While our neighborhood appears nowhere as bleak as Diana Lind's description, I have to admit that when I first came to live in the city, I took a rental in the southern part of Kensington and was shocked at first by the viscerality of Philadelphia's urban decay. Of course, up until my arrival here, my Philadelphia was represented by its historic and tourist sights, the vibrancy of Center City, and the grand design of the Parkway, a perspective defined primarily by my interest in the city's museums. The only forays I had made beyond this comfort zone were navigated, during a short house-hunting visit, in the censoring cocoon of a realtor's car, so, the experience of actually being here came as a jolt that displaced my former image of the city and replaced it with a picture of a gritty reality that was intensified by my sudden immersion in it.

While my image of it is now quite different, in those early months, as I walked each morning to the train or spent time in the evenings and weekends strolling the neighborhood to acquaint myself with its geography, the bleakness west of Frankford Avenue felt almost Dickensian. For this newcomer, it looked like a patchwork of decaying brick buildings interspersed with huge empty lots and, while I seemed to observe few people milling about in amongst this blight, their presence was all too visible in the urban trash that lay strewn across the neighborhood. It reminded me of a cityscape from my childhood in a northern English industrial city during the 1960s, where my friends and I would play among the rubble of sites where urban development had yet to

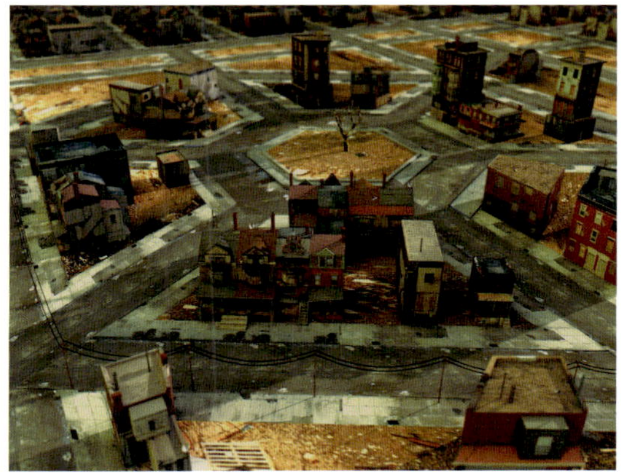

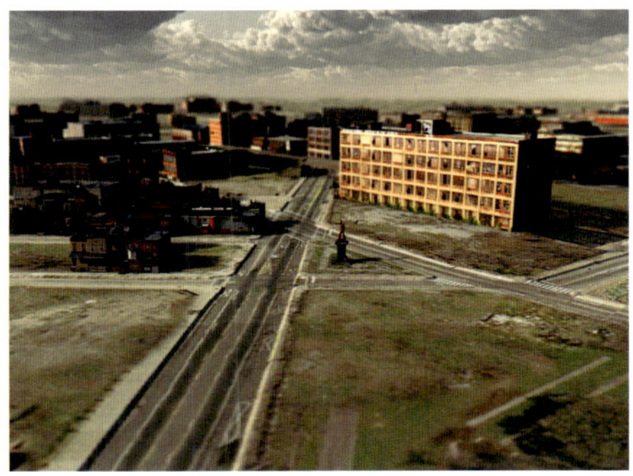

Figure 1. Tim Portlock, *Ghost City 1*, 2008,
Ink jet print, 54" x 72", Image courtesy of the artist

Figure 2. Tim Portlock, *Ghost City 13*, 2009,
Ink jet print, 54" x 72", Image courtesy of the artist

fully replace the scars of wartime bombing. Now here, in Philadelphia—a city that, for almost a century after the civil war, had boasted its status as "the Workshop of the World"—a similarly disheveled patchwork of architectural relics and empty urban lots in my neighborhood now spoke to the ravages of industrial collapse.

I clearly remember my first encounter with Tim Portlock's work in an exhibition at Vox Populi.[3] In this show, the atmospheric fictions of his *Ghost City* pictures, (Figs. 1 and 2) representing curtailed blocks of row-houses and factories surrounded by empty lots, seemed, at first sight, to be a shorthand for my own first impressions of Kensington. Portlock's large scale, richly pigmented inkjet prints, resemble aerial views of a fictionalized Philadelphia, where orderly layouts of roads and sidewalks criss-cross half barren landscapes, creating a framework of broken down groups of buildings and the occasional statue or dead tree. Seamlessly collaging photographs of Philadelphia's architecture with the aid of computer technology, the atmosphere of Portlock's vivid vistas seemed to me to be part documentary photograph, part science fiction film, and part video game; a post-urban sublime, not bustling with human activity but silent with dissolution (see page 138). It was reassuring then, on my first studio visit, to discover he too is also a transplant to Philadelphia and that, even though we live in different neighborhoods, his first impressions of the citybore similarity to mine. Arriving in the birthplace of the nation, a city that during the second half of the nineteenth century was transformed into an engine of industry by the acumen of its entrepreneurs and skills of its labor force, he could not help but be surprised at the "contrast between the ideals of the historical Philadelphia and the scale of the grossly deteriorated material condition of the city."[4] If you land in among the empty factories and broken down housing stock of areas like Kensington, the decay is bewildering, casting a long shadow over the impressions the outsider takes away from the more up-tempo and salubrious parts of the city.

Time, of course, dampens this effect and just as a growing familiarity with a place shrinks its geography, it also opens up its communities and their histories, enriching the newcomer's relationship to the city. As Portlock says of himself, he has now "grown to greatly appreciate some of the city's aspects that can only be known after living here for some time." Yet, while his first perspective is clearly muted by time as it recedes and transforms in memory, it is, as Portlock would have it, refreshed each time he returns from a trip—a connection that he admits continues to inform the images he makes.

Of course, Portlock's reconstructed images of the city are not simply his personal musings on Philadelphia's ruins. The city, rather, forms the particular center around which he is able to weave ideas relating to broader issues of urban decay, the rundown conditions that are familiar to the citizens of many cities lying across the rustbelt of the nation. Like Philadelphia, these are places that have grown prosperous with industrialization and then suffered immiseration and collapse; places that now struggle to retain populations with new inner city developments, which then seem to stutter and stall with the cycle of economic expansion and contraction that accompanies the vicissitudes of capitalism.

In some ways, Portlock's giant representations of the post-industrial city are a disquieting counterfoil to the dreams and fantasies of the contemporary city that are sold by developers. In particular, these works

keeping its fabric alive by filling in empty lots and replacing old and derelict homes. On the other, it is a sign that threatens the familiarity of the neighborhood, less through the visual changes it effects than through the transformations of community that accompany gentrification and often drive longer established residents away. It is a subject that Jennifer Levonian takes up in her new short film *The Oven Sky* (2011), which tells the story of a long-time resident of the neighborhood who ends up struggling with the needs and wishes of the newcomers (see page 130).

Levonian's animated films have frequently been autobiographical in nature, reflecting on the communities that surround her and often including her as a character in their narratives. Using the medium of watercolor to tell stories of the ordinary and the everyday, the images of people, animals, and objects she paints are cut out and brought to life through stop-motion animation. The sensual delicacy of Levonian's medium conveys a familiarity on the objects and situations she depicts but, as her narratives unravel, this intimacy serves to magnify the ambiguities and absurdities she observes in the quotidian. For instance, based on the artist's experiences in Mexico, *Take Your Picture with a Puma* (2010) (Fig. 5) reflects upon a female tourist's search for the authentic Mexico experience that her guidebook promises, yet, "as she visits unconventional tourist spots she inadvertently travels the well-trod path of other Lonely Planet-style tourists."[6] In *Her Slip is Showing* (2010) (Fig. 6), the narration of a bridal shower explores the loss of youthful dreams and their replacement with the comforts of suburban living. Here, the niceties of social restraint elevate and magnify triviality, creating a world of alienation that smothers the idealism these women shared in their former years. Funny, smart, and well crafted, Levonian's films sharply observe how, in appearing to search for the real, her characters' expectations of fulfillment are continually thwarted and left wanting by consumer culture's promise to satiate the desires it initiates in us. As Jeffrey D. Gower puts it, "even if they sometimes go along with all the nonsense taking place on the surface, [they] struggle to find a more authentic place in their world and with others while being hemmed in by the narrow sense of life that this surface, this facade, demands."[7]

Engaging the authentic by celebrating the things that occupy the reality of the everyday is part of the project of *Megawords* magazine, the centerpiece of a collaboration that Philadelphia artists Dan Murphy and Anthony Smyrski began in 2005. It is a publication that refuses to conform to the norms of periodical production, changing its format each time the artists publish an issue, and it is distributed free in bookstores, galleries, and record stores—

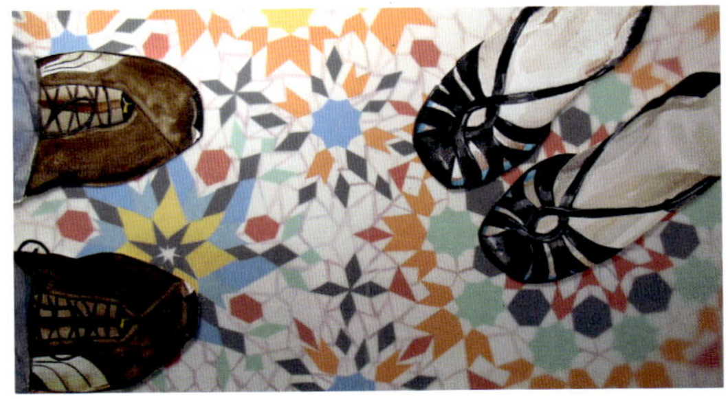

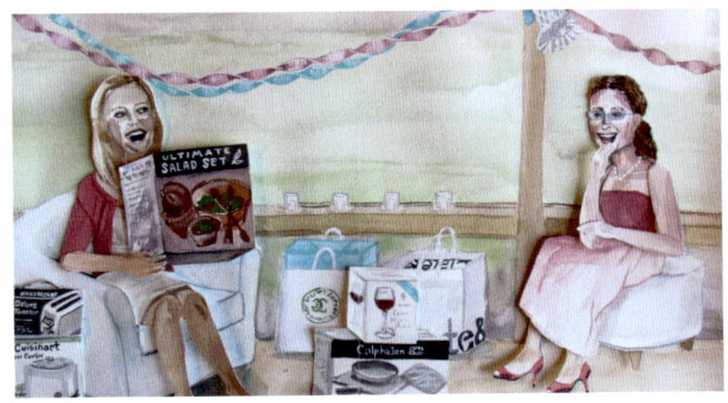

Figure 5. Jennifer Levonian, Video still from *Take Your Picture with a Puma*, 2010, Cut-out animation using watercolor and collage, Image courtesy of the artist and Fleisher/Ollman Gallery, Philadelphia

Figure 6. Jennifer Levonian, Video still from *Her Slip is Showing*, 2010, Cut-out animation using watercolor and collage, Image courtesy of the artist and Fleisher/Ollman Gallery, Philadelphia

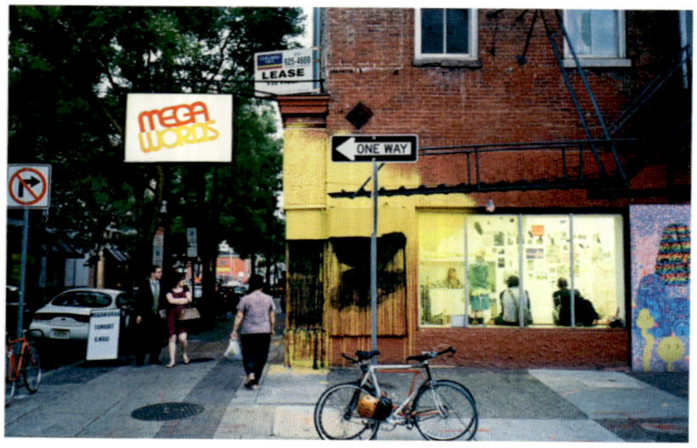

Figure 7. Megawords, Megawords storefront exterior, 2008, Image courtesy of the artist

among other places. Despite its title, *Megawords* features few words, but it does speak volumes through the host of photographs it contains, which are shot by Smyrski, Murphy, and their many collaborators. Taking a leaf out of the DIY culture that characterizes a lot of the art activity in Philadelphia, Megawords is self-published and has been mostly funded by the artists own resources—augmented more recently with arts institutional grants—in order to keep the pressures of commerce at bay and allow the publication to remain free from outside editorial interference.

While pictures of Philadelphia form its staple—for instance, issue number 4 was a focused portrait of a family living in west Philadelphia—Megawords also looks outward to encompass a broader conception of community. Its compiled juxtapositions of photographs taken here, and in other cities in other parts of the world, are laid out in ways that visually democratize them, so that the reader's attention is drawn not just to the particularities of localities but also to the commonalities that are shared by different places. Here, everyday Philadelphia finds visual conjunction with elsewhere in straightforward images of daily urban life. The Megawords website declares, "Megawords has a simple purpose: to document our surroundings, experience, to have a voice free from the noise of commercialization and competing novelties, and to create an open and active dialogue between Megawords and the community at large."[8] Embracing the idea that their project can be a vehicle to spark recognition and thereby engender discussion, the shared qualities perceivable in the imagery of *Megawords* magazine seem to suggest that the potential to bring communities together lies in the celebration of the commonplace, in reclaiming what we take for granted. As Smyrski says, "Generally, magazines are all about telling people what they're not, like, 'Look at these beautiful people who you will never meet, these products you'll never be able to afford.' ... We want people to look at their own lives and see them as valid. Maybe more than valid, maybe something completely sublime."[9]

While Smyrski and Murphy planned originally to make only one magazine, their commitment to Megawords has seen them publish sixteen issues and develop Megawords into a multifaceted project. The magazine remains at the core of their activities, but they now also work with internet radio shows, videos, music, readings, and installations; activities that allow them to organize direct interactive contact with diverse audiences. Among their so-called "pop-up" events, *The Megawords storefront project and exhibition* saw them occupy an empty store at 1125 Cherry Street in Philadelphia for the month of September 2008 (Fig. 7). Here, and following Smyrski's belief that "people are most interesting exactly where they are, doing what they're doing,"[10] they created an environment of changing activities that included rotating art installations, talks, musical performances, workshops, and film-screenings, that were open and free to the passing public. A subsequent manifestation was held during the Art + Soul Food festival in June 2009, in the Brewerytown neighborhood of Philadelphia. A part of the city that has also suffered economic decline, over the past few years Brewerytown has been revitalized by an influx of new, young professional residents. Finding an abandoned news kiosk at 27th Street and Girard Avenue, Smyrski and Murphy employed it as a place to launch an issue of *Megawords* magazine and, with the aid of volunteers, manned the kiosk and engaged directly with people in the street (see page 132). Furthering this commitment to Philadelphia's communities, Smyrski and Murphy are now developing a project called the Mobile Publication Studio, which will take the form of a mobile media production lab. From this facility, they will be able to document the environments of the city's neighborhoods, interacting with and interviewing residents in a variety of racially, socio-economically, and culturally distinct neighborhoods with the ambition to make "a catalog of Philadelphia; a body of work that can be used both as a reference and a point of departure."[11]

No doubt some of the neighborhoods that Smyrski and Murphy's project is going to document will be places like Kensington and Fishtown. Here the social dynamics are changing as established blue collar families find themselves sharing space with the creative classes and young professionals who are repurposing old buildings and regenerating the housing stock. However, while renewal refreshes this place positively with new blood, it also forges an asymmetrical relationship of power that privileges the newcomers' desires to recast place in their own image and which, in turn, poses the threat of displacement to older communities as rents and property taxes rise. In Levonian's *The Oven Sky*, rather than be driven out from her neighborhood, a long-time resident submits to the wishes of those who newly colonize her neighborhood, and gives up the things that have helped define her identity thus far. There is no initiative to ignite an open and equitable dialog between her and the gentrifiers, and there is no conversation about what a collective idea of community can be. So, instead, she is persuaded and then directed to let her garden become a dog park and, as the lawn ornaments that have been removed from her garden find their way into someone else's art, she reluctantly accepts her lot. Could it be otherwise? Somehow, I can't help but wonder how things might have been different had the Mobile Publication Studio passed by.

From where I live in Fishtown I can hear the rumble of the El as it arrives and leaves the local Berks station, which lies about six blocks away. After work, going home from this stop is a short five minute walk that takes me along Front Street, under the highline architecture and alongside the Kensington High School for the Creative and Performing Arts, a new "green roof" building erected on a former brown field site and opened just over a year ago. A few blocks north and to the east of the school, young professionals have been building small infill houses, energy efficient homes with modernist lines that challenge the existing architecture of brick row-houses, while warehouses and factory buildings across this area are being used as lofts and studios and, like the former factory I live in, renovated into condominiums. The changes in my neighborhood are marked, and while this process of renewal may be slow and subject to the faltering fortunes of the economy, the results are nonetheless beginning to surface. The weave of established and newer residents is at times—like all places and by its very nature—sometimes awkward, and in this context the ongoing desire to build an integrated community is not simply a consideration of the present and the everyday, it is also a struggle involving both the history of place and divergent ideas about its future potential. The challenge posed by this struggle is what is alluded to in the gentrification narrative of Jennifer Levonian's film, where the submission of the long time resident gives the colonizer the upper hand. Equally, it is a challenge that is figured in Lewis Colburn's installation, except that here the signifiers of past and present seem locked together in a self-conscious and discontinuous coalition of form. Complementing these perspectives, Megawords' mediating social practice can be seen to act out this challenge by creating environments and events that will open up dialogue and encourage exchange.

At dawn, the sunrise casts light from behind my apartment and across Kensington to the west, reflecting against the red brick of the many factories and warehouses I can see from my window. It is a gradual coming to life that starts with a warm and ever changing glow that almost imperceptibly intensifies into the sharp brightness of day. I revisit the memory of this effect in the image of *Sunrise* (2011) (see pages 66/67), a large new work by Tim Portlock, where the fictional city no longer seems lost and melancholic but open to future possibilities that are not yet fully visible. It's a work that captures the moment when night fails and is replaced by a sublime luminescence that rises over the urban landscape. It is a picture of stillness that breathes with anticipation. Like the works by other Philadelphia artists in ***here.***, Portlock's image speaks to the neighborhood I live in, where I see potential and feel optimism. And as I consider the way these artists' works engage questions of identity, history, and community, it makes sense to own up that my choosing them has been influenced by where I live because it is a place that saturates my experience. I still live in Fishtown and it has changed, both in itself and in my perceptions; it has taken on a quality of place and I now feel I'm *here*.

[1] Diana Lind, "The Bright Side of Blight," *New York Times*, January 24, 2011.

[2] For a discussion of how Fishtown came to be named see Kenneth W. Milano, "Earliest known use of the name Fishtown" in *Remembering Kensington and Fishtown* (Charleston: The History Press, 2008), 76.

[3] Vox Populi is one of the best-known artist collectives in Philadelphia, founded in 1988.

[4] Unless otherwise noted, all quotations from the artists can be found in the artist pages of this publication.

[5] John Lewis Gaddis, *The Landscape of History: How Historians Map The Past* (Oxford: Oxford University Press, 2002), 1.

[6] Jennifer Levonian quoted in Edith Newhall, "Critic's Pick - Jennifer Levonian," *Art News*, Summer 2009, 144.

[7] Jeffrey D. Gower, "Mehr Licht / Mehr Nicht," *Machete Magazine*, June 2011, 6.

[8] See http://megawordsmagazine.com/about/.

[9] Anthony Smyrski quoted in Jessica Pressler, "Local Talent: Anthony Smyrski and Dan Murphy," *Philadelphia Magazine*, July 2006.

[10] Anthony Smyrski quoted in www.e-flux.com/shows/view/5795.

[11] See www.pcah.us/the-center/grants-awarded/philadelphia-exhibitions-initiative-2011-grantee-megawords.

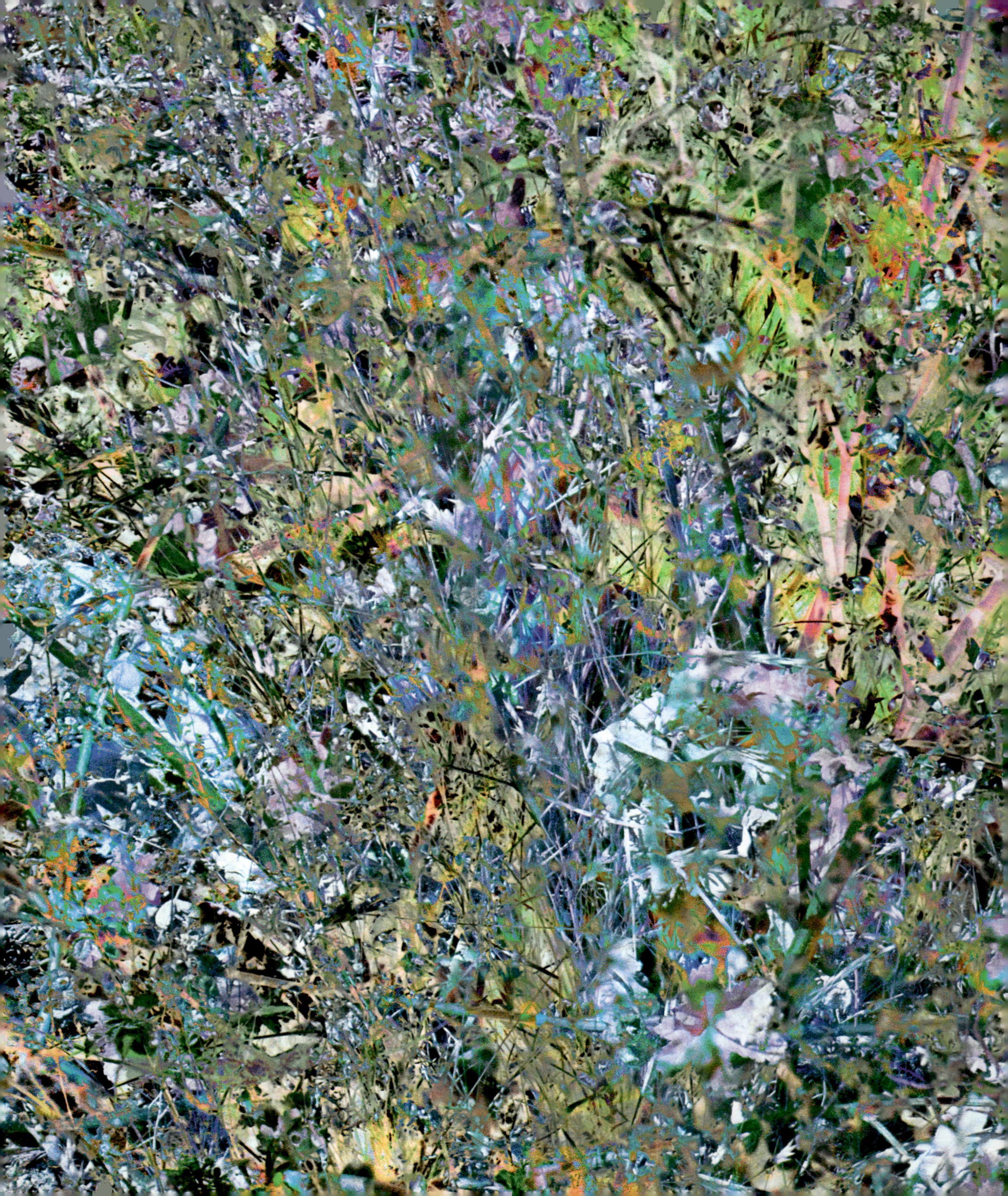

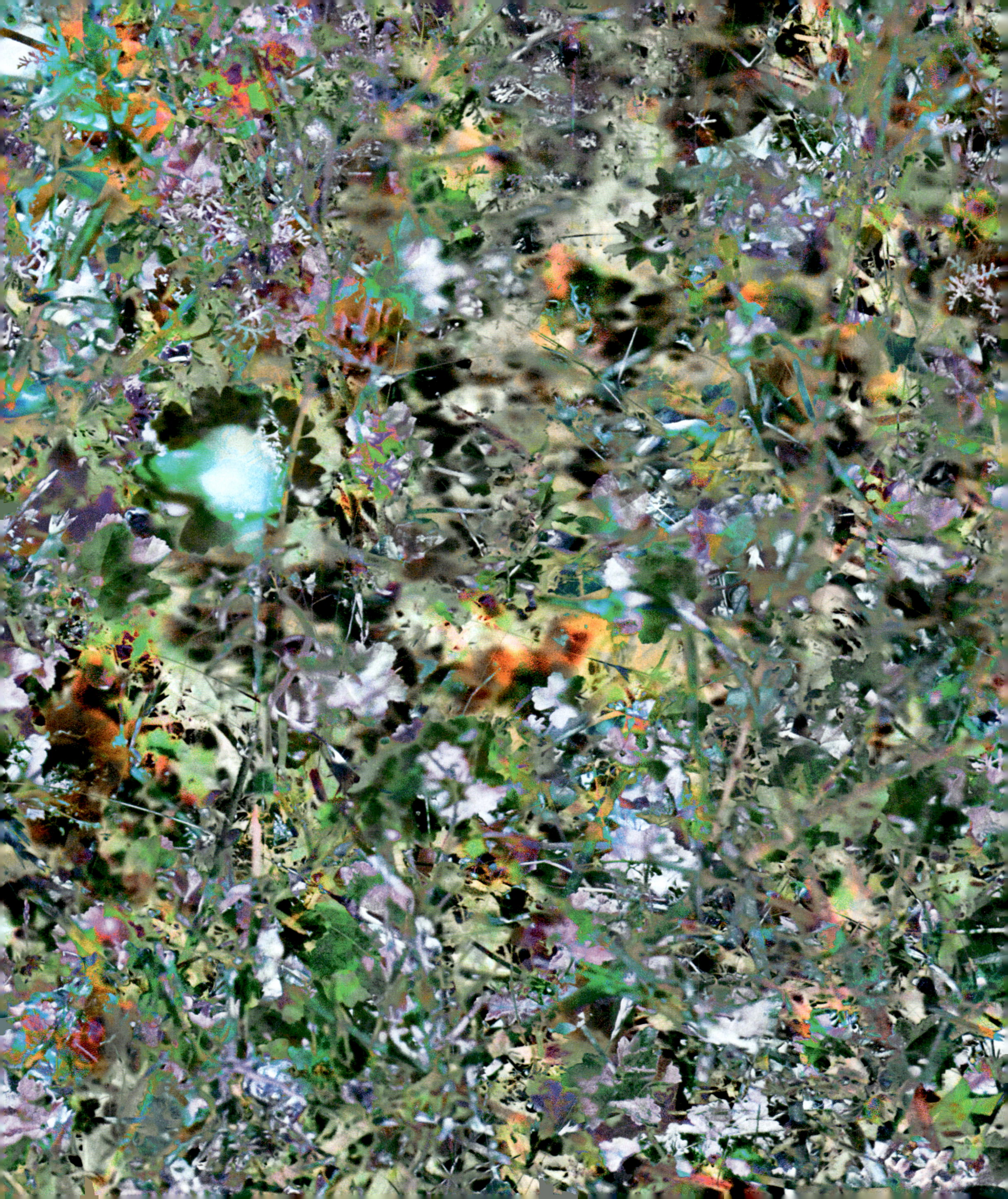

Greater America

BY CLAIRE SCHNEIDER

Previous spread:
Aaron Rothman
Idle Speculation 7, 2011 (detail)
Archival inkjet print
40" x 50" (image)
Image courtesy of the artist

My intent in selecting artists from Phoenix was to spotlight ambitious work and artistic practices that have not had sufficient exposure outside the region. I wanted to highlight *visibility* as much as *locality*. Aaron Rothman, Sue Chenoweth, Gregory Sale, and Postcommodity are all engaged with the international art conversation—they just happen to live and work in a place less visited by the art world. Consequently, I was more concerned with how place might alter contemporary art practice, than with finding artists whose central interests revolved around a specificity of place.

Commenting recently about how there is so much contextualization of experience on the high and low end of society, *Artpapers* editor Sylvie Fortin was prompted to ask why we ignore the middle, places, for instance, like Atlanta and Phoenix.[1] Like Fortin, I want to know what exists in *Greater* America and what can we learn from these places. What about the rest of America? What is happening where the Whitney Biennial doesn't touch down, or does so too briefly and infrequently, and what do artists have to say about our world there?

But I am biased. I have lived my whole life in non-"art centers" and have always felt that those confined to the major hubs had missed out on the richness of America. My experience of growing up in middle Tennessee was one of lush greenery, expansive trees, a spring that seemed to unfold forever with forsythia, tulip poplars, daffodils, redbuds, tulips, dogwoods, irises, crab apples, and magnolias. As the daughter of a born-and-bred Southern Jew, my experience of the South was not temple bombings, as a later colleague's husband once suggested, but of a liberal education in the first de-segregated school in Nashville. Buffalo, New York, a later home, has snow and urban blight like other Rust Belt cities, but also marvelously designed parkways, with livable, walkable, and affordable neighborhoods. It also functions as a de facto museum of early and mid-20th century architecture, with one of the best modern and contemporary art collections in the country. There is more to America than most people have taken the time to see, much less consider. While this seems an almost too obvious claim to make, the fact remains that those in the major art centers largely view the art "peripheries" with a benevolent paternalism.

Yet, there is a trend to embrace places outside of the main art centers. Artadia recently published its first book, *5 Cities / 41 Artists / Artadia 08/09*,[2] which documents artists who have won their award in "second tier" American cities they support: Atlanta, Boston, Chicago, Houston, and the San Francisco Bay Area. There is also the *California Biennial, Prospect New Orleans,*[3] *Beyond/In Western New York,*[4] *inSite* in San Diego/ Tijuana, *The Desert Initiative*,[5] and the exhibition *Heartland*.[6] These new American biennials and surveys are a part of the ever-expanding biennial game, whose number internationally reaches over 100. With these exhibitions, the "periphery" globally promotes its sophistication, encourages cultural regeneration, economic growth, and competes for visibility.[7] The desire to do this within America is, likewise, expanding.

Sometimes, however, this wish to understand or experience art in Greater America, while well-meaning, can feel condescending. People presume a lack of sophistication outside the main centers and thus go looking there for "homespun," colloquial, or "outsider" art. *The People's Biennial*'s goal to show "significant contemporary work originating from often overlooked locales by artists who have not had significant exposure" was an attempt, as the organizers stated, to counter the "often-isolated" biennial model in

America.[8] The curators, however, were more interested in finding amateur artists working outside the art world. These individuals can be found just as easily in New York and Los Angeles as Haverford, Portland, Scottsdale, Rapid City, or Winston-Salem. Likewise, the Walker Art Center's recent exhibition, *The Spectacular of Vernacular*, does much the same thing, but with a focus on well-known international artists whose practices embrace the "rustic," localized craft, or tourist aesthetics of out-of-the-way places. This very methodology reinforces a hierarchy where one inevitably is looking down when looking out from the "center."

It may be that we simply need a semantic shift to discuss art that engages with the international art world but speaks from a particular *here* in the rest of America. The word vernacular is too focused on folk and localized popular culture traditions. The word regional is too connected to nostalgic notions of the American heartland, and an artistic movement that spurned innovation, city life, and technology. I prefer Localism.

Localism is about place in a way that embraces sophistication and diversity. It focuses on supporting the uniqueness of place, without being nostalgic. Eating or buying locally when one is in Phoenix does not mean only tamales, cactus jelly, or cowboy boots (very likely made in Texas, China, or Italy). Rather, it is about tomatoes that have enjoyed the same intense sunlight as their consumers, music from around the globe selected by an independent store, or clothes made by a designer living in the area who may have been educated in London. Localism opens its doors to the world, while at the same time is grounded in a particular environment and community.

"Locavore" may have its roots in the food world, but is a word that has broadened its meaning to encompass local businesses, arts, and culture.[9] Art in a locavore ideology would be connected to the place it comes from and be steeped in the larger international art discussion. It would make sense of place for the people living there, not reaffirm stereotypes and expectations. It would demand respect for artists who call these places home, are invested in their communities, and make art on par with the work coming out of Los Angeles, Berlin, or Johannesburg. It would celebrate diversity.

In locavore spirit, rather than describe the Southwest or Arizona, I want to introduce Phoenix. Better known as Phoenix/Scottsdale/Tempe (Mesa/Glendale/Gilbert/ParadiseValley/Guadalupe/Carefree/Chandler/Goodyear/Surprise/Sun City/Peoria), greater Phoenix covers over 2,000 square miles, and has over 4 million residents,[10] one of the lowest density urban areas in the country. In 1950, the City of Phoenix, the center of this metropolitan area, had 107,000[11] residents and compared to its present 1.45 million.[12] In 2007, it was the second fastest growing city in America (after Las Vegas).[13] The sun shines over 310 days,[14] with 106 days over 100°F and a whopping 17 over 110°F annually on average.[15] The sense of newness, the apparent lack of history, the heat, the desert landscape, and the sprawling cityscape make Phoenix unlike any other place I have lived or visited. Not surprisingly, the city/land-scape and sense of community affect the art and how it grows here. It is marked by extremes, as is almost everything about Phoenix.

The stark, majestic vistas, the towering saguaro cacti, and the big, eternally blue sky are Phoenix's face to the outside world and itself. The city's identity comes from nature: not monuments, the built environment, or cultural history. Camelback Mountain, Papago Butte, and Piestewa Peak dominate the horizon. But, Phoenix's other distinctive characteristic is the cheap, new, single family home in endless suburban developments. Space is big, wide-open and expansive. Open desert butts up to the city emphasizing again the feeling that Phoenix goes on forever. And like the desert, the city is neither empty nor dull. It's just different. It takes awhile for eastern eyes to acclimate. The brightness affects you.

Aaron Rothman (see page 142), like many, has become seduced by the possibilities offered by this unique ecology. However, his love of Phoenix did not happen quickly.[17] It grew over time and was facilitated by Arizona State University (ASU) and its strong photography department. Filled with renowned professors, ASU is a mix of traditions in process, landscape, and conceptual approaches. Rothman initially studied photogravure, a technique that allowed him to mine the space between photography, printmaking, and drawing. Professor Mark Klett, taught Rothman rigor, in the traditional sense that has been handed down by generations of precise landscape photographers. With photographer/professor Bill Jenkins, he studied how photographs communicate "the mechanics of how meaning is created."[18] Like his mentors, Rothman was interested more in the how of the pictures, than the what; in work, he says, "that embodies an experience of the landscape in a broader sense."[19]

Phoenix is a good place to do this. Somehow, as a result of a size and scale that feels beyond our comprehension, we are more aware of "being"—both where we are and our temporary presence.[20] As Rothman says, it is "the awareness of being in relation to time—both in the immediate present and the geologic past and future."[21] It's almost as if the natural and manmade environments have been reversed, and all the new, anonymous buildings evoke potential and dread all at once—a kind of suburban sublime. Rothman sees these "ruins in reverse" mirroring "the feelings of beauty and fear instilled by the vast spaces of the American west."[22] (Fig. 1)

In 2009, Rothman was included in *Looking Through the Other End of a Telescope* at the Scottsdale Museum of Contemporary Art (SMoCA) alongside Jon Fisher and Jeff Shore, Mungo Thomson, and Jennifer West. Despite working in different mediums and in distinct ways, all these artists are trying to evaluate our place on the earth and how technology affects that understanding.[23] For this exhibition, Rothman created *Where You Are and Where You Can Never Be* (2009) (Fig. 2), an installation that exposed the museum's skylights, from which he produced a series of photographs and videos that documented the light as it moved across the room. This work was then shown in conjunction with the actual light of the open skylight and earlier sky studies, which forced the viewer to slow down, notice, and consider that specific place in relation to the outside world (Fig. 3).

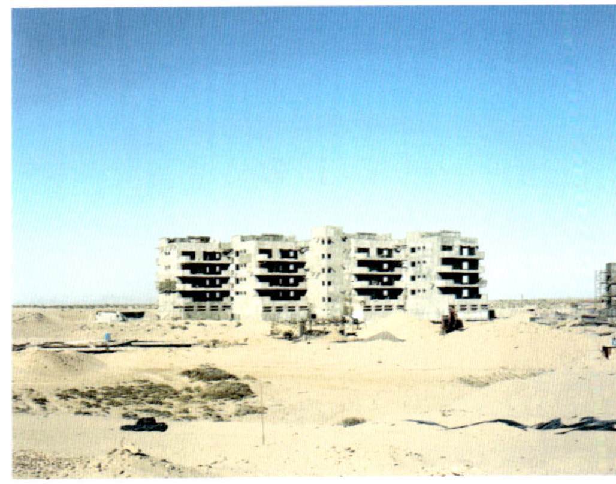

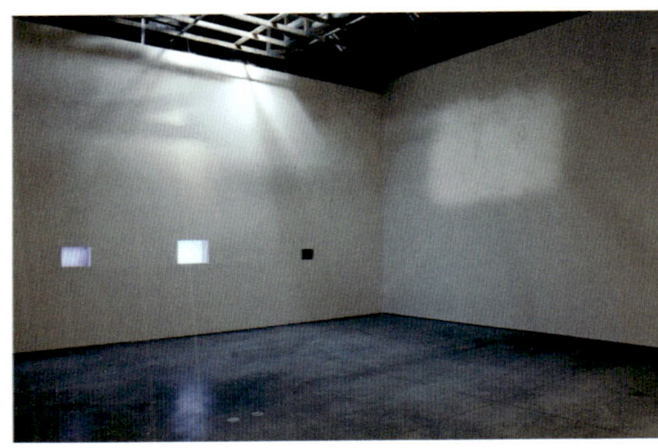

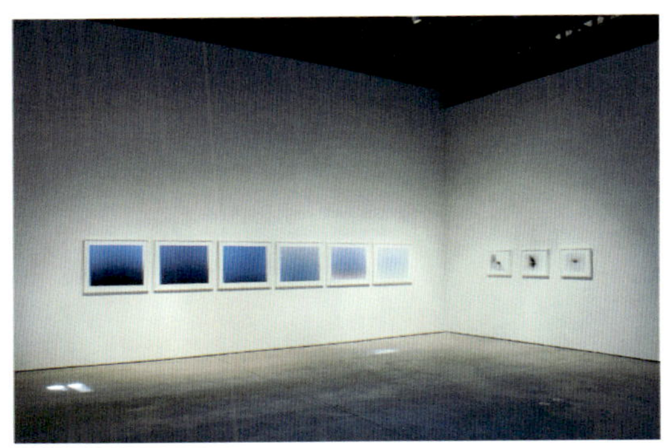

Figure 1. Aaron Rothman, *Ruin*, 2007, Archival inkjet print, 30" x 37.5", Photo courtesy of the artist

Figure 2. Aaron Rothman, *Where You Are and Where You Can Never Be*, 2009 (installation view), Scottsdale Museum of Contemporary Art, Scottsdale, AZ, Photo courtesy of the artist

Figure 3. Aaron Rothman, *Where You Are and Where You Can Never Be*, 2009 (installation view), Scottsdale Museum of Contemporary Art, Scottsdale, AZ, Photo courtesy of the artist

While Rothman draws heavily from his experience in the natural and urban desert, he shares much with other artists working with perception and abstraction. Similar to Luisa Lambri's photographs of modernist buildings, his images of beams of light, flowering weeds in a forgotten parking lot, the open sky, or corners of a room abstract the experience of the physical world. Both owe much to mid-century painters and "light and space" artists—Lambri to Barnett Newman and Mark Rothko, and Rothman to Agnes Martin and James Turrell. In these traditions, Rothman creates suggestive, rather than descriptive, images that allude to place rather than describe it explicitly.

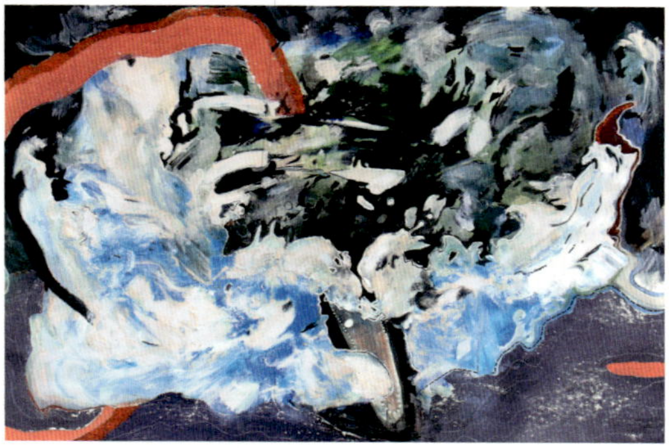

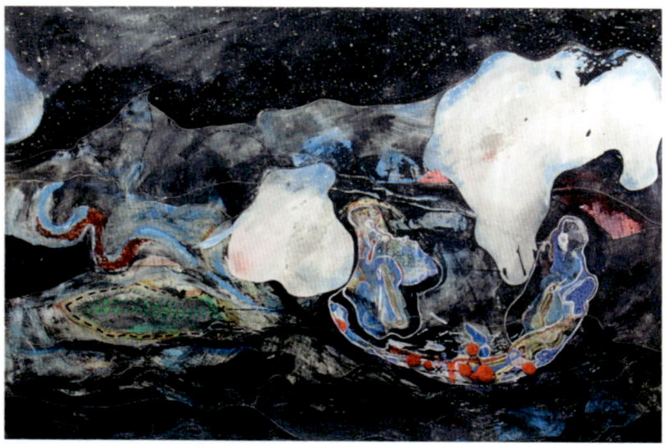

Sue Chenoweth (see page 108), like so many, moved to Arizona for health reasons. One of Phoenix's early attractions was the comfort it provided to thousands because of its dry, warm, and allergy neutral climate. Many of the area's storied patriarchs first moved here to cure the likes of respiratory problems or typhoid fever and left an indelible mark: Doc Holliday (dentist, gunfighter), Dwight Heard (landowner, cattleman, and citrus farmer turned arts patron), Del Webb (a revolutionary in retirement living and developer of Sun City), and Frank Lloyd Wright (who established Taliesin West).[25] Chenoweth's family followed in 1958, when they left Plainview, Texas, to find relief for their four-year-old daughter's myriad medical problems.

Like many, they drove West and stopped in El Paso, Tucson, and finally, Phoenix. Knowing no one, her father got a job as a salesman of architectural hardware, a field in which he would eventually have his own very successful business. They soon bought a single-family home on an irrigated Phoenix lot and lived there for over fifty-five years.[26] Chenoweth's family story is a classic, almost too-perfect, American Dream.

Chenoweth still lives in the Phoenix you don't expect, with its tall trees, some fifty to sixty feet tall, and shaded backyards with expansive swaths of green. On one-third to two-acre lots, ash, evergreens, eucalyptus, and citrus trees flourish from the regular flooding of carefully sloped lawns.[27] Central Phoenix is an oasis with temperatures five to ten degrees cooler than the rest of the Valley. This artificial landscape mirrors the lush surroundings people left back east. It has made real their ability to create a new world for themselves. Here the desert becomes a literal clean slate on which to build one's dreams—one's landscape, one's house, and one's story.

Figure 4. Sue Chenoweth, *Ramming of the Whale Ship Essex*, 2007, Gouache, graphite, Letraset, model railroad flocking, and pantone paper on paper, 30" x 44", Photo courtesy of the artist

Figure 5. Sue Chenoweth, *Pollard and Ramsdell on the 94th Day, February 23, 1821*, 2007, Gouache, graphite, Letraset, model railroad flocking, pompom, and pantone paper on paper, 30" x 44", Photo courtesy of the artist

The long languid summer days spent dreaming and reading in this environment fostered Chenoweth's process of transforming the everyday into the extraordinary. *Alice in Wonderland*, the poetry of A.A. Milne, Fedor Rojankovsky's illustrations in *Froggie Goes a Courtin'*, Anne Frank's *The Diary of a Young Girl*, William Golding's *Lord of the Flies*, and eventually the works of southern writers like William Faulkner and Carson McCullers[28] furthered her quest for real-life magic. In her series *Predator and Prey* (2007-2008) (Figs. 4, 5 and 6), Chenoweth drew on Herman Melville's novel *Moby Dick*, and the true story that inspired the tale involving the 19th century American whaling ship the *Essex*, its attack by a sperm whale, and the cannibalism that resulted from the shipwreck. The work was also formed of her own experiences and interests: her obsession with Timothy Treadwell,[29] a childhood close-encounter with a black bear, and diving with great white sharks as an adult.[30] Additionally, teaching at a charter arts high school further allows Chenoweth to discover her true self by finding inspiration in young, less constricted imaginations.[31]

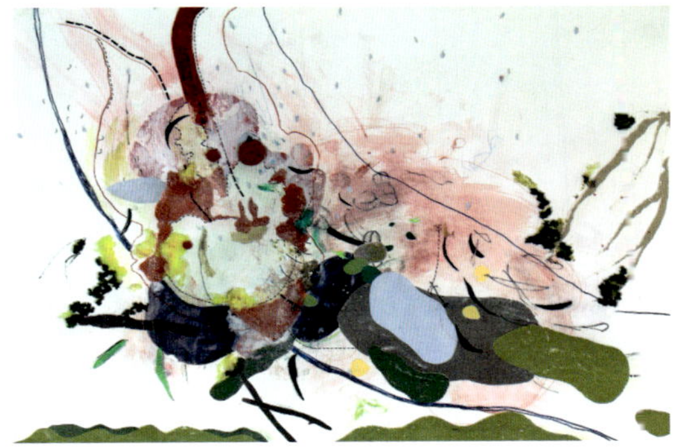

With work that is full of "sophisticated artistic awareness," yet "confident enough to throw caution to the wind," as Susan Krane, former director of SMoCA, stated,[32] Chenoweth is a kindred spirit to many contemporary painters and draughtsmen/women struggling to find individual voices in mediums weighed down by history that draw only intermittent interest from curators. Akin to Laura Owens, Chenoweth indulges in pure fantasy and creates work that appears casually made, but is really deeply layered and complex. Both had an intense and rigorous training in drawing. Chenoweth also shares an unsteady balance between childlike narrative and abstraction with Amy Sillman, a curiosity and a fascination with dismemberment with Dana Schultz, an interest in primal narrative with Kiki Smith, and a non-linear understanding of time with Lari Pittman.

Unlike Rothman and Chenoweth, Gregory Sale's perspective is that of a critical outsider (see page 144). His work not only attempts to understand community but to build it. Community is an odd word for Phoenix for, while it is a big city in terms of numbers, in other ways it is a conglomeration of inward-facing small towns. As a place to start over and live your dreams, "neighborhoods" are formed around personal desire—retirement, vacation, fitness, and job opportunities—rather than grown through years of organic settlement. Each community separates itself and prioritizes its own needs, finding safety and economic security in avoiding civic engagement. Sun City not only popularized active retirement, it withdrew from its respective local school district, claiming its residents had already paid for their children to be educated back in their hometowns.[33] Immigrants from Texas, Chicago, or Buffalo root for the Cowboys, the Cubs, or the Bills first over the Arizona Cardinals or Diamondbacks. Why invest in urban life if you are new to a place, know that you might leave anyway, or only live here part-time?

Figure 6. Sue Chenoweth, *Timothy Treadwell*, 2007, Gouache, graphite, Letraset, model railroad flocking, pompom, and pantone paper on paper, 30" x 44", Photo courtesy of the artist

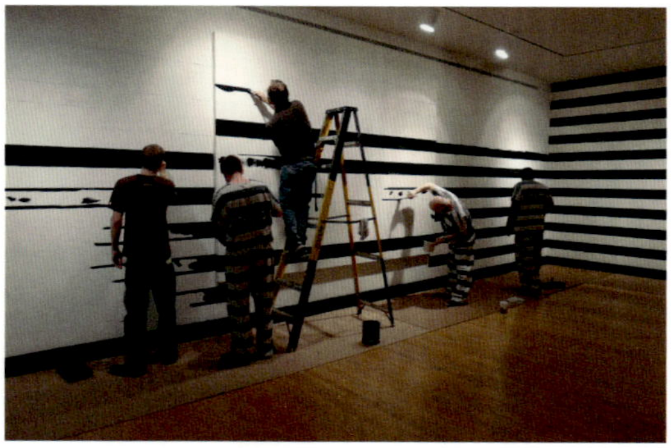

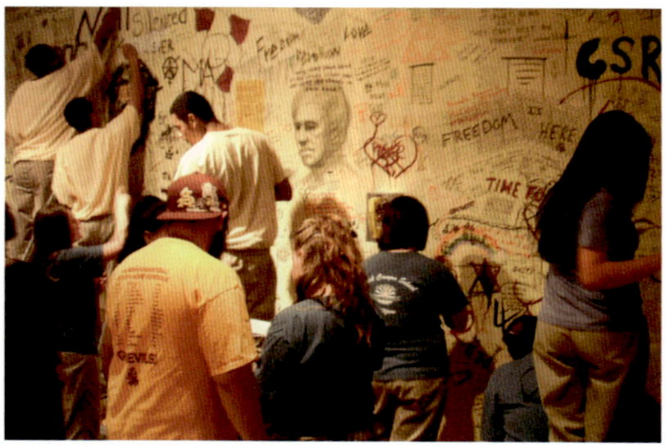

Figure 7. Gregory Sale, *It's not just black and white*, 2011, Photo by Stephen Gittins

Figure 8. Youth on temporary escorted furloughs from Adobe Mountain and Black Canyon, Arizona Department of Juvenile Corrections, 2011, Photo by John Spiak

This feeling of a fractured community is heightened even further by Phoenix's desire to maintain its identity as an outpost of Midwestern culture, while being on the cusp of becoming a Latino city. Phoenix today mirrors Los Angeles in the 1980s, with a third of the population now being Hispanic.[34] This ethnic diversity is not new for, like other Western cities that grew up in the late 19th century, early Phoenix was a mix of Mexicans, Chinese, Native Americans, and African Americans. Yet, unlike other cities in the Southwest, because it has no history of Spanish or Mexican periods, early Anglo-European settlers reframed the city's image as one of a prosperous, progressive American town. They physically and culturally segregated minorities in ethnic communities and schools, such as the Phoenix Indian School, in an attempt to erase cultural histories.[35]

While Sale probably did not know about Phoenix's complex sense of community when he and his partner left New York City in 1992 looking for an adventure, this contextualization of the place has been important to both his development as an artist and to a fuller understanding of his work. When he arrived in Phoenix, in addition to being an artist, he worked as a Curator of Education at the ASU Art Museum, a public art project coordinator for the Phoenix Office of Arts and Culture, and the Visual Arts Director at the Arizona Commission on the Arts. Sale's ability to be a driving force in his community was exemplified by his collaborative efforts with his colleagues to bring the Creative Capital Foundation to Arizona to conduct professional development training for artists from 2006 – 2008.[36] All of this work has been representative of and formative for his artistic practice.

Sale has a gift for bringing people together, establishing trust in difficult places, and engendering an open-ended, organic dialogue. For his most recent project, *It's not just black and white* (2011), Sale delved into Arizona's criminal justice system and the complex cultural fabric that determines the practices of punishment and discipline. Maricopa County's Sheriff Joe Arpaio has become nationally known for his Hollywood/cowboy methods and ideas. Sale brought the multiple constituencies of this world into the apolitical space of the ASU Art Museum over the three-months of his residency. For fifty-two different events, everyone from incarcerated men and women and their families, parolees, ex-inmates, corrections officers, elected officials, government employees, members of the community, media representatives, activists, artists, and academic researchers gathered in the museum for both discussions and activities.[37]

At the start of the project, Sale, together with inmates (participating in the only rehabilitation-reentry program offered in Maricopa County's harsh, punitive system), painted stripes on the gallery walls (Fig. 7). His new collaborators were also provided with an "open" graffiti wall within the space where they could take the design lead (Fig. 8). Aided by a streaming live-video feed, daughters danced in the museum for and with their imprisoned mothers, while community members stood as witnesses (Fig. 9). Interested citizens signed up for tours to see Tent City Jail first hand, a place where short-term inmates live outside even in extreme heat. The prisoner-rights activist Angela Davis spoke to a standing-room-only crowd of 500 during finals week, receiving two standing ovations.[39] Most importantly, a widely diverse range of people got to know each other, develop relationships, gain new respect for one another, and find informal ways to connect in a community known for fragmentation and segregation (Fig. 10). Fortuitously, five of the men, who had been paroled by the end of the project, returned to paint out the stripes in a closing event; one of these men proposed to his future wife in front of the wall.[39]

Sale wants to see behind the "toughest sheriff in America" and to work with the community to diffuse the power of images appropriated from old Hollywood films (chain gangs in striped uniforms working on the highway) and military style humiliation (pink underwear) that have gotten Arpaio elected for the last twenty years. Sale hopes that by providing an extended forum for direct and mediated experience, we can start to form our own conclusions about crime and justice, the effects of its rhetoric on our public resources, freedom and democracy, and most simply, how we relate to our fellow human beings.

Sale explores relational aesthetics in a particularly engaged and sustained way that moves beyond simply bringing human relations to the center of art practice as a point for inspiration or general investigation. In so doing, he answers Claire Bishop's critique of this new art direction, when she asks "what *types* of relations are being produced, for whom, and why?"[40] Sale's work is truly transformative, synthesizing Tim Rollins' community collaboration, Suzanne Lacy's performance and activism, and the transformative healing of Linda Montana's work. It is at once specific, committed, and open-ended.

Any discussion of Phoenix must include Native American culture and history. While the city itself (like all of America) has erased all traces of an Indigenous past, it does retain trace connections to it through kitsch and history museums. It is, however, the most important "Red City" in America. As artist Kade L. Twist describes it:

> Indians have always been here. It's central. It's where many rivers once came together, draining from the surrounding mountains. It's located along historic trade routes. It's home to one of the largest ancient civilizations in America.[41]

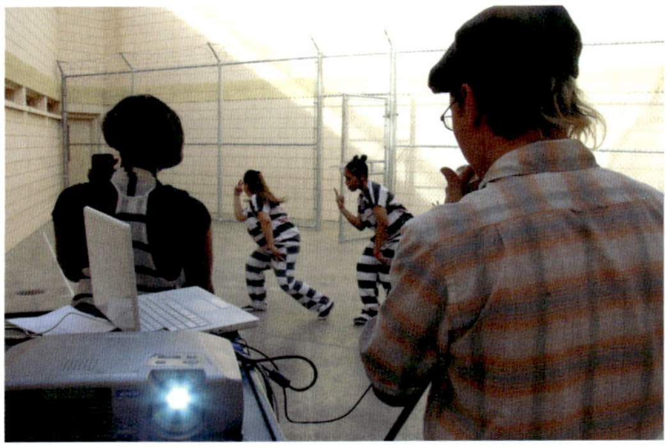

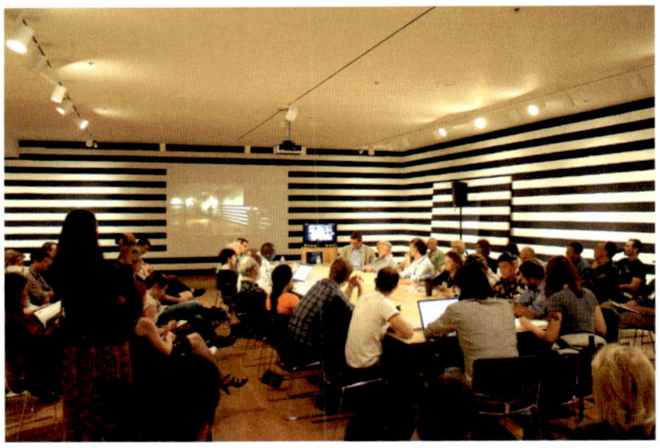

Figure 9. Mother-Daughter Distance Dance, 2011, Choreography by Elizabeth Johnson with Teniqua Broughton and Gregory Sale, Photo by Gregory Sale

Figure 10. Roundtable Discussion, 2011, Photo by Josh Loeser

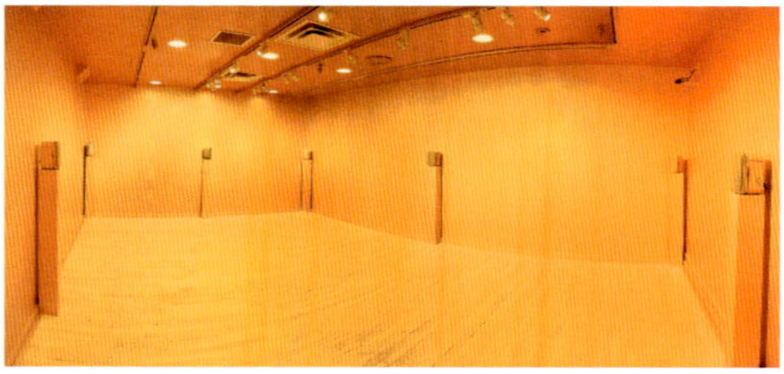

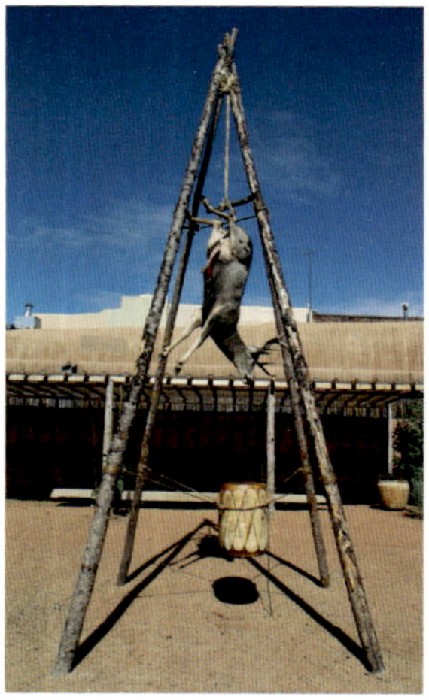

Because of this history of convergence, Native Americans have long used Phoenix as a place to connect. Indigenous leaders like Ben Hanley, Joy Hanley, Sid Beane, and Phyllis Bigpond have been coming to the city for over 60 years to advocate for social justice, self-determination, and tribal sovereignty.[42] The 1970s and 80s ushered in a golden era of philanthropic, religious, and federal support as a response, in part, to decades of egregious and devastating treatment. The current generation is building on this foundation, and Phoenix is currently at the forefront of the Native American intellectual discourse and social, political, educational, and community development work, in part through ASU's Law School and its new American Indian Policy Institute.[43] With the third largest Native population in the country, after New York and Los Angeles, but with a far greater Native identity, Phoenix is the urban Indian center to watch in the 21st century.[44]

Nationally, seventy percent of Native Americans live in urban areas.[45] This is the contemporary experience of the Native American, despite the stereotype of an "Indian" on a reservation. As a central city for Indigenous artists and thinkers to gather, Phoenix played a key role in the formation of Postcommodity (see page 140). The Indigenous collective is made up of: Raven Chacon (Albuquerque), Cristóbal Martínez (Phoenix), Kade L. Twist (Phoenix), and Nathan Young (Albuquerque). Operating out of different cities, the collective's geographical dispersal reflects the historical displacement of their forebears, representing the experience of Indigenous peoples and advocating for their interests.[46]

Postcommodity poetically captures the disjointed experience of the contemporary Native American. Their sometimes aggressive, revolutionary-spirited installations condense the visceral dislocation of being ripped from one's homeland. Their installations are visual, auditory, and spiritual, while their writings recall early modernist manifestos in their spirit and urgency. The disruption of time and space is amplified in Postcommodity's *If History Moves at the Speed of Its Weapons, Then the Space of the Arrow Is Changing* (2010) (Fig. 11), where a sonic "ambush" filled a gallery with sounds of Pueblo Revolt era weapons.[41] *P'oe iew naví ûnp'oe dînmuu (My Blood is in the Water)* (2010) (Fig. 12) memorialized Anglo-European settlers' total disrespect for the land, the symbolic blood of a mule deer dripped on an amplified Pueblo drum as an act of resistance against colonization, economic supremacy, and convenience.[48] In *Do You Remember When?* (2009) (Fig. 13), they cut a hole into the ASU Museum's floor to create a spiritual, cultural, and physical portal between an Indigenous worldview and the mainstream discourse on sustainability. The block of concrete that was removed was, in their words, "a trophy celebrating Indigenous intervention in opposition to a Western

Figure 11. Postcommodity, *If History Moves At the Speed of Its Weapons, Then the Shape of the Arrow is Changing*, 2010 (installation view), 3D sound sculpture (9 audio channels, loudspeakers, gold acrylic paint), 29'x16', Museum of Contemporary Native Arts, Santa Fe, NM, Photo by Will Wilson

Figure 12. Postcommodity, *P'oe iwe naví ûnp'oe dînmuu (My Blood is in the Water)*, 2010 (installation view), Mixed media installation, sculpture with sound (mule deer taxidermy, wood poles, water, amplifier, drum), Dimensions variable, Museum of Contemporary Native Arts, Santa Fe, NM, Photo courtesy of Postcommodity

scientific worldview."[49] Postcommodity's practice at its heart is about reclaiming spiritual space, pointing out that the real transgressions are not individual or policy decisions but modernity itself and the loss of understanding interdependent life cycles.

Postcommodity's work resembles other artists' practices, which explore violence against a specific culture. Like Kara Walker, Glenn Ligon, and Mona Hautom, Postcommodity takes horrifying cultural histories and documents their impact through powerful aesthetic and emotional forms. With their commitment to utilizing found, repetitive, and manipulated sound, they follow in the footsteps of John Cage and Christian Marclay, and at times resembling a noise band, their disruptive spirit mirrors Bruce Nauman's *Clown Torture* and its insatiable screaming "nos." The spiritual sons of the Cherokee, Chicano, Delaware, Kiowa, Navajo, and Pawnee tribes from which they descend, these tricksters combine critical questioning and formal transformation in the spirit of contemporary Native American artists Jimmie Durham and Rebecca Belmore.

The extremes that define Phoenix itself also define the artistic community as a whole. On the positive end, the metropolitan area boasts three institutions devoted to cutting-edge contemporary art. A handful of grassroots, artist-run, and smaller spaces present thoughtful projects on a regular basis. National and international speakers frequently come to town. 10,000 people converge monthly for a First Friday gathering of open studios, gallery exhibitions, and a general outdoor art fair in a revitalized section of central Phoenix. Significant collectors of contemporary art and their collections spend part of their time here. Foundation initiatives over many years from inside and outside the community have had a major impact. Public art is able to thrive at a level unheard of in the East. The percentage of artists who own their own homes and studios exceeds the national average. ASU has an active and engaged art school, and there is a general acceptance of the new, of wanting to take risks. Possibility is de rigueur.

Yet, you would not know about the wealth the Valley of the Sun's contemporary art scene has unless you went looking for it. Phoenix does not embrace a sophisticated cosmopolitan persona. Most galleries sell traditional or contemporary Southwestern art and share sidewalks with tourist shops. Only one commercial gallery consistently embraces the international contemporary art scene. The Phoenix Art Museum actively supports purchases of significant contemporary works, built a new contemporary art wing five years ago, and has a large and engaged patron group for contemporary art. Nevertheless, the museum's best fundraiser is the *Cowboy Artists of America Exhibition and Sale*, the most anticipated Western American fine art event in the country.

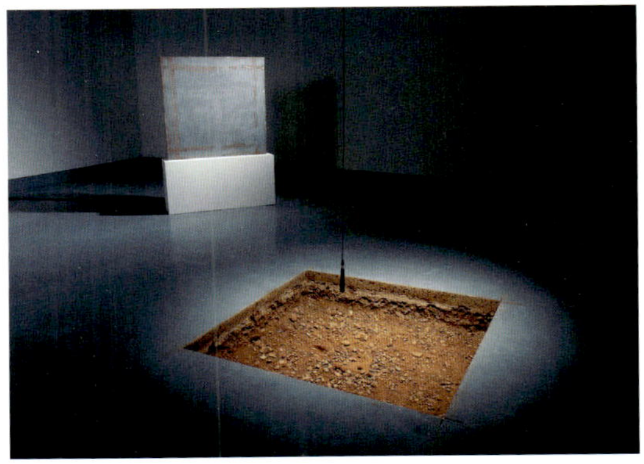

Figure 13. Postcommodity, *Do You Remember When*, 2009 (installation view), Site-specific intervention and mixed media installation (cut concrete, exposed earth, light, sound), Dimensions variable, ASU Art Museum, Tempe, AZ, Photo courtesy of Postcommodity

Eighth-generation followers of Frederic Remington share space for a month every year with a Cornelia Parker burnt "house," a Yayoi Kusama infinity room, and a Lawrence Weiner site-specific text piece. While national contemporary collectors with homes in the area are engaged with the local scene, their first allegiances and largest gifts are to their home cities. Mid-career artists, serious young gallerists, and start-up art magazines struggle to sustain themselves.

Future Arts Research, or F.A.R. @ ASU, was created to host leading international and national artists to work in collaboration with university departments and the surrounding community. But like many things in the Valley, active funding for F.A.R. dwindled just two years after it was founded. More than elsewhere, in recent years Phoenix has been dramatically affected by city, state, and local institutional arts de-funding. Consequently, the arts tend to mirror the real estate community; while full of promise and potential, economic investment can quickly evaporate.

Nevertheless, while established traditions are few, the spectacular can bloom more easily in Phoenix. For instance, the ASU Art Museum's Social Studies program is breaking important ground on experimental discourse and audience engagement. The museum has a venerable history of presenting first exhibitions in the United States by Central and Latin American artists. They took Bill Viola to the Venice Biennale in 1994. The museum enthusiastically supports local artists and, in 2007, documented the expanding contemporary art scene in *New American City: Artists Look Forward*. In 2001, just two years after the museum was founded, SMoCA hosted an important survey of James Turrell's work and has supported fantastic commissions by Nick Cave, Song Dong, Lyle Ashton Harris, Nina Katchadourian, and Jean Shin and Brian Ripel. SMoCA's legacy of creating and supporting original architecture and design exhibitions and commissions is unparalleled in the Southwest and rare nationally. They regularly give local artists significant opportunities to show and create new work, often side-by-side with national and international stars. Likewise, the Phoenix Art Museum recently presented *Locals Only*, their first Latino exhibition.[50] They also give generous grants to local artists working at all stages of their careers. Today, artists working in the region could not find better institutional advocates, exhibition opportunities, or recognition for their work. Yet, despite all this support, what is lacking, both here and in other "peripheral" cities, is not artists or institutions but the marketplace—a Chelsea, a Culver City.

Artists in Greater America are not so much expressing their "cultural identity," but rather, as Nicolas Bourriaud noted about globalism's effect on artists, they are "projectiles" that start from a general shared understanding of culture, aesthetic developments, and critical inquiry and figure out what that means wherever they happen to land. Bourriaud calls these people, whom he is most interested in and who resist the standardization that happens with globalism, "radicants."

> [Radicants] produce their roots as they move forward. They invent themselves as human beings and as artists through the territories with which they enter into negotiation, through the forms they use. In other words, what globalization introduced is the possibility for an artist to start at a global level of culture and arrive at specific and vernacular forms, in opposition to this postmodern figure of the artist putting forward his "cultural identity," his "origins" and pedigree.[51]

Stephanie Smith reaches a similar conclusion about the dance between the global and the local, but approaches the discussion from the opposite end. She speaks about an "aerated provincialism," where one takes advantage of local resources, conditions, and circumstances while reaching out for "global relevance." It is "regularly refreshed by the movement of people and ideas, in and out." Importantly, she notes that this "aeration" helps weed out the downsides of provincialism, "boosterism," and an ignorance of the world outside of the locale. Smith listed a few of the ingredients these "provincial" art centers have to use to their advantage: cheap real estate, supportive close-knit communities, and an open and unmonitored territory within which to develop. Additionally, artists working from these places benefit from easy connectivity provided by cheap air travel, the Internet, and solid local art infrastructures.[52]

The four artists selected to represent Phoenix perfectly illustrate these new understandings of global and provincial influences on contemporary art practice; they are true to the locavore spirit. They are all actively engaged with Phoenix, the region and its history, but are decisively part of a larger dialogue within contemporary international/global art practice. In that sense, the only thing that differentiates them from artists in New York and Los Angeles is visibility and the hierarchy of the art world.

It is time that we recognize art in "Greater America" at a global level. The Whitney Museum of American Art is continually reassessing its definition of what constitutes American art and sees a responsibility to understand it within an international context. Today this means they are exhibiting and collecting American art by "non-Americans who live in the U.S., Americans born in the U.S. who live abroad, [and] Americans who were born and live abroad with U.S. passports."[53] They collect work by non-Americans who make work about America in America. Why not include more American artists living in other parts of America who are engaged in the international discussion? Why not take the time to know these places in a real and sustained way, as they do artists in Basel or Bejing? In our locavore times, a time when globalism is inversely creating a heightened awareness of local food, culture, and consumerism, artists in the overlooked locales of America deserve to be a part of an expanded discussion of American art. Their work here demands our respect.

1 Sylvie Fortin, "Insight? Outta Site! lecture series" (presented by Nashville Cultural Arts Project, Nashville, Tennessee, October 2, 2010).

2 Franklin Sirmans, ed., 5 Cities / 41 Artists / *Artadia 08/09* (New York: Artadia, 2011).

3 Prospect New Orleans has reconfigured itself, after the initial international splash, to be more focused as part of its mission on Louisiana artists.

4 *Beyond/In Western New York* is a regional biennial presented in 2010 by twelve Buffalo arts institutions. See http://beyondinwny.org.

5 Housed at the ASU Art Museum, the Desert Initiative is composed of a network of arts institutions throughout the Southwestern United States and in other global desert regions with a vested and active interest in the desert as a point of creative investigation. See http://asuartmuseum.asu.edu/news/press_release.php?id=871.

6 Charles Esche, Kerstin Niemann, and Stephanie Smith, *Heartland* (Chicago: Smart Museum of Art, University of Chicago, 2009). It should be noted that this catalogue was published to coincide with an exhibition held at the Van Abbemuseum in Eindhoven, Netherlands, Oct. 4, 2008-Feb. 8, 2009 and at the Smart Museum of Art in Chicago, Oct. 1, 2009-Jan. 17, 2010.

7 Bruce W. Ferguson, "Beyond/In Western New York: Alternating Currents," in *Beyond/In Western New York: Alternating Currents*, ed. Albright-Knox Art Gallery et. al. (Buffalo: The Buffalo Fine Arts Academy, 2010), 9.

8 "People's Biennial," Independent Curators International," accessed June 3, 2011, http://www.curatorsintl.org/index.php/exhibitions/peoples_biennial/.

9 Phoenix has a strong non-profit organization, called Local First Arizona (LFA), dedicated to "supporting, maintaining, and celebrating" locally owned businesses throughout the state. http://www.localfirstaz.com/. A large group of cities nationally have similar organizations, often with strong "Buy Local" campaigns.

[10] "Fun Facts," Visit Phoenix, accessed August 5, 2011, http://www.visitphoenix.com/about-phoenix/facts/index.aspx.

[11] "Table 18. Population of the 100 Largest Urban Places: 1950," U.S. Census Bureau, accessed August 5, 2011, http://www.census.gov/population/www/documentation/twps0027/tab18.txt.

[12] "U.S. Census Bureau Delivers Arizona's 2010 Census Population Totals, Including First Look at Race and Hispanic Origin Data for Legislative Redistricting," United States Census 2010, accessed August 5, 2011, http://2010.census.gov/news/releases/operations/cb11-cn76.html.

[13] In 2007, the City of Las Vegas since 2000 has grown 29.2% and the City of Phoenix 24.2%. "In Pictures: America's Fastest-Growing Cities," Forbes.com, accessed August 8, 2011, http://www.forbes.com/2007/10/31/property-cities-growth-forbeslife-cx_mw_1031realestate_slide_3.html?thisSpeed=undefined. It is also interesting to note that the City of Phoenix is the sixth most populous in America. Phoenix Facts," City of Phoenix, accessed August 5, 2011, http://phoenix.gov/citygovernment/facts/index.html.

[14] "Fun Facts."

[15] "Fact about 100 Degree Temperature at Phoenix," National Weather Service Forecast Office, accessed June 18, 2011, www.wrh.noaa.gov/psr/general/history/index.php?page=100deg.

[16] Dr. Patricia Gober, "Phoenix: The New American City", in *New American City: Artists Look Forward*, ed. Heather Sealy Lineberry, (Tempe: Arizona State University Art Gallery, 2007), 12.

[17] In fact, Rothman's attraction to Phoenix surprised him, calling him back several times, despite first escaping to San Francisco and then teaching in Memphis. He missed the open sky, saying that over time the initially unappealing city grows on you. Information from Rothman, email message to author, June 10, 2011. See also Rothman, "50 States Project," http://www.50statesproject.net/aaronrothman.html.

[18] Aaron Rothman, email message to author, June 10, 2011.

[19] Ibid.

[20] Rothman, "Artist Statement" in email message to author, June 10, 2011.

[21] Rothman, "Artist Statement, February 2009" in email message to author, April 14, 2010.

[22] Ibid.

[23] Cassandra Coblentz, *SouthwestNET: Film & Video: Looking Through the Other End of a Telescope* (Scottsdale: Scottsdale Museum of Contemporary Art, 2009), 11.

[24] Rothman, unpublished interview with the author, May 4, 2010, for *Temporary Contemporary: Aaron Rothman: The Far Field* (Nashville: Cheekwood Botanical Garden and Museum of Art, 2010).

[25] Gober, "Phoenix," 11.

[26] Sue Chenoweth, email message to author, June 9, 2011.

[27] Utilizing irrigation canals from the Salt Water Project and built when the area was still citrus groves, yards are flooded on request at a preset time. Homeowners are required to be there to open the valves and anyone can opt out. During the summer it's every other week, in fall once a month, and during the winter not at all.

[28] Chenoweth, email message to author, June 15, 2011.

[29] Born April 29, 1957 in Long Island, New York, Timothy Treadwell was a self-taught grizzly bear expert, wildlife preservationist and documentary filmmaker. He lived among the coastal grizzly bears of Katmai National Park in Alaska, USA, for approximately 13 summers. In October 2003, Treadwell's remains, along with those of his girlfriend Amie Huguenard, were discovered near their campsit. They had been mauled and devoured by a grizzly, the first- known victims of a bear attack in the park. Treadwell's life, work and death were the subject of the 2005 documentary film by Werner Herzog titled *Grizzly Man*. For more information see: http://animal.discovery.com/tv/grizzly-man-diaries/timothy-treadwell/timothy-treadwell.html.

[30] Chenoweth, studio visit with author, April 15, 2011.

[31] Chenoweth, email message to author, June 15, 2011.

[32] Susan Krane, "Curator's Statement," in *Sue Chenoweth* (New York: Cue Art Foundation, 2005).

[33] Gober, "Phoenix," 14.

[34] Ibid, 14. Phoenix's Hispanic population rose from 20% to 39% between 1990 and 2004.

[35] Ibid, 14-15.

[36] Gregory Sale, email message to author, June 24, 2011.

[37] "It's not just black and white: Gregory Sale – Social Studies Project 6," ASU Art Museum Blog, accessed June 15, 2011, http://asuartmuseum.wordpress.com/2011/01/31/it's-not-just-black-and-white-gregory-sale-social-studies-project-6.

[38] Sale, Skype call with author, June 14, 2011.

[39] Ibid.

[40] Claire Bishop, "Antagonism and Relational Aesthetics," *October* 110, (Fall 2004): 65.

[41] Kade L. Twist, email message to author, June 17, 2011.

[42] Twist, email message to author, June 9, 2011.

[43] Twist, email message to author, June 17, 2011.

[44] Twist, "Urban Indians and the New American City," in *New American City: Artists Look Forward*, ed. Heather Sealy Lineberry, (Tempe: Arizona State University Art Gallery, 2007), 55.

[45] Ibid.

[46] Twist, email message to author, June 17, 2011.

[47] *If History Moves at the Speed of Its Weapons, Then the Space of the Arrow Is Changing,* Postcommodity, accessed June 18, 2011, http://postcommodity.com/?page_id=156.

[48] *P'oe iew naví ûnp'oe dînmuu (My Blood is in the Water)*, Postcommodity, accessed June 18, 2011, http://postcommodity.com/?page_id=154.

[49] *Do you Remember When?* Postcommodity, accessed August 8, 2011, http://postcommodity.com/DoYouRemember.html.

[50] Sara Cochran, *Locals Only* (Phoenix: Phoenix Art Museum, 2009), exhibited in tandem with *Phantom Sightings: Art after the Chicano Movement* from the Los Angeles County Museum of Art.

[51] Nicolas Bourriaud, "Globalization. So What Is It?" Art Press 379 (2010), accessed June 27, 2011. http://en.artpress.com/mobile/index.php?a=8123.

[52] Stephanie Smith, "Chicago: Beyond the Big Shoulders," in *5 Cities / 41 Artists / Artadia 08/09*, ed. Franklin Sirmans (New York: Artadia, 2011), 61.

[53] Adam Weinberg, director of the Whitney Museum of American Art, quoted in Dorothy Spears, "Curators Wanted: Must Love Art and Travel," *New York Times*, November 26, 2006, accessed June 25, 2011, http://www.nytimes.com/2006/11/26/arts/design/26spea.html?scp=1&sq=%22Curators%20wanted%22&st=cse.

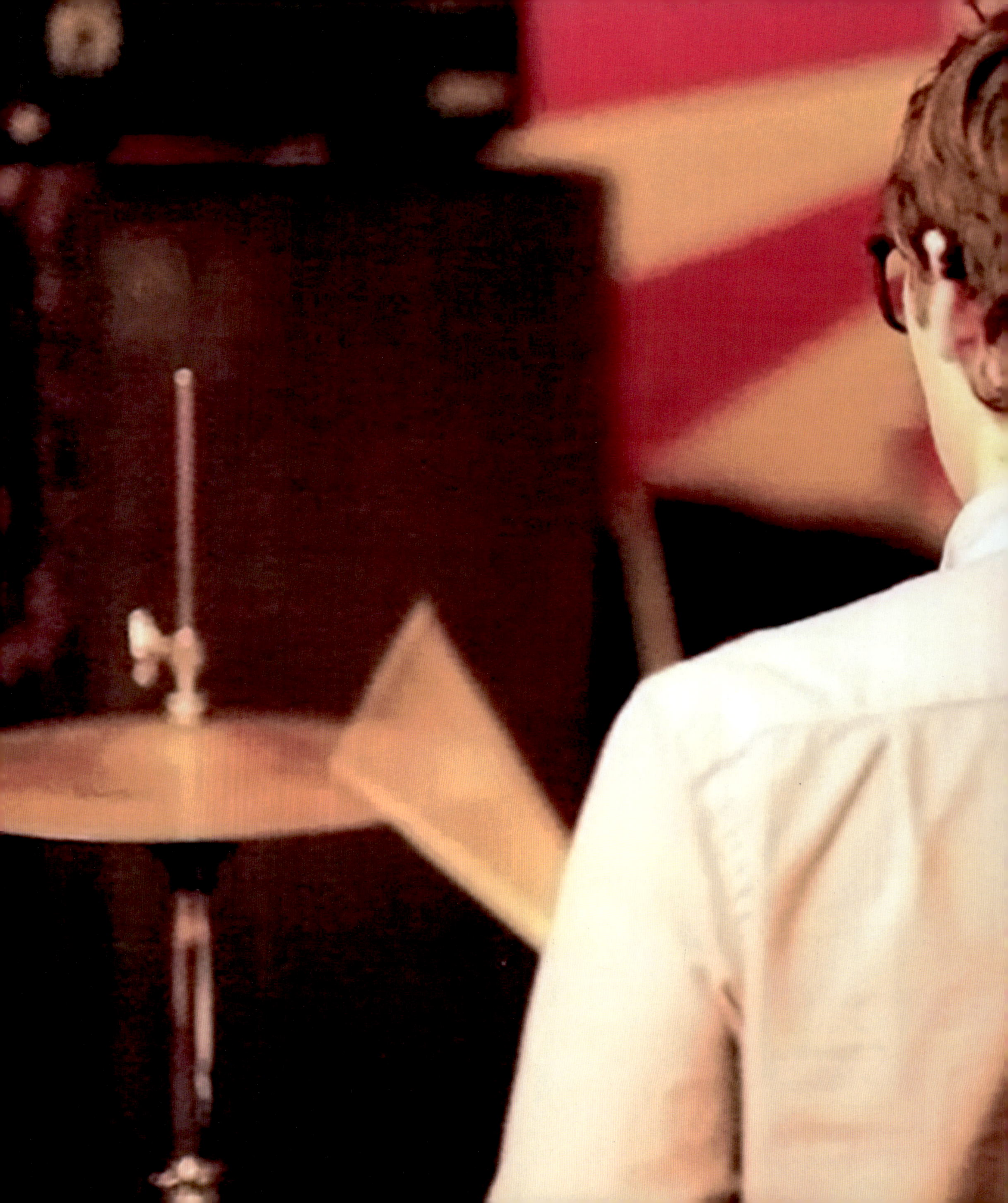

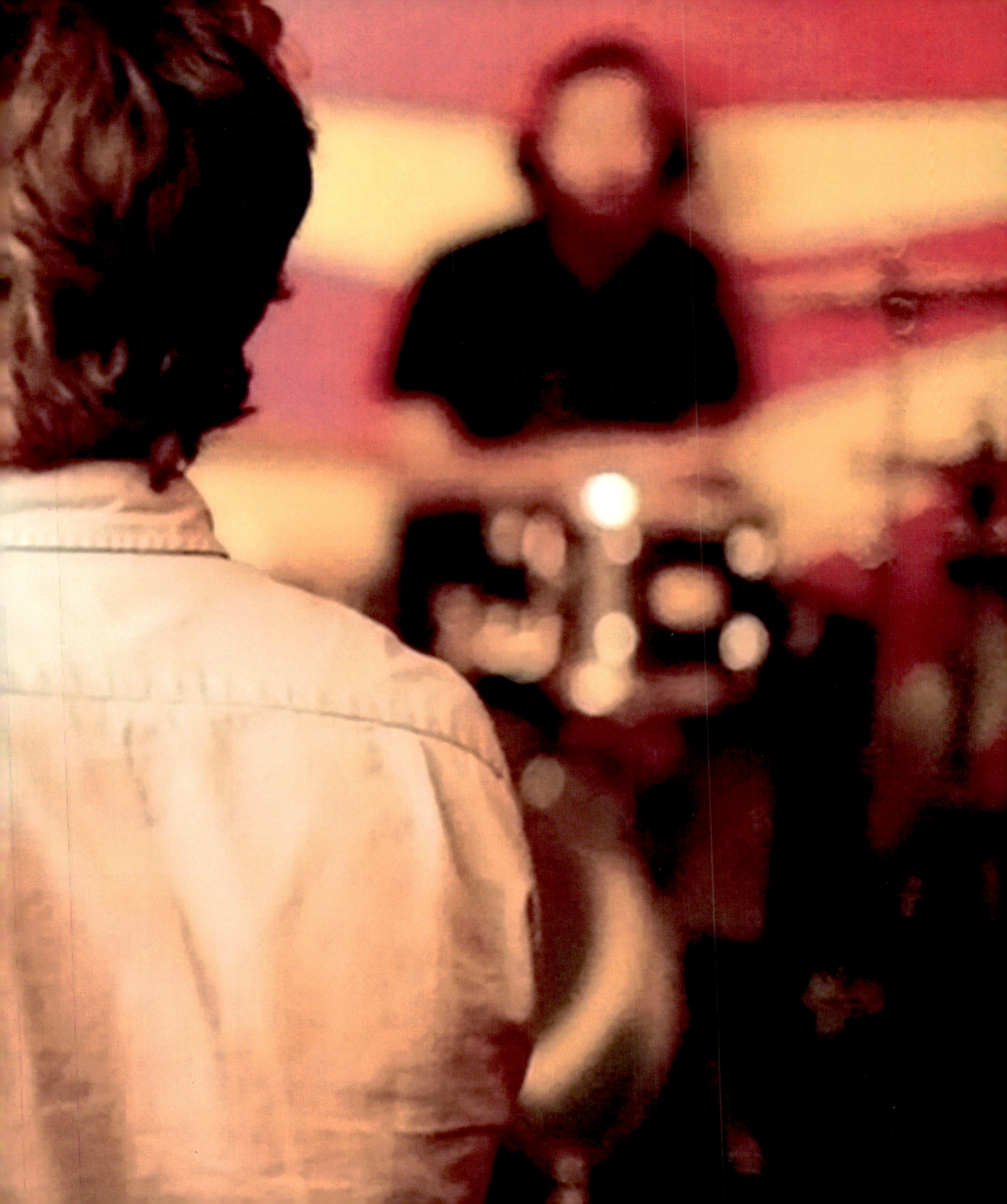

Carolina At Close Range

BY TEKA SELMAN

Previous spread:
Harrison Haynes
LRLL RLRR (Screen Test), 2011
Video still
Image courtesy of the artist

The Bull City, as Durham is sometimes known, is one of three points of the North Carolina Triangle region, which also includes Raleigh and Chapel Hill. The city's minor league baseball team—the Durham Bulls—was made famous by the eponymous 1988 movie, *Bull Durham*, starring Kevin Costner, Susan Sarandon, and Tim Robbins. Though the team's well-worn baseball park was a major—if unbilled—character, the film did little to showcase the city, perhaps because at the time some felt that there was little to flaunt. A rough and tumble city with a history in manufacturing intimately tied to big tobacco, Durham historically lacked the gloss attributed to its more cosmopolitan neighbor and the state's capital, Raleigh. But more recently, Durham and the surrounding area have become well-known as a hub of the slow-food movement, home to a booming indie music scene, as a high-ranking place to retire, and host to a legendary college basketball rivalry. The baseball team has moved to new digs in an upgraded stadium downtown, and the old ballpark is used by high-school teams for practice, visited by the occasional tourist in search of an iconic photograph. Even with these changes, Durham has retained much of the character for which it was once known, as a place in-between town and country. Both rural and industrial all at once, Durham is a city in the trees with air that once smelled of drying tobacco and now smells mostly of pine, the sky often glimpsed through breaks in the green canopy that fills the landscape.

All of this was new to me when I moved to Durham five years ago from Brooklyn, New York. Like most people who live or have lived in "the city," as Manhattan and its surrounding boroughs are so often designated, I came there from somewhere else, venturing to a large city from a smaller one. After college, I moved from my relatively small suburban hometown outside of Detroit, Michigan to Chicago, then to London before I eventually settled in New York, my professional Mecca as the then non-disputed arts capital of the world. When the time came to move again—in my case to North Carolina, where my partner would begin a new job—I could anticipate little more than a lower cost of living and a chance to own a home. Though no stranger to living outside of a major metropolitan area, newly married to a native North Carolinian and having visited before, the state was in many ways a mystery. Like most things unknown, it was easy to both romanticize and fear a place new and foreign, especially for me, an African-American northerner. Long held, well-worn generalizations about the South that fit so comfortably can be hard to shed. Yet like most things, from a distance the landscape appears less complex than when examined at close range.

Perhaps because it is both where I live and in many ways the nexus for my deeper engagement with the state, Durham became the starting point for thinking about artists living and working in North Carolina for ***here.*** As a partner from 2006 – 2009 in the now-defunct Branch Gallery, a local commercial gallery in Durham, I found myself in a unique position to learn about artistic production in the state. Two of the artists represented in ***here.*** are connected to Branch: Harrison Haynes and Stacy Lynn Waddell. In addition to Durham and the Triangle region, the other main area of engagement was the Piedmont Triad, which—though it has a similar geometrical regional designation to the Triangle—refers to the north west corner of the state that includes Winston-Salem, Greensboro, and High-Point. Glenda Wharton and Elsewhere Collaborative hail from Winston-Salem and Greensboro respectively; coincidentally, my husband grew up in the former and his mother in the latter, making both familiar to me in some sense.

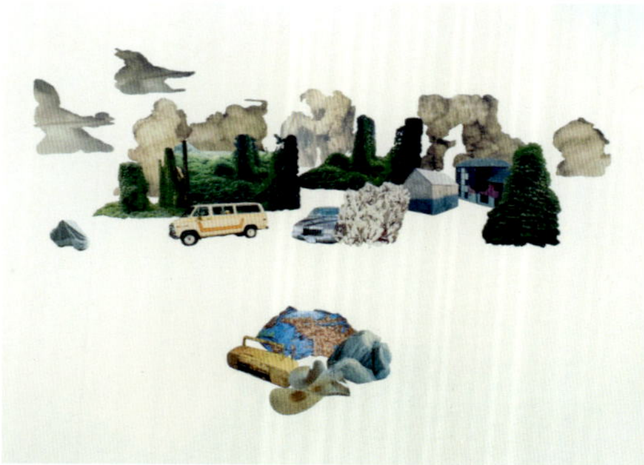

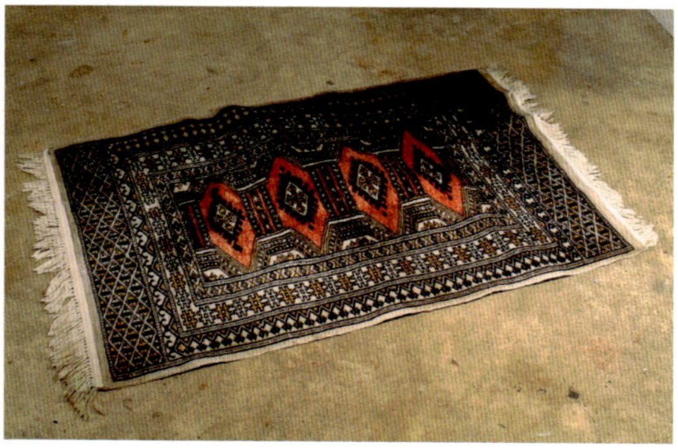

For most of the 20th century, both the Triangle and Triad have been known for their connections to manufacturing—particularly tobacco, textiles, and pharmaceuticals. As a legacy of the history of wealth and prosperity that industrialization brought to the region, it is not surprising that both philanthropy and thus the arts have long had a home there; the bulk of the state's contemporary arts institutions and hence, it could be argued, many of North Carolina's contemporary artists are based in the Triangle and Triad. Still, my selection of four artists from these areas is by no means an attempt to encompass, represent, or define all of what is happening in the arts in North Carolina. My contribution—I would suggest, like all curation—is a purely subjective snapshot, reflective of only some of the things I've seen in my short five years here.

Beyond the geography that links them together, what Elsewhere Collaborative, Harrison Haynes, Stacy Lynn Waddell, and Glenda Wharton share is work that is deeply personal, often tied to their experiences and memories, their lives that happen to be lived in North Carolina. I would hesitate to insist that their work is a direct reflection of this place; rather, geography is at times a part of, but does not define, their work. Just as the energy of major cities is built on the diversity of their populations and the experiences, histories, and traditions they bring with them, so are the areas outside of major cities multifaceted, complex, and full of multiple points of view. In the case of the work presented by these four artists based in North Carolina, the same is true. Each has its defining characteristics and all have things in common.

When we first met in 2006, Haynes was exploring the literal and metaphorical landscapes of his life so far, mining his childhood in paintings of reworked family photographs and, more compellingly, in quietly spare collages of the complex topography of the Triangle. The success of the latter series of works—entitled *Disruptive Patterns* (2006 - 2008) (Fig. 1)—lay in their ability to recreate an ambiance of evocative contrasts that mirrored Haynes' own environmental history: kudzu juxtaposed with high-rises, late model cars, amplifiers, drum kits, and houses. In these works, Haynes seamlessly combines fragments from magazines, books, and family photos into a new landscape floating within empty space. The jarring mix of familiar images that seem to hover above a vast plane gives the work a surrealist, dream-like quality, which renders elements of everyday life concurrently recognizable and alien. The resulting images seem to speak to the tension between "truth" and "memory"; objects emerge from blinding whiteness or perhaps the depths of the subconscious, floating dreamily to the surface to coalesce.

Figure 1. Harrison Haynes, *Disruptive Patterns #39*, 2008, Collage on paper, 22.5" x 30", Photo courtesy of the artist

Figure 2. Harrison Haynes, *Untitled (Drum Rug)*, 2010 (installation view), Hand-cut archival pigment print, 62" x 39", Photo courtesy of the artist

In some ways, these works mirror Haynes' own experiences. As a North Carolinian who is also a drummer in a post-punk band that tours frequently, he understands that memories of home while away take on a surreal, disjointed quality, and the return home can be jarring. Thus, the *Disruptive Patterns* series in some ways considers the tension between memory and reality; the inventive space between departure and return.

Haynes' most recent work more explicitly explores the slippage between his two professions—drummer and visual artist—while expanding his interest in photography, video, and performance. He once again turns to representation as a tool for toying with notions of truth, this time considering the spatial experience of being a musician. Now, the plastic elements of life as a musician—their mundane object-hood—are explored: an oriental rug to sit a drum-set on, a pile of cymbals ready to be put into a case, a piece of foam batting used to muffle sound in a recording studio (Fig. 2). The photographed objects are blown up to life-size proportions and either hung on the wall or placed on the floor, resulting in a hyper-realistic yet strangely flat, two-dimensional image that yields the surreal quality familiar in Haynes' work.

In ***here.***, Haynes moves to the experiential in the video work and performance *LRLL RLRR* (2011) (see page 122). The performance consists of two drummers—Haynes and a local musician—playing in a public space for an extended period of time. Facing each other yet physically far apart, they repeat the same beat in unison, the basic "left right left left, right left right right" hand motion taught to all beginning drummers. With time and the physical strain of repetition the beat speeds up or slows down, shifting in quality and intensity. The resulting interaction between the artists and audience transforms into an endurance test or a metaphysical experience, depending on one's perspective. In contrast, the video work puts the viewer in the place of the drummer so that the point of view is the same as the performer, where the viewer hears the staccato beat while looking at the drummer opposite. Both works give insight into the transcendent quality of rhythm through the meditative state of drumming, where synchronicity leads to fellowship in the physical reverberations of pounding rhythm. In *LRLL RLRR*, Haynes achieves the rare success of bringing the viewer into his interior space, closer than ever to the process of artistic creation itself.

Haynes' interest in immersive visual and aural experience is shared by Glenda Wharton, whose film *The Zo* (2010) (see page 150) is a striking example of the labor-intensive practice of hand-drawn animation. The making of the work was marked by a return home to Winston-Salem to be near an aging family member. Five years later, what was planned as a brief sojourn had turned into

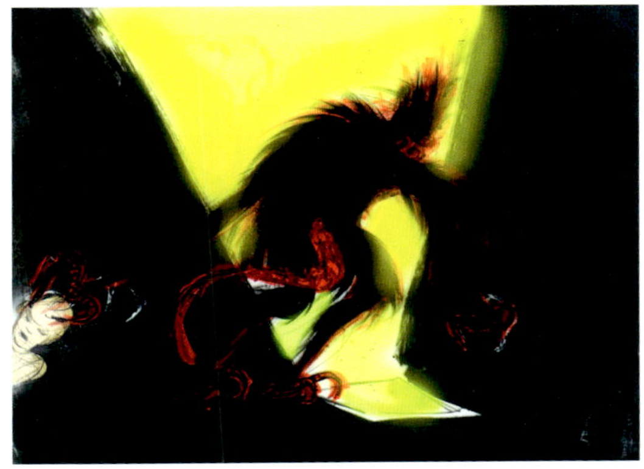

Figure 3. Glenda Wharton, *Zo takes her down*, 2011, Still from the hand-drawn animated film, *The Zo*, Pencil on animation cel, Image courtesy of the artist

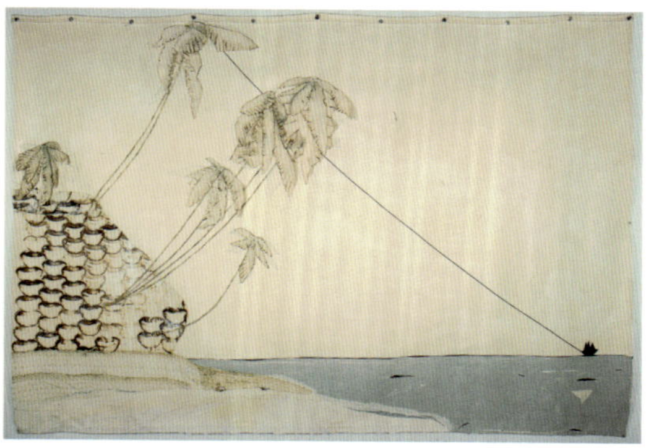

Figure 4. Stacy Lynn Waddell, *Ardeidae*, 2010, Singed and burned paper with watercolor, 96" x 51", Photo courtesy of the artist

Figure 5. Stacy Lynn Waddell, *Untitled (Bye Bye)*, 2009, Burned, branded, singed, and collaged canvas and muslin with string and lace, 84" x 120", Photo courtesy of the artist

something more permanent, manifesting with it a significant work of art. Wharton describes *The Zo* as "a lyrical journey into the dark night of the soul ... a tale of abuse and escape ... dedicated to all who have or do live with monsters." A loose compilation of scenes without dialogue, the animated work—composed of over 5000 hand-drawn cels—is a dreamlike adventure in another world, where the narrative unfolds in a richly layered succession of images and sound. An energetic series of delicately rendered images references fairytales and folklore, building a bridge between the known world and a parallel universe. What seems at first non-linear and chaotic coalesces into a gripping narrative that tells a story of youthful discovery, heartbreaking abuse, and an eventual path to freedom.

The protagonist is a young girl who goes to sleep and "wakes" to discover a portal to another world. When she enters, she encounters a cast of characters, both joyful and menacing. At times bound by restraints that move with her even as she struggles against them and, at others, free to run and be amazed by the new world around her, the girl is trapped in an unstable yet captivating dream world. Like a nightmare lurking on the edges of a dream, the menacing, shadowy character "the Zo" dominates the work, his threatening presence seeming to lurk at every corner of the frame. The resulting portrayal of the Zo, as a hulking figure that might emerge to cause harm at any time, speaks to the psychological torture faced by victims of abuse—no matter their age—conveying the sense that safety and security are impermanent (Fig. 3).

Notable in Wharton's execution is her deft and multifaceted approach to draftsmanship. *The Zo* continually shifts from color to black and white, while the quality of line and weight evolves from frame to frame—with stylistic references that recall everything from Goya to Disney. As a result, each element of and character in the story is linked not only to a progressing narrative but also to specific visual markers, which become familiar as the story evolves. The girl, for example, is drawn in a soft, shadowy style in black and white, evoking a certain tenderness that prompts both the viewer's intrigue and empathy. Moments of joyful play burst forth in cinematic color, only to fade away again into shadowy, gray darkness. Like the dream that the girl wanders through, the experience of watching *The Zo* is disjointed—at times vibrant and at others murky, but always breathtaking. In the tradition of Lewis Carroll's novel *Alice's Adventures in Wonderland*, Wharton's *The Zo* explores the rabbit hole of our subconscious, where humor mingles with dark fantasy, making room for play in a rich inventive space.

Stacy Lynn Waddell's work also engages storytelling at the intersection of memory and invention. Since graduating with an MFA from the University of

North Carolina in Chapel Hill in 2007, Waddell's work has explored the spectacle of history and the viewer's contribution to it. While she is accomplished in photography and installation, much of Waddell's two-dimensional work uses heat and flame as tools for drawing on paper or canvas (see page 148). Employing fire directly, indirectly, or by using implements for branding, Waddell creates landscapes, portraits, and installations that mine history as a means of exploring collective cultural memory.

An avid researcher, Waddell finds her source material in everything from James Audubon's groundbreaking taxonomic book, *Birds of America*, to vintage 20th century snapshots purchased from thrift stores. Most of the photographs she collects are images and portraits of African Americans at important moments in their anonymous lives: graduations, proms, pageants, and family gatherings. Waddell then removes these items from their contexts, remaking and reassembling them in a multilayered visual collage that uses a range of materials and methods, including collage, branding, drawing, painting, and sewing. Regardless of the medium, the same motifs reoccur across her work, building a unique language of signs, symbols, and methods that link the diverse objects together. In her large-scale canvas works, for example, ships, water, and tropical flora and fauna might stand alone in a landscape inhabited only by gracefully rendered waterfowl and lone cursive letters. The suggestive "B" is a favorite—might it stand for "bold," "beautiful," or "black"? In other instances, the same elements found in these monumental canvases form the backdrop for large works on paper; full-scale vintage portraits of anonymous African-American women from the 1950s and 1960s, smiling and resplendent in feathered prom dresses or graduation caps and gowns (Fig. 4). Unknown faces and places of the past are muses for the creation of a phantasmagorical playground in Waddell's work. By removing language, geography, and portraiture from their familiar contexts, Waddell creates poetic visual juxtapositions that make room for the telling of new stories.

Visually, Waddell's work projects an ephemeral air. Her use of fire as a primary medium results in a blanched sepia color palette and surfaces that bring to mind skin, marked by scars that fade but never fully disappear. When color does come into play, it is most often blue, hinting at the ocean or perhaps the indigo textiles of the Gullah.[1] The resulting works seem to be fading before our eyes like antique photographs, even as they are punctuated with bursts of color that hint at a brighter image than the trace that is left behind. The sense of ephemerality is augmented by Waddell's method for displaying these works. Her large canvases are usually hung loose on the wall with railroad ties, calling to mind early 20th century stage backdrops, easily taken down and rolled up when the show is over (Fig. 5). In these works, language, too, is fleeting; Waddell employs words as fragments, leaving the viewer to divine their purpose and meaning. Without explanation from the artist and robbed of context from within a sentence, language becomes both poetic and problematic.

With a lush visual topography that calls to mind the antebellum South—as portrayed in romantic landscape paintings or, in contrast, the bitingly ambiguous works of artists like Kara Walker—one could easily find things to say about the historically violent collision of black bodies with fire and the sea. Yet while aspects of Waddell's work seems to reference the landscape of coastal North Carolina, or at the very least the American South, it is ambiguous in its engagement with local landscape or history. In landscapes, bodies are absent, and when they appear in portraits, they are relatively contemporary representations of people, so that any easy associations with slavery slip away. It could also be posited that Waddell's experience as a black woman in the South is also embedded in the work—yet it seems more accurate to suggest that the work engages with black experience as a reflection of the artist's cultural history, rather than as a modus operandi or explicit objective. Even as it hints at an inventive back-story, Waddell's project is open ended, allowing any such associations to add another layer to the work—rather than define it. In this sense, she creates a starting point for a larger and open-ended conversation about the formulation of cultural memory and how it is reflected in contemporary society, revealing the disconnect between what is real and what is imagined: the actual past and what we as contemporary viewers project onto it. As such, the work leaves room for contemplation of the role of specificity in historical zeitgeist, a concept that by its very nature tends to be generalized.

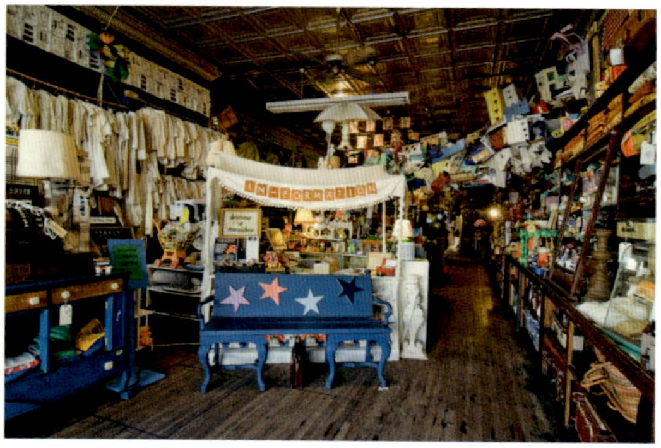

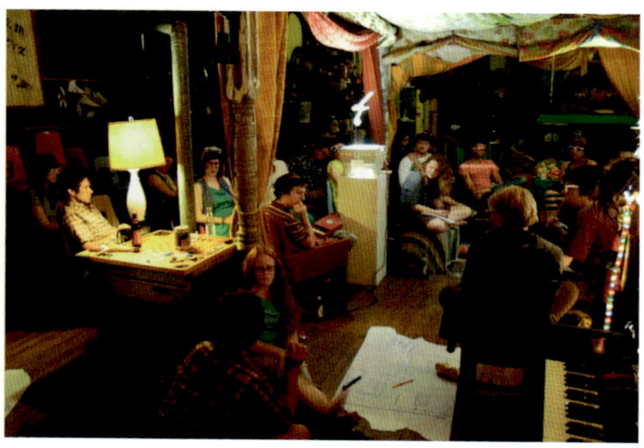

Distinguishing itself from a collective, Elsewhere Collaborative is a group of artists interested above all things in how engagement with artistic practice breeds community. Founded in 2003 by George Scheer and Stephanie Sherman, Elsewhere is based in a 12,000 square foot building in downtown Greensboro, in a once vibrant area that—having seen hard times—is now revitalizing. Indeed, the history of downtown Greensboro is intimately tied to the Civil Rights Movement of the 1960s, as the location of the pivotal Woolworth lunch counter sit-ins that were the nexus for desegregation in North Carolina. Occupying a building with its own rich history, the collaborative emerged out of unique circumstances. For almost 60 years, Elsewhere's space was a store run by Scheer's grandparents, Joe and Sylvia Gray, first specializing in army surplus and eventually (after Joe's death in the 1950s), general thrift. As it happened, Sylvia Gray was both frugal and fairly eccentric, being selective as to what from the store's inventory she actually sold and to whom. The result is that when she died in 1997, the building was filled with the remnants of half a century of unsold inventory, ranging from army mess kits and clothing to bolts of fabric and boxes of buttons.

All of this material forms the basis for the interactions and engagements staged by Elsewhere, and while all of the items that make up this part of the Gray's material legacy may be employed in all forms of artistic practice, none may actually leave the store. Instead, artist collaborators create new works and installations from a rich treasure trove of odds and ends, perpetually remaking and reconfiguring the building and its contents (Fig. 6). As an institution interested in civic engagement through creativity, Elsewhere's artist-in-residence program engages all aspects of artistic practice. Musicians, writers, painters, sculptors, chefs, gardeners, architects from across the country and the world—the program is open to anyone who can find new and interesting ways to engage the public (Fig. 7). Thus, Elsewhere describes itself as "a living museum designing collaborative futures from old things."

Figure 6. Elsewhere, Museum Interior, Photo courtesy of Elsewhere

Figure 7. Elsewhere, Idea Meeting, Photo courtesy of Elsewhere

What comes out of these collaborations blurs the boundaries between art and education, where a collective endeavor becomes both a work of art and an act of civic engagement. Even as Elsewhere is most often rooted in one space—their storefront in Greensboro—so are they literally everywhere and elsewhere, via an international cadre of collaborators. Whether their practice is based in their building, on the streets of Greensboro, in Berlin (as they have been recently), or in Philadelphia, engagement with an audience as participants and fellow collaborators is central to both their mission and their work. Both as an artist cohort and a self-sustaining non-profit organization, Elsewhere's engagement with the art market and the museum are less benchmarks for success than additional opportunities to engage community.

To that end, the viewer/participant is a central player in Elsewhere's endeavors—the discreet works they produce happen *with* and *because* of audience. And when the works themselves are not directly collaborative, then they facilitate conversation and dialogue between the viewer and artist. In ***here.***, for example, Elsewhere's *Cabinet of Wonder* (2011) is a museum on wheels, an activated object that literally requires the viewer's participation to function; where the opening of drawers and cabinets and the handling of elements found inside create the work (see page 118). During the opening reception of ***here.***, Elsewhere artist collaborators from North Carolina and Philadelphia took the *Cabinet of Wonder* outside of the Academy's walls and into exterior public space, where they employed it as a starting point for multiple interactions with viewers and passersby. In this sense, the artificial separations between the artwork and the viewer were erased. Elsewhere, there is no audience; there are only participants.

Perhaps it is a similar sense of open-ended possibility—of the potential to contribute to something in the making—that draws people to the region and causes them to stay, invites some to return, and convinces others not to leave. Elsewhere, Haynes, Waddell, and Wharton may have other reasons. Regardless, it remains that there is something extraordinary and inspiring about being here, in this place where we are, home.

[1] The term "Gullah" refers to a group of African Americans historically living on a series of islands spanning an area along the coast of North and South Carolina, continuing south to Georgia and ending near Jacksonville, Florida. Descendents of slaves who came primarily from West Africa by way of the ports of Charleston, South Carolina and Savannah, Georgia, the Gullah—or "Geechee" as they call themselves and their language—worked primarily on rice and indigo plantations. Because of their relatively sustained isolation, even following the abolition of slavery, they have been able to preserve many aspects of their African cultural inheritance, particularly as relates to language and community life.

artists.

BUNK NEWS ARTS COLLECTIVE

Founded 2005
Members include visual artists based in Cincinnati, with other members residing in Cleveland and San Francisco. Includes frequent collaborations with various other local artists, musicians, and performers.

BUNK NEWS represents our specific "HERE" as an aesthetic reflection of our location in the grittiness of Cincinnati; by utilizing and re-purposing the residues of urban and cultural decay, we create a means for social interaction. By focusing on collaboration, many minds—reflecting a similar "HERE"—work together to create an experience to share with other minds. By bringing together artifacts from past BUNK events, our "HERE" is compressed with the "NOW" into an experience we would like to share with you.

Bunk News is a collective working in Cincinnati engaged in a range of creative practices that include music and art shows, installations, performances, and the creation of art objects. The initial Bunk Spot venue closed in November 2009 and soon reopened in a nearby preexisting space called the Mockbee. They continue to incorporate mediums such as painting, drawing, video, and sculpture in works created by individual members and through the collective. They also collaborate with other local artists and touring musicians. The collective operates with a strong DIY mentality, and they seek to build an art community that brings people together to enable a less traditional engagement with viewing and making art. As co-founding member Ben Brown stated, they are "a collaborative group of friends and artists where each person is bringing different media, styles, skill sets, and perspectives into one somewhat focused direction."

For ***here.***, Bunk's installation is an environment employing materials from past installations that simulates a stage with visual props consisting of the *Tao Twins* (2011) and a painted, wooden floor work called *Mandala* (2011). Within this framework, they are also presenting a variety of photocopied posters relating to previous projects. During the exhibition, Bunk are staging a multi-media event that includes a music set, spoken word, and performance featuring author and vocalist Jim Swill performing with Evolve, a contemporary electronic punk and hip-hop group.

Opposite left:
Tao Twin Red, 2011
Acrylic and india ink on wood
141" x 72" x .5"
Photo by Arlie Trowbridge

Opposite right:
Tao Twin Blue, 2011
Acrylic and india ink on wood
141" x 72" x .5"
Photo by Michael Englender

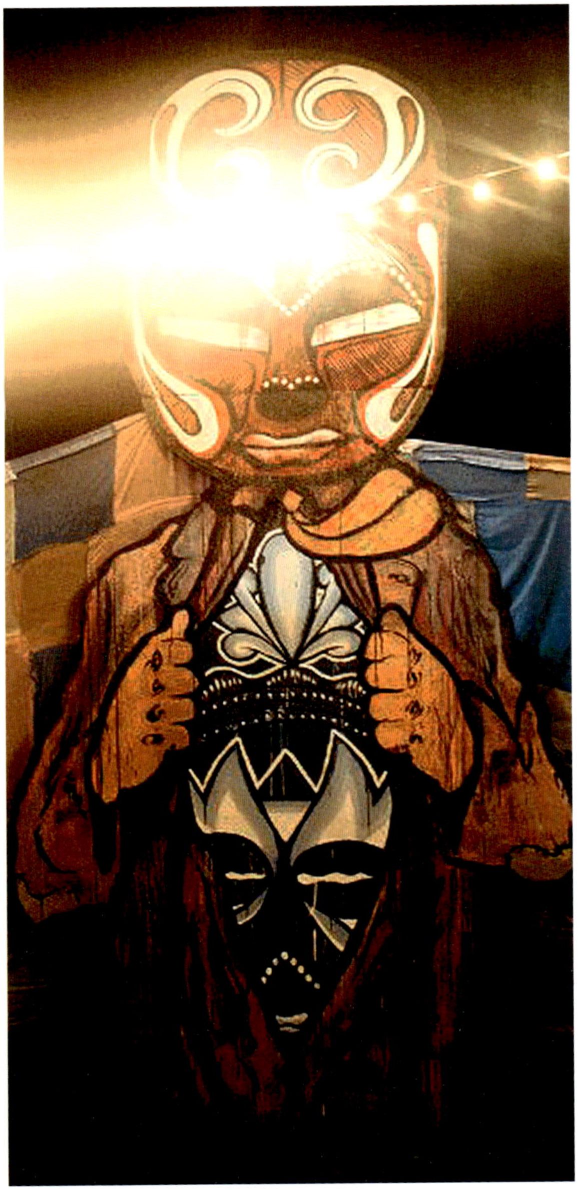

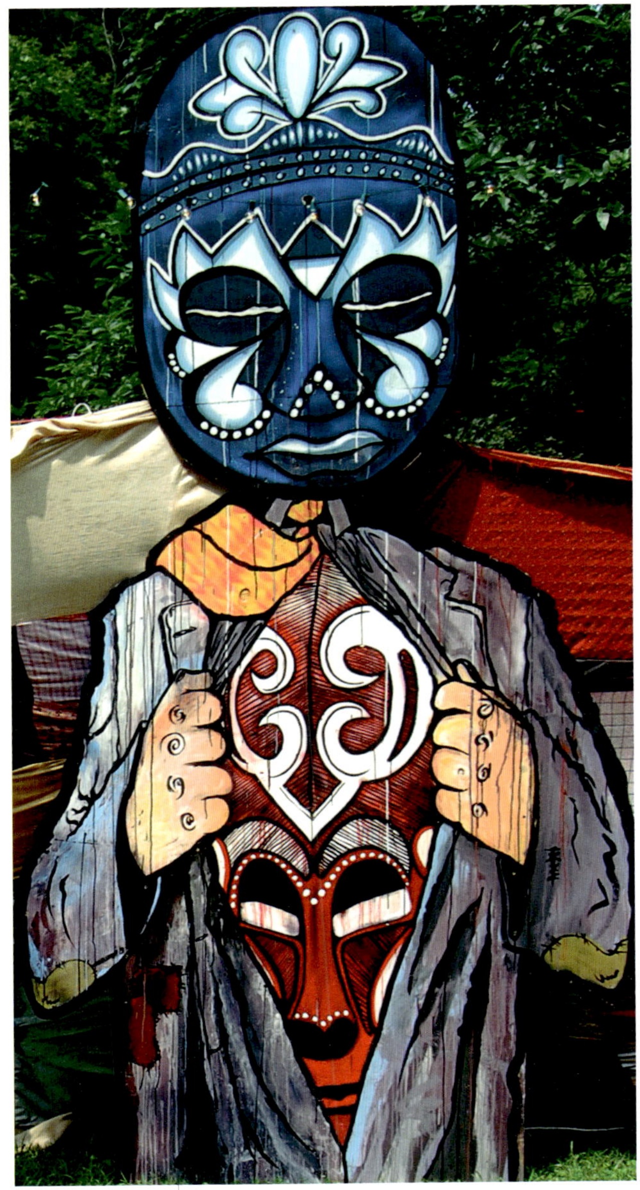

SUE CHENOWETH

Born 1953, Plainview, Texas
Lives in Phoenix, Arizona

Home is Phoenix, Arizona, where I live and have lived for more than 50 years. But, my real home rides around with me. My home is in my head. It is my own history and memories. I am 'here' and cannot experience anything but that. There is no way I could objectively look at how this city in the desert has influenced my art making because this city is my constant, and it is ingrained into who I am.

I live in the center of Phoenix, Arizona, where the irrigated grass is a deep green and enormous trees shade the homes. It is an artificial oasis that was created when people moved west with their families. These fine folks tried to recreate the lush land of their history. Central Phoenix is a welcoming and picturesque place and not at all what is expected when one first experiences it.

Phoenix just happens to be my home. My home is exploring memory, myth, and place through paintings inspired and informed by historical narrative, architectural forms, and zoological studies. I try to recreate what it is like to be alive. By blending these intuitions, premonitions, and realizations, I try to capture with my work certain archetypes, common human experiences and the surprising emergence of the extraordinary from within the everyday experience of being human. Home is the grand tale every human experiences by being alive. We only see what we see.

In reaction to the Post-Minimal whitewash of current museum programming, Roberta Smith recently lamented that "what's missing is art that seems made by one person out of intense personal necessity, often by hand."[1] Sue Chenoweth, a beautiful seed that has thankfully not been hybridized, is an artist whose work displays these qualities. The granddaughter of an oil painter and the daughter of a craftswoman, Chenoweth has forever been living in her imagination. An inherently talented draftsperson, she declined acceptance to California Institute of the Arts in 1971 claiming that she "didn't like the way [Los Angeles] smelled, too smoggy."[2]

Chenoweth has allowed her innate curiosity and creativity to bloom as she chronicles the joy, tragedy, insanity, and wonder of being alive. She brings the viewer into a mythological world, where predator and prey meet, archetypal heroes face archetypal nature, and childhood magic becomes an epic physiological landscape. Indulging a free association of sources, Chenoweth's dynamic and large-scale works on paper coalesce diverse techniques and disparate images. In compositions that, simultaneously, are explosively energetic and tautly executed she sustains a tension between figuration and abstract form.

The series presented in ***here.*** draws on sources from Plato's "Allegory of the Cave," cloisonné, analytic cubism, and the mosaics of Ravenna to develop and express an understanding of center and periphery. The "center" is Plato's Cave, while the "periphery" is the fragmented artistic devices she references. It is, she says: "Shattered. Cordoned off but at the same time stepping over boundaries. Life."[3] In *To Climb the Highest Peak* (2011), the confusion of the world is referenced in opposing perspectives. Mt. Everest emerges in the corner as the entire space becomes a puff of smoke or a mirage. She says, "It is a portrait of everyone trying to get to the top of their world. Or not!"[4]

[1] Robert Smith, "Post-Minimal to the Max," *New York Times*, February 14, 2010, http://www.nytimes.com/2010/02/14/arts/design/14curators.html.
[2] Sue Chenoweth, studio visit with artist, April 15, 2011.
[3] Ibid., email correspondence, August 8, 2011.
[4] Ibid., email correspondence, June 7, 2011.

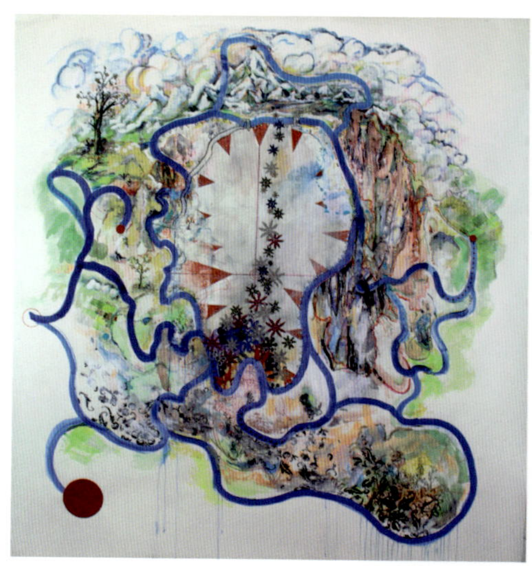

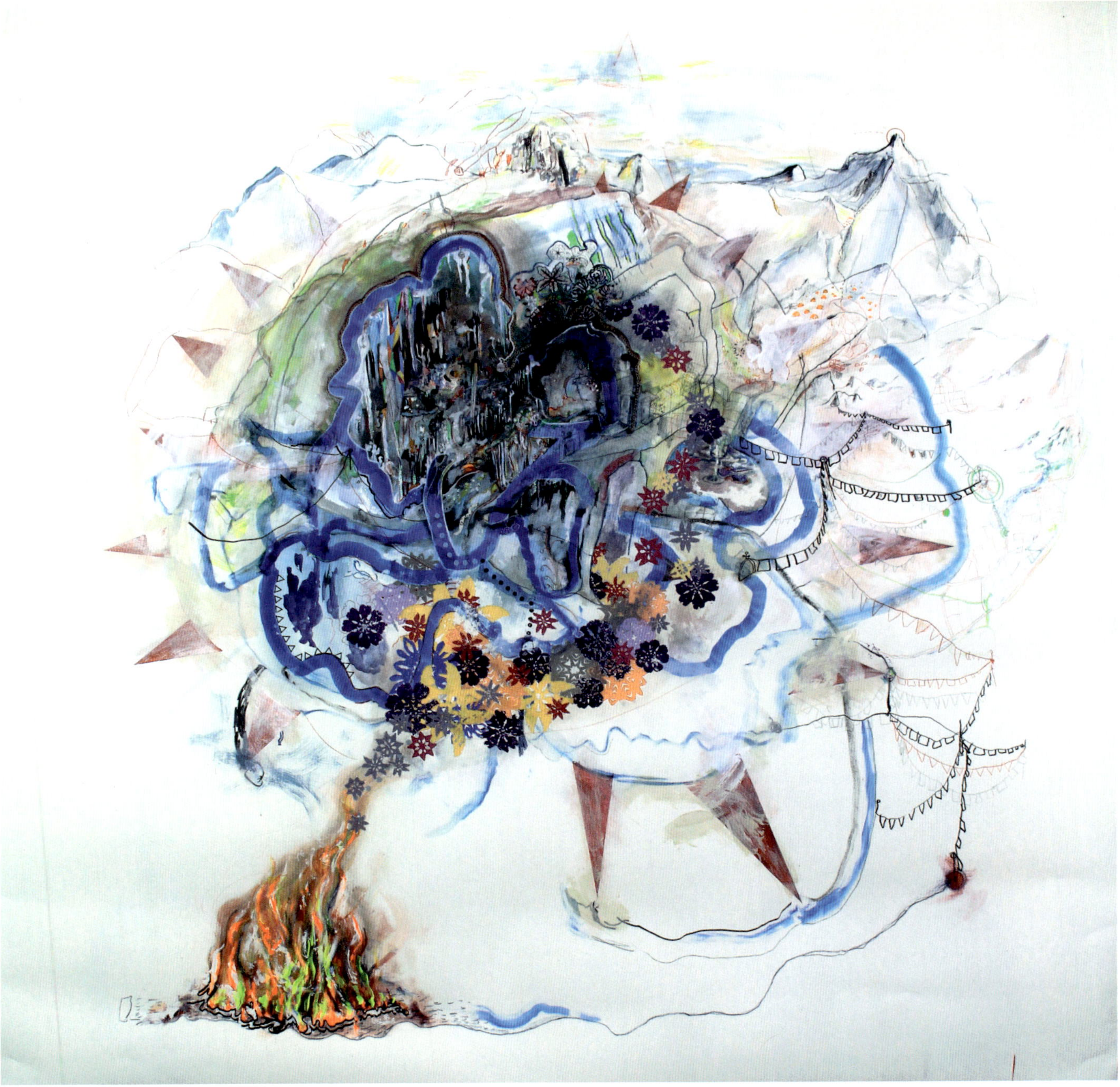

Opposite:
Wouldn't He Remember his First Home? What Passed for Wisdom There?, 2011
Gouache, acrylic, ink, graphite,
Letraset and Flocked paper on paper
80" x 80"
Photo courtesy of the artist

Above:
To Climb the Highest Peak, 2011
Gouache, acrylic, ink, graphite,
Letraset and Pantone paper on paper
80" x 80"
Photo courtesy of the artist

LIZ COHEN

Born 1973, Phoenix, Arizona
Lives in Bloomfield Hills, Michigan

In 2008 I moved from the West Coast to Detroit for the completion of my Trabantamino, a project that transformed an East German automobile, the Trabant, into a General Motor's El Camino. The build involved eight years of apprenticing at auto body and fabrication shops. I deconstructed the vehicle (and my life) piece-by-piece, slowly learning trade skills, negotiating shop culture, and becoming the model that would represent the car.

The Trabantimino and I arrived in Detroit at the cusp of GM's collapse and worked through the time when GM was rebuilding a leaner self by leaving behind thousands of workers, denying people their pensions, suppliers their receivables, and, consequently, custom car shops of their paying customers. As the Trabant became an El Camino, I witnessed some defiant and resourceful people mourn the loss of their identities as solely "car guys" and adapt to circumstances beyond their control by retuning their shops and skills to serve an expanded customer base including the film industry, food and beverage, and the military.

Building the Trabantimino was an experiment in transformation to see what happens when one object or person sets out to become another. When the goal is unattainable in the conventional sense—a Trabant can never truly be an El Camino—something beautiful happens: innovation. The Trabantimino is not a Trabant, an El Camino, a lowrider because of its hydraulic transformations, or a muscle car because of its engine. It's something else. Chrome covers hardship and reflects the optimism that there is construction after deconstruction.

Over eight years in development, Liz Cohen's *BODYWORK* series simultaneously explores two types of transformation: the production of a custom car, *Trabantimino* (2002 – 09), and the creation of a sexualized persona as the artist donned bikinis and posed with her automotive creation. The inspiration for her project developed while Cohen was photographing transgender sex-trade workers in Panama. In an attempt to create an analogue for such extreme physical transformation, she engineered a hybridized car that, when operated, can morph from an East German Trabant into an American Muscle Car. She installed in this vehicle a larger engine and custom hydraulics that expand the shell of the sub-compact Trabant to mimic the dimensions of the 1973 Chevrolet El Camino. In photographs and videos, she documented her Trabant in transition, posing with it clad in a variety of bikinis and holding tools that have a sexual or political valency. This project took Cohen from the Latino low-rider culture of California to Detroit where, despite setbacks, the automobile industry remains the primary manufacturing base.

BODYWORK has strong conceptual underpinnings and an elegant structural trajectory. Cohen bookends the project with two videos: *Bikini Car Wash* (2002) and *Hydro Force* (2011). In the first video, she appears as a nubile model who coaxes and teases drivers, imploring them to allow her to hand wash their cars. The performance was staged near the Castro district, linking the project to the LGBT community in the isthmus that inspired it. Her most recent video records Cohen, eight months pregnant, riding astride the *Trabantimino* as it bucks up and down. About the series she comments, "I'm the car's builder, the vehicle's owner, and the bikini model who will show it off. There's usually a disconnect between all three, yet I'm embodying them all."

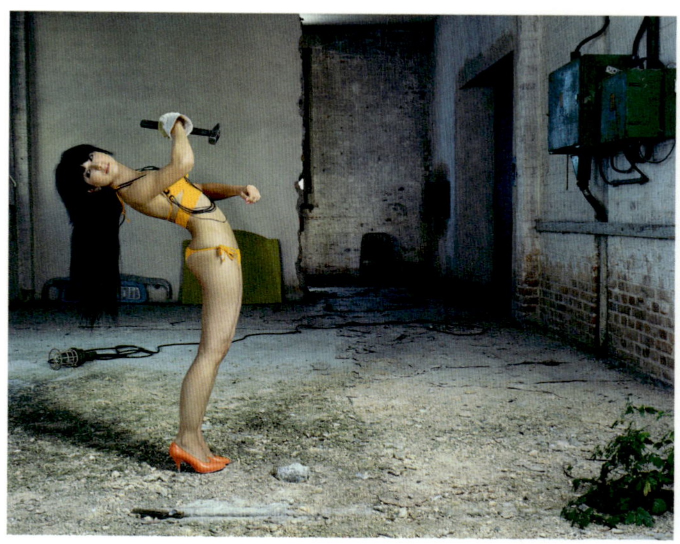

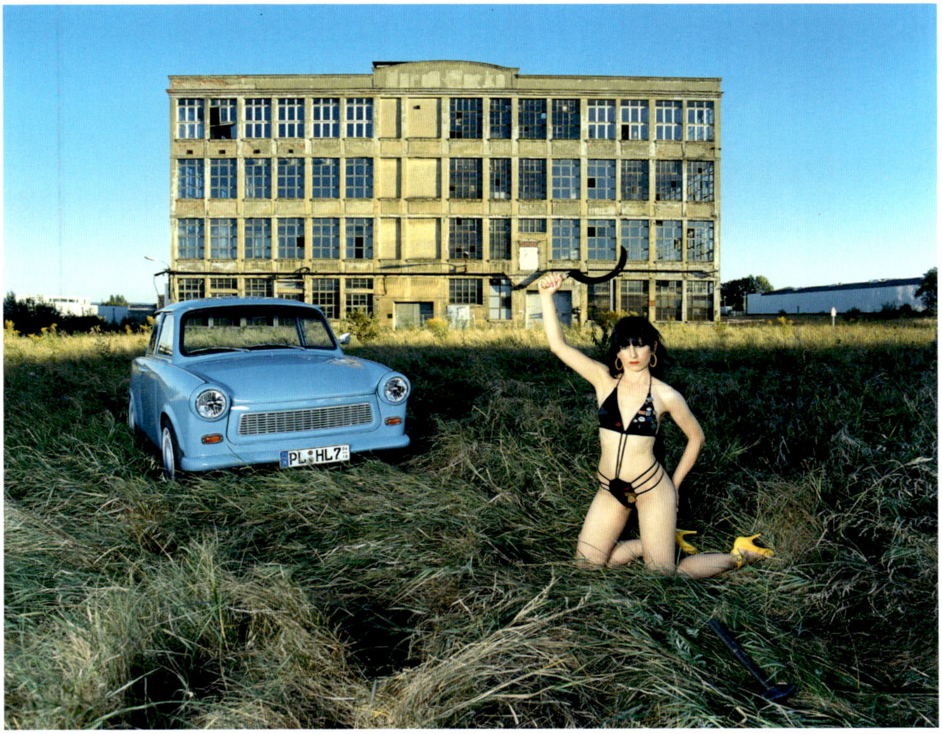

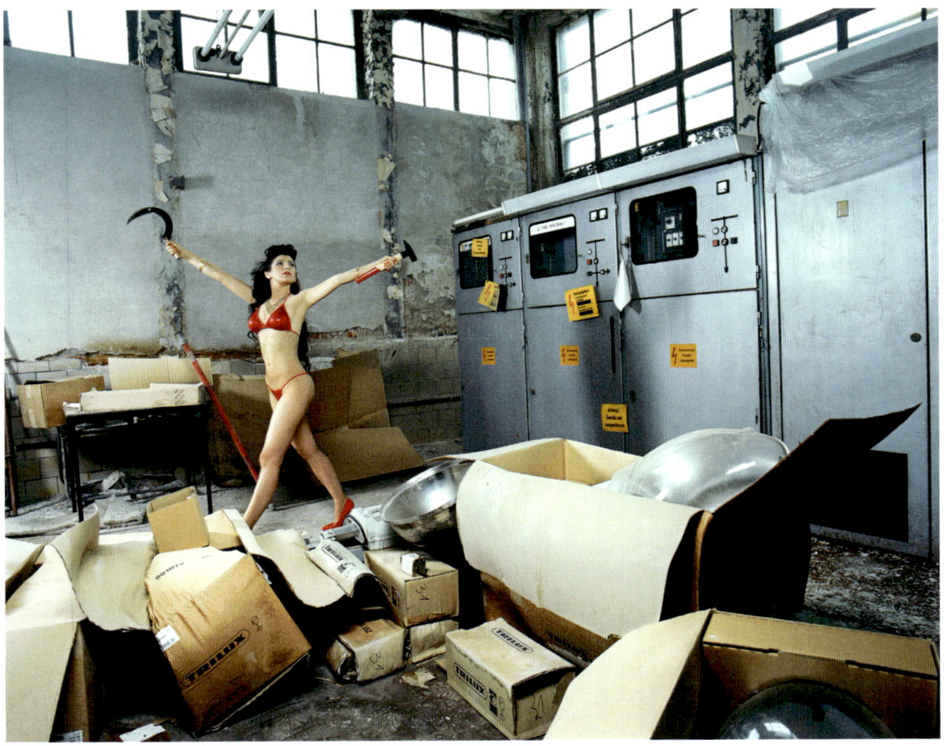

Top:
Zwickau Routine:
Black Execution, 2010
C print
16" x 20"
Image courtesy of the artist
and David Klein Gallery

Bottom:
Zwickau Routine:
Red Cossack, 2010
C print
16" x 20"
Image courtesy of the artist
and David Klein Gallery

Opposite:
Zwickau Routine:
Yellow Inward Turn, 2010
C print
16" x 20"
Image courtesy of the artist
and David Klein Gallery

LEWIS COLBURN

Born 1982, Cedar Falls, Iowa
Lives in Philadelphia, Pennsylvania

To be honest, I have always used my location as a backdrop, as a scene in which to deploy myself in order to make my work. In this sense, I can make use of many locations, from a solitary stretch of road in Utah to a busy train station in Philadelphia. Still, when I consider my relationship to these places, it stays on the surface, at the level of an actor on a set.

As of now, my relationship to place is changing. I came to Philadelphia two years ago, from New York State. Both of these places contrasted sharply with the Midwest, where I grew up. The first work I found in Philadelphia was with a costumer for the Mummer's parade (a local tradition akin to Mardi Gras). Soon after, my car was stolen and burned.

Despite this abrupt introduction to Philadelphia, I now see the city and my neighborhood shaping my work. Kensington, where I live, is changing rapidly. The new buildings look like flimsy theater sets compared to the decaying warehouses and row homes. This collision of cheap new construction with the old infrastructure of the neighborhood creates the same clash of historic and contemporary imagery that drives my work. Now the collision happens daily just outside my studio.

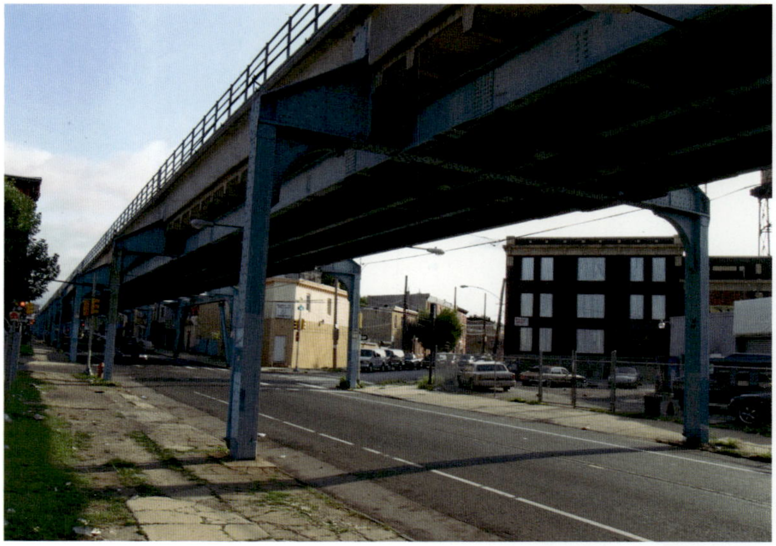

Lewis Colburn is an artist who is interested in the way our experience of history is mediated for consumption. Working in sculpture and performance, he simulates objects and re-enacts events in order to explore how identities are formed and to "interrogate our longing for a past that never was."

Untitled (Set for a Homestead) (2011) elaborates Colburn's interest in history's translations by making visual reference to the eclectic collection of architectural styles that can be found in the Kensington neighborhood that surrounds his studio. The main framework of this sculpture is a scaled-down replica of a section of the Market-Frankford rail line—the El—that has been meticulously crafted in paper covered plywood. High up on this platform the artist has mounted an arrangement of rectangular vertical panels that have been painted in bright primary colors. Making reference to the industrial and engineering architecture that gave life to this neighborhood until the 1950s and blending it with allusions to the geometry and color that adorn the façades of new row-houses in the area, Colburn fuses images of past and present in a hybrid that speaks to the mutable nature of the city, where the productivist tropes of Modernism collide with the non-objective appropriations of gentrification.

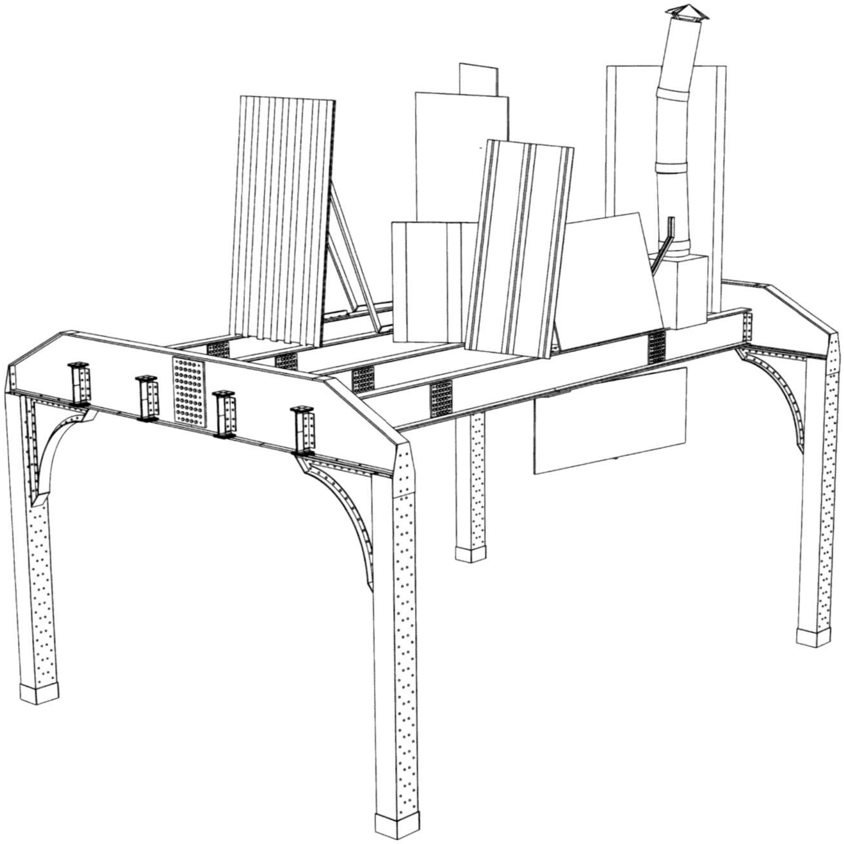

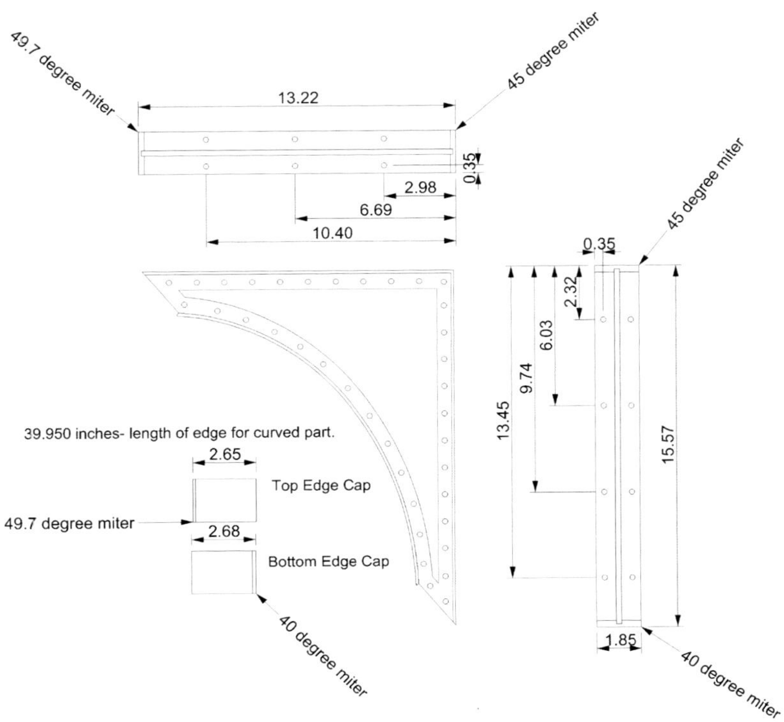

Untitled (Set for a Homestead), 2011
Plywood, steel, acrylic, found objects and mixed media
180" x 148" x 180"
Renderings and photos by Lewis Colburn

Opposite:
Reference image of Philadelphia's Market-Frankford Line elevated train tracks

Top:
CAD rendering of *Untitled (Set for a Homestead)*

Bottom:
Construction drawing for *Untitled (Set for a Homestead)*

PAUL COORS

Born 1982, Cincinnati, Ohio
Lives in Cincinnati, Ohio

For the past 7 or so months, I've been slowly converting a portion of my apartment into a show space. Ironically, I used to operate a different "artist-run" gallery inside my last apartment here in town. That space lasted exactly 5 years and really bore the mark of youthful ambition. Since that ended, a few years ago, I've been exhibiting around town quite a bit and mostly at spaces of the "alternative" variety. I guess I prefer those types of spaces, although I sort of wish I didn't have to make objects at all. I can almost imagine a futuristic sociality where all my friends, past, present, and future, collaborate on the type of cultural work I try to address in my current practice (although that changes every day). I'll send out some emails. Lots of friends have moved elsewhere, some never even lived here to begin with. But I'm trying to get everyone to move back, even if only spiritually. After all, rent is so cheap in Cincinnati! It seems almost irresponsible to NOT operate your own creative-type space. This new thing I'm doing though, in *my* place now, I wouldn't call a gallery. It's just my house. And I'm way younger than I used to be.

Paul Coors is a printmaker and designer who currently lives and works in the west end of Cincinnati. He co-founded and directed Publico, an art space located in his loft, for 5 years until its closing in 2008. He has collaborated with musician C. Spencer Yeh as a designer for What The...? Records and is co-founder with poet Dana Ward of Perfect Lovers Press. He is in the process of converting a portion of his current residence into an exhibition space for future in-house collaborations with various artists.

Coors' works come in many forms, such as posters, books, album covers, postcards, typography, and mixed-media installations. His most recent works combine objects and images that force the viewer to question the works' themes, creating discrepancies in communication. ***here.*** includes *Stonehenge* (2011), an installation comprised of thirteen yard signs affixed to wooden supports, and five fake movie posters that weave together different source images, such as in *Spiderman Uncivilized* (2010 – 2011) where references are made to film icons Spiderman, *Looney Toons*, and Dick Tracy. It is left to the observer to untangle these images and participate in his exploration into the intersecting meanings of adolescent and adult experiences with mass culture imagery.

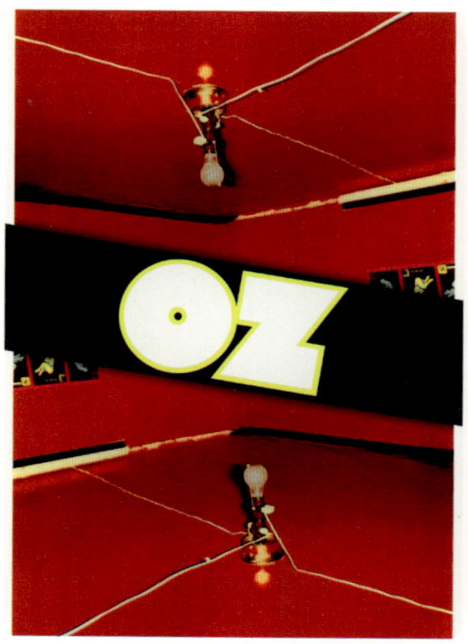

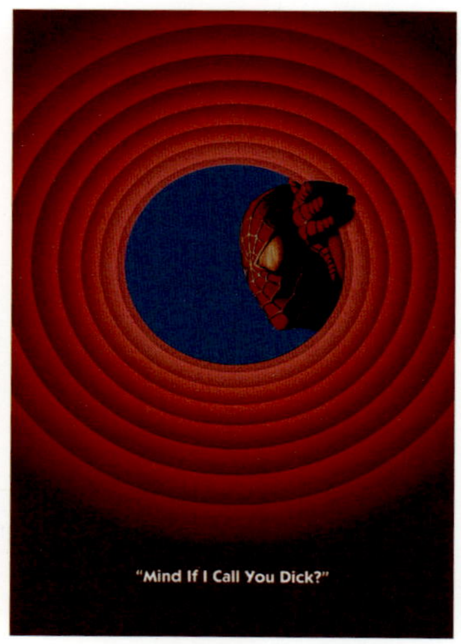

Left:
Oz & Them, 2010 – 2011
Offset print on paper, edition of 100
27" x 39"
Photo courtesy of the artist

Right:
Spiderman Uncivilized, 2010 – 2011
Offset print on paper, edition of 100
27" x 39"
Photo courtesy of the artist

Opposite:
1 Day, 2010 – 2011
Offset print on paper, edition of 100
27" x 39"
Photo courtesy of the artist

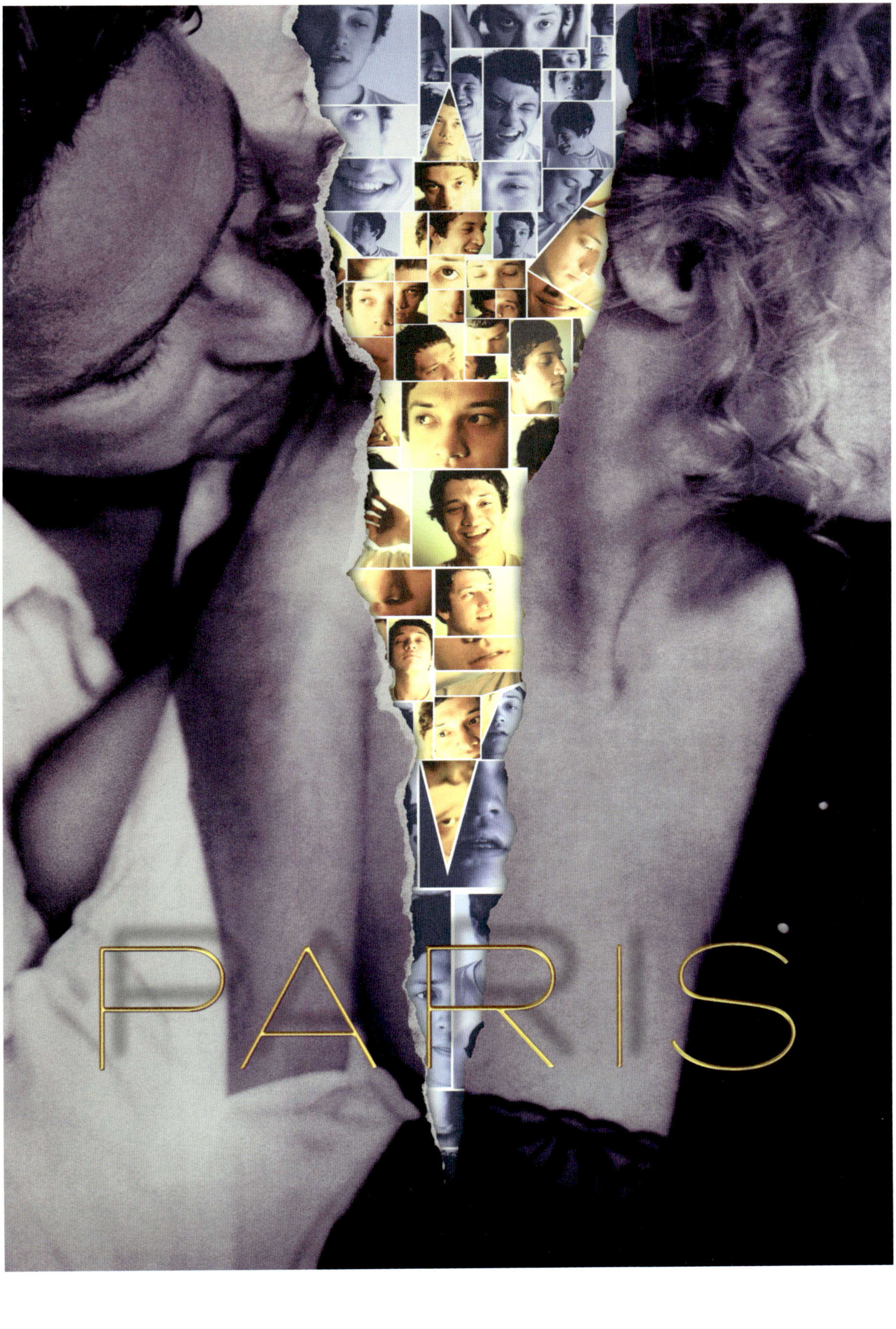
PARIS

GUY MICHAEL DAVIS AND KATIE PARKER

Guy Michael Davis and Katie Parker
Future Retrieval
Founded 2009
Guy Michael Davis: born 1978,
Bartlesville, Oklahoma
Katie Parker: born 1980,
Jonesboro, Arkansas
Live in Cincinnati, Ohio

Being HERE means having access. Access to a variety of industrial processes, situated on either end of the technological spectrum. There is an abundance of overlooked materials, leftovers and detritus from a booming river town. Cincinnati has a rich history in the production of fine things: silver, furniture, print, and ceramics to list a few. We can comb through junk shops and antique malls, estate sales and flea markets, searching for subjects that fit within our aesthetic.

There is an appreciation for our practice and how it straddles the space between art and design. Work is not classified by media, but judged on a case-by-case,space-by-space basis. Cincinnati has a thriving art scene within a tight knit community, allowing plenty of opportunities for artists to exhibit a wide range of projects.

Guy Michael Davis and Katie Parker, who work under the collective name of Future Retrieval, create works that combine new technology with traditional craft. Their creative process merges the strengths of their individual studio practices and often involves making three-dimensional scans of organic forms that are then rapid-prototyped, processed in the studio, molded into porcelain and then often painted with china paint, in a way that mimics traditional European decorative arts.

Hy-que Monkey in Captivity (2011) involves five painted porcelain monkeys, each cast from a rapid prototype of a clockwork toy monkey. Placed on matching sconces, each object is mounted in front of a panel of hand-printed wallpaper whose motifs are derived from the fifteenth-century tapestry series *The Lady and the Unicorn*. In this work, they seek to comment on the ways in which the natural world can be interpreted and its representations distorted. A second series in the exhibition is titled *Still[ed] Life* (2011), and it includes three portrait busts of William Taft's father that are covered in decorative motifs and patterns inspired by works from the Taft Museum of Art's permanent collection. Combining the idealized beauty of historical decorative arts with vibrant organic details, which seem to grow freely across the ceramic surface, both works display the artists' fascination with the relationship between the natural and the manufactured.

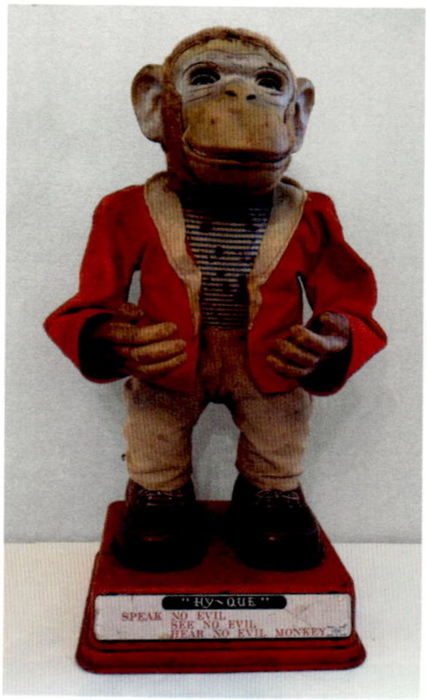

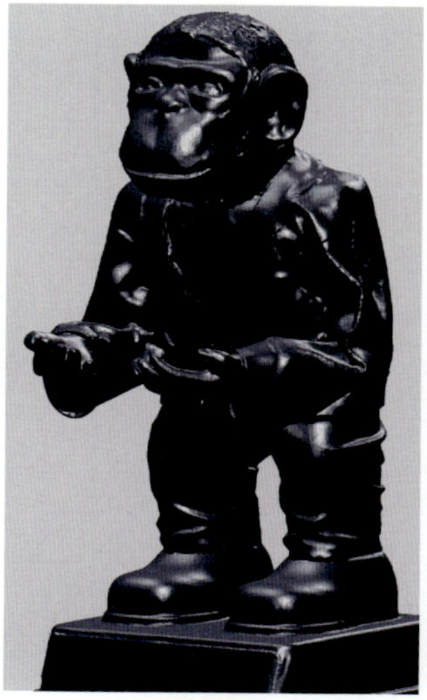

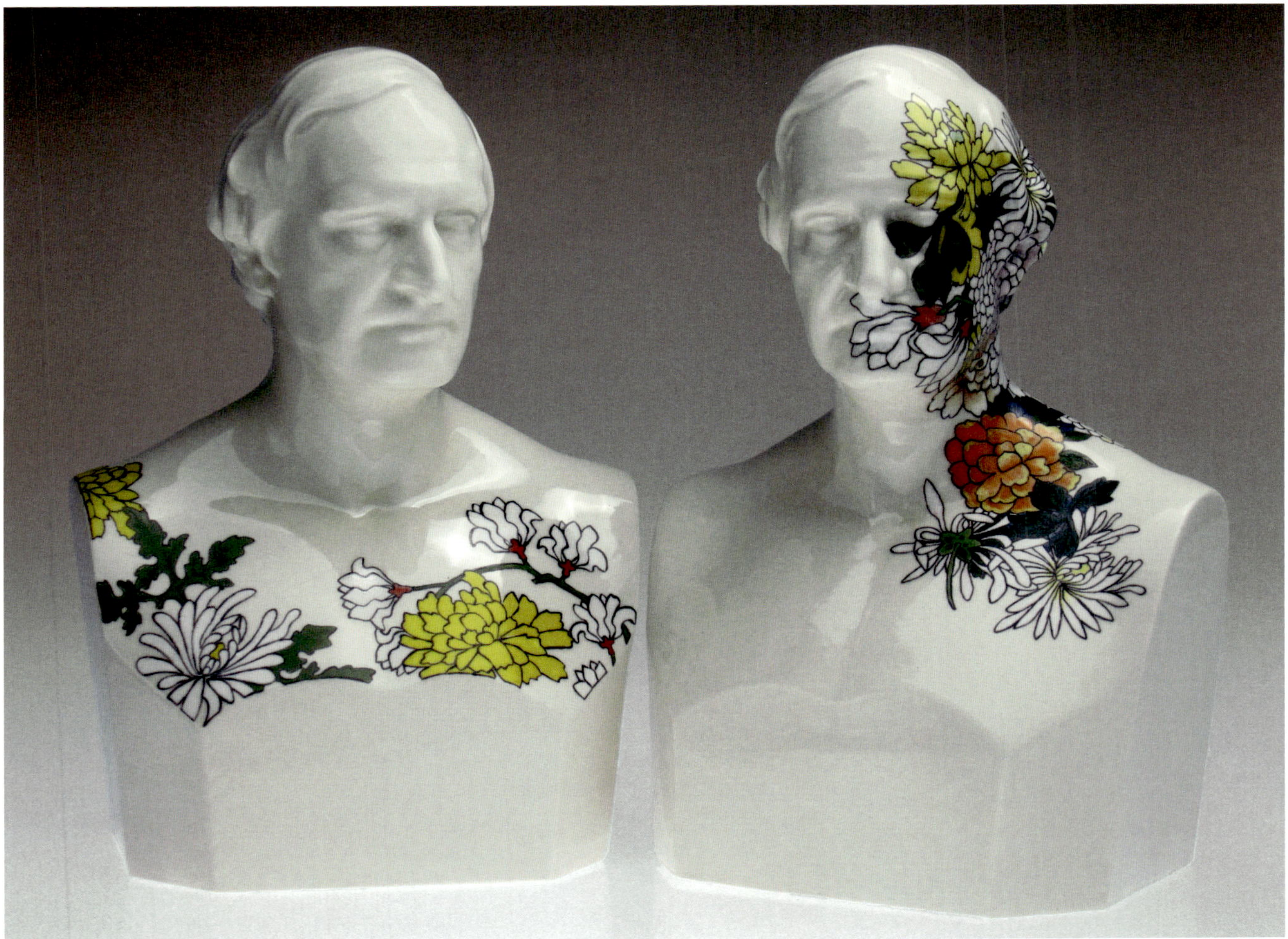

Opposite:
Clockwork toy monkey and 3D scan used to create porcelain casts for *Hy-que Monkey in Captivity*, 2011
See exhibition checklist
Photo courtesy of the artists

Above:
Porcelain busts from *Still[ed] Life*, 2011
See exhibition checklist
Photo courtesy of the artists

ELSEWHERE

Founded 2003, Greensboro, North Carolina

Elsewhere is both here and there, a place and presence. It is a site where formations are emerging. It is an idea that everything is re-forming all at once. Elsewhere, everything seems close and distant, ordinary and extraordinary, historical and contemporary, remembered and forgotten. Here, inventions are arranged and discovered from facts and fictions. We find ourselves beside ourselves.

Our aim is to unfold cultural commons where the environment speaks, listens. By repurposing cultural remnants as creative elements, we activate new stories, tales, and echoes from our material past. From these spaces, we create playgrounds for experiencing concepts. We invoke interactions between things and people to notice what is here—merging our senses of place and time.

Our approach is a radical openness towards process. We are all always changing all at once. We navigate whereabouts. We animate environments. We construct experiences for more present tomorrows.

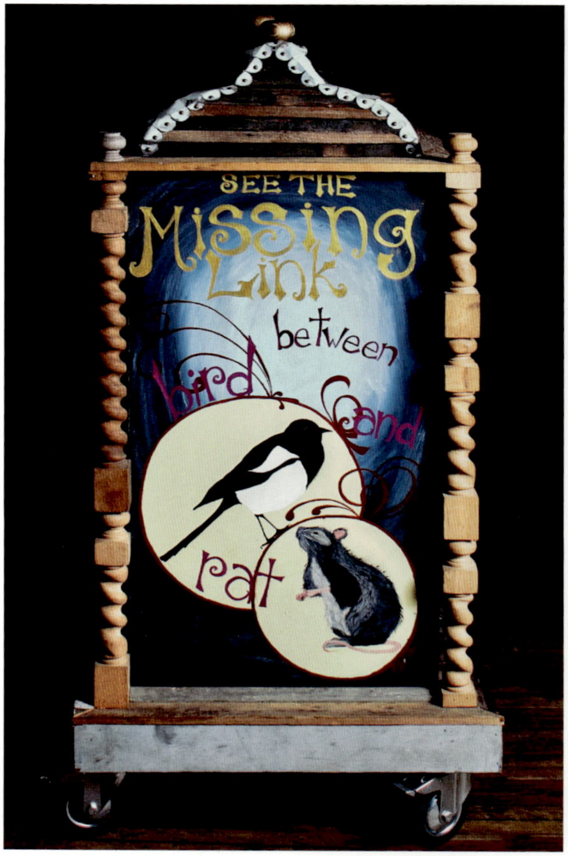

Elsewhere is a living museum, experimental residency, and laboratory for collaborative education located in Greensboro, North Carolina. Founded in 2003 by writers George Scheer and Stephanie Sherman, Elsewhere is set within a former second-hand store containing the 58-year collection of former proprietress Sylvia Gray. Nothing in the store is for sale; instead, Elsewhere invites creative individuals working in a wide range of media (such as writing, music, textiles, photography, sculpture, installation, and other forms of artistic practice) to utilize the collection to create works for the living museum.

The *Cabinet of Wonder* (2010) is part of Elsewhere's mobile museum, a flexible series of themed carts built by Elsewhere's team and alumni artists that invites interactions with concepts, materials, and tools that activate creative re-search and playful imagination. The work is a large, rolling cabinet with drawers, doors, and miniature tableaus that audiences are invited to explore, touch, and transform. Reconfigured with mini-exhibits that are adjusted to be salient for audiences at its destination site, the Cabinet is largely made from materials and artifacts from Elsewhere's space in North Carolina. Interaction with the Cabinet's imaginative contents invites viewers to consider the socio-cultural residue held by artifacts from the real, yet fantastical world of a living museum, as well as how these objects might shift and evolve as Elsewhere goes elsewhere.

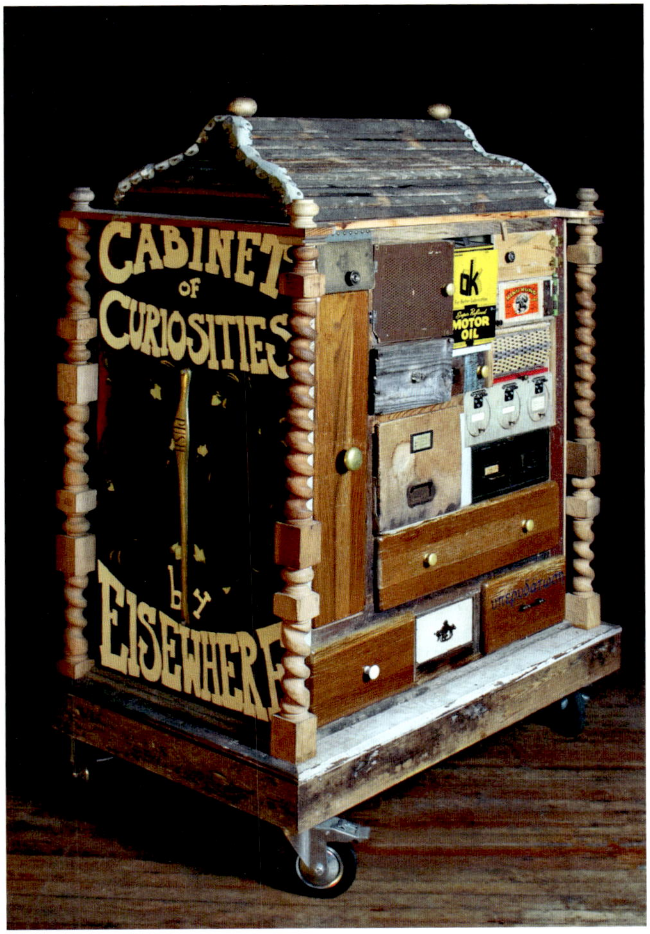

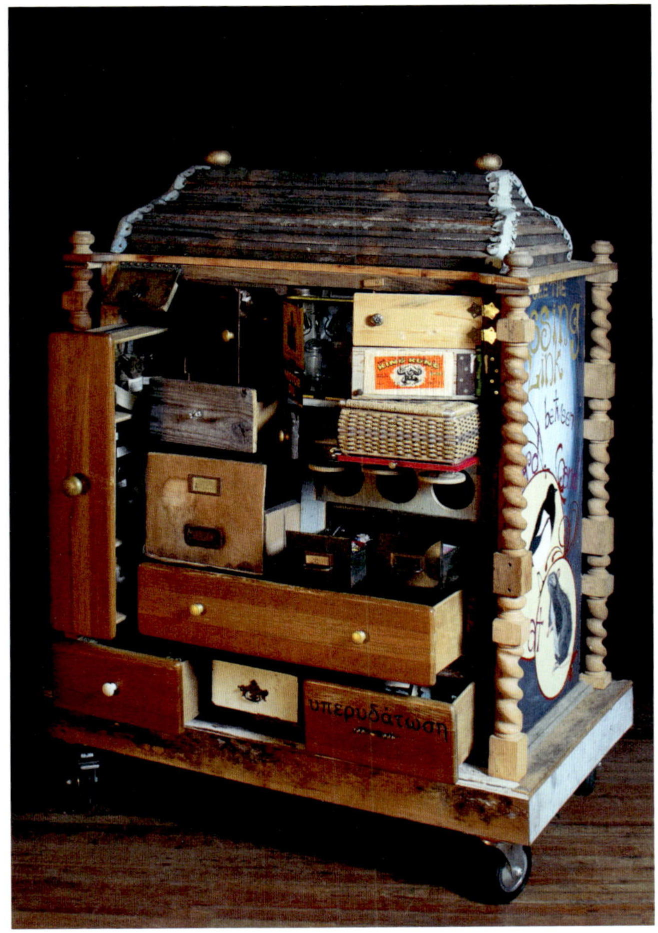

Cabinet of Wonder, 2010
Mixed media sculpture
Approximately 3' x 5' x 6'
Photos by Norah Hoover

TERENCE HAMMONDS

Born 1976, Cincinnati, Ohio
Lives in Cincinnati, Ohio

I live and work in the neighborhood that I was born and raised in. A neighborhood rich in beautiful historic buildings. Many of them are neglected and run down, be it from "white flight" or economic downturn, run down but still beautiful. I couldn't help but to be influenced by this place, from the ornate architecture to the city's long printmaking history. Lately, I have been particularly interested in the ways this place tries to reinvent itself ten years after riots rocked and reshaped it. What happens when the lower income families, like the one I was born into, leave and are replaced by young people, artist, students, and then gentrification (again)? It is a pattern that is all too familiar in Cincinnati. I think of these patterns, the buildings, the beauty, and the history, both good and bad, as family heirlooms.

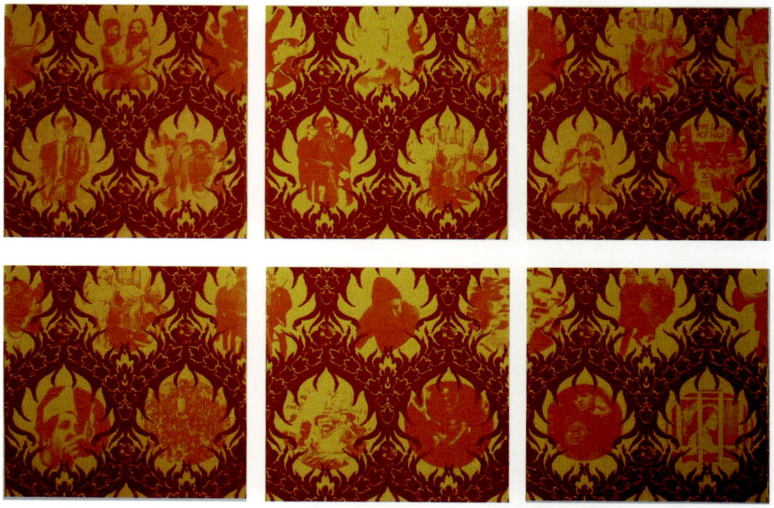

Above and opposite:
Stand Up! Organize!, 2010 (details)
21 screen prints on paper
Each 24" x 24"
Photos courtesy of the artist

Terence Hammonds, a native of Cincinnati's Over-the-Rhine neighborhood, creates works that intertwine images drawn from popular culture and civil rights history and motifs characteristic of the city. Although his work is informed and inspired by the struggles and determination of African Americans seeking equality during the Civil Rights Movement of the 1960s, he seeks to make works that are universally identifiable. As Hammonds states, "I think they're American stories, not just African American stories."

Hammonds' installation works for ***here.*** include *Stand Up! Organize!* (2010) and *Cincinnati Goddamn* (2011). Each series is comprised of twenty-one screen prints on paper that are then organized into grids. The rich imagery incorporates historical newspaper clippings arranged in ornate patterns and printed motifs evoking nineteenth-century design. Through Hammonds' appropriations and print processes, he merges contemporary experiences and historical memory to "create heirlooms of cultural transgression."

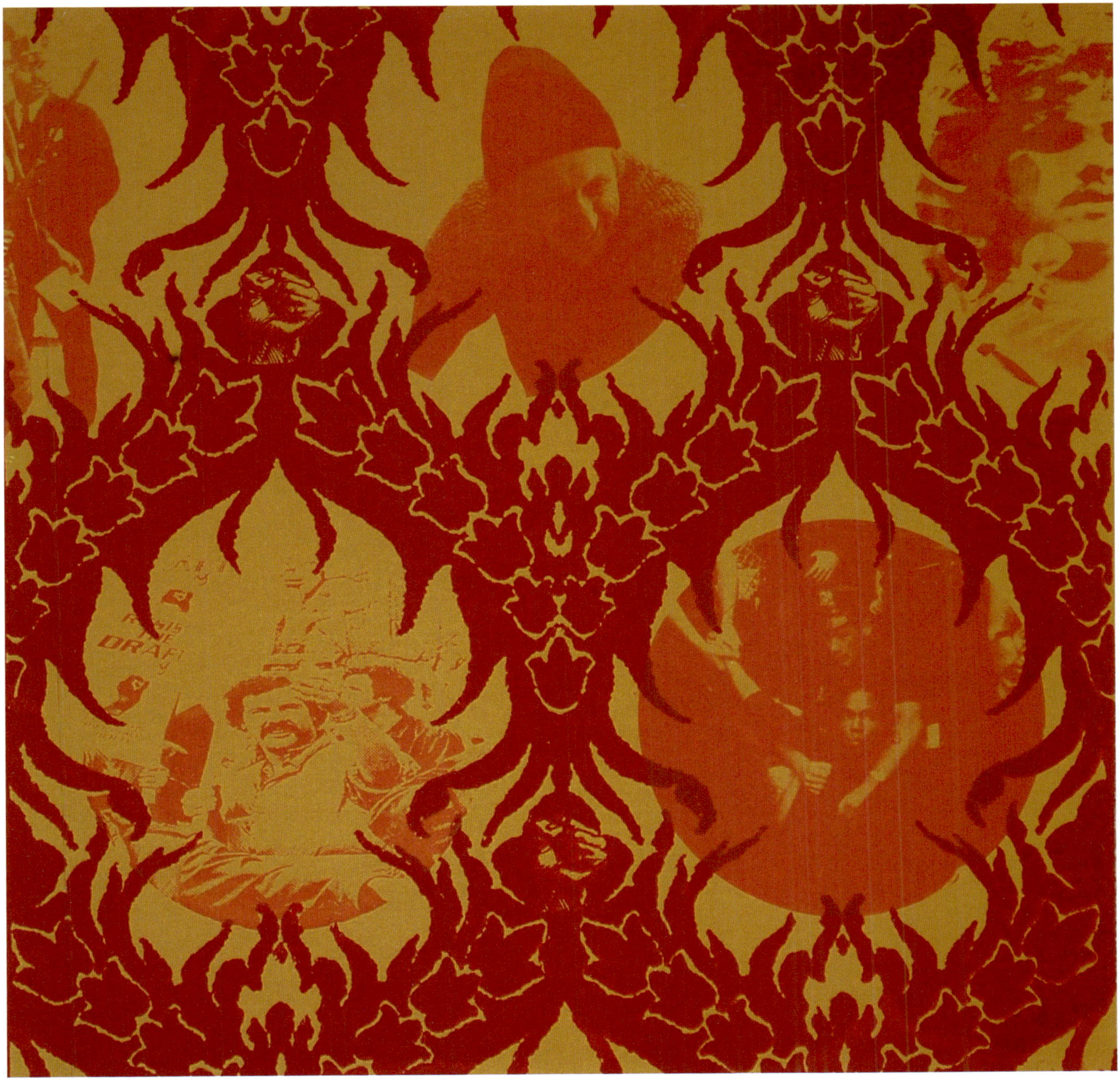

HARRISON HAYNES

Born 1973, Durham, North Carolina
Lives in Durham, North Carolina

Living in the same area of North Carolina as where I grew up has afforded me a dependable stream of autobiographical content. At one time I accepted bits of this material as ready-made subject matter for visual art. More recently, though, I've come to regard my practice's relationship to my locality as a resist, as a layer of impermeability that challenges the absorption of intuitive gestures, and thereby generates a counterpoint within the work.

As a musician, I have traveled extensively throughout the world, rarely staying in one place for more than 24 hours. However, at each stopping point, I make an effort to seek out endemicity. In my artistic practice, too, engaging a native citizen as a collaborator brings perspective on what it means to be "here." We, the two performers, salute the moment in unison but from very different points of view.

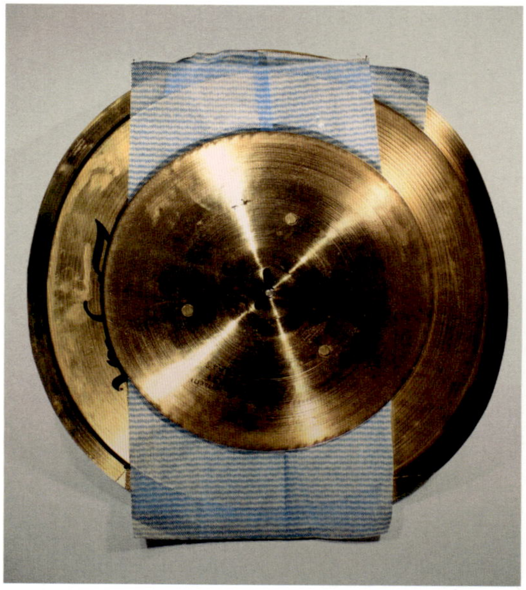

Harrison Haynes describes his work as having a "preoccupation with decontextualization." Haynes works in a range of media, from painting, photography, collage, video, and performance, as a means to explore the mundane objects of his life as well as the landscape of his North Carolinian environs. Removed from their contextual associations and examined up close, the objects that populate Haynes' work reveal a world both ordinary and surreal.

In the video installation *LRLL RLRR* (2011), Haynes considers the notion of "here" from the perspective of both origin and itinerancy. The work is based on a 74-minute serialized, site-specific performance, where every iteration occurs in a different locality and invites a native collaborator to join as the second drummer. Filmed in Haynes' home state of North Carolina, the video features Haynes and North Carolina-based drummer and artist Casey Cook. In its exhibited form, the video makes reference to the layout of the live performance, with the video monitors approximating the positions of the musicians' opposing drum sets. As viewers sit on drum stools and don headphones to watch the work, they become virtually immersed in the drummer's audio-visual experience, implicating the viewer as both a voyeur and participant. During the exhibition opening, Haynes staged the work in its original form, as a collaborative performance with a Philadelphia based-drummer, presenting the experience of being "here" in a more finite state.

Untitled (Cymbals & Cloth), 2010
Hand-cut archival pigment print
37" x 38"
Photo courtesy of the artist

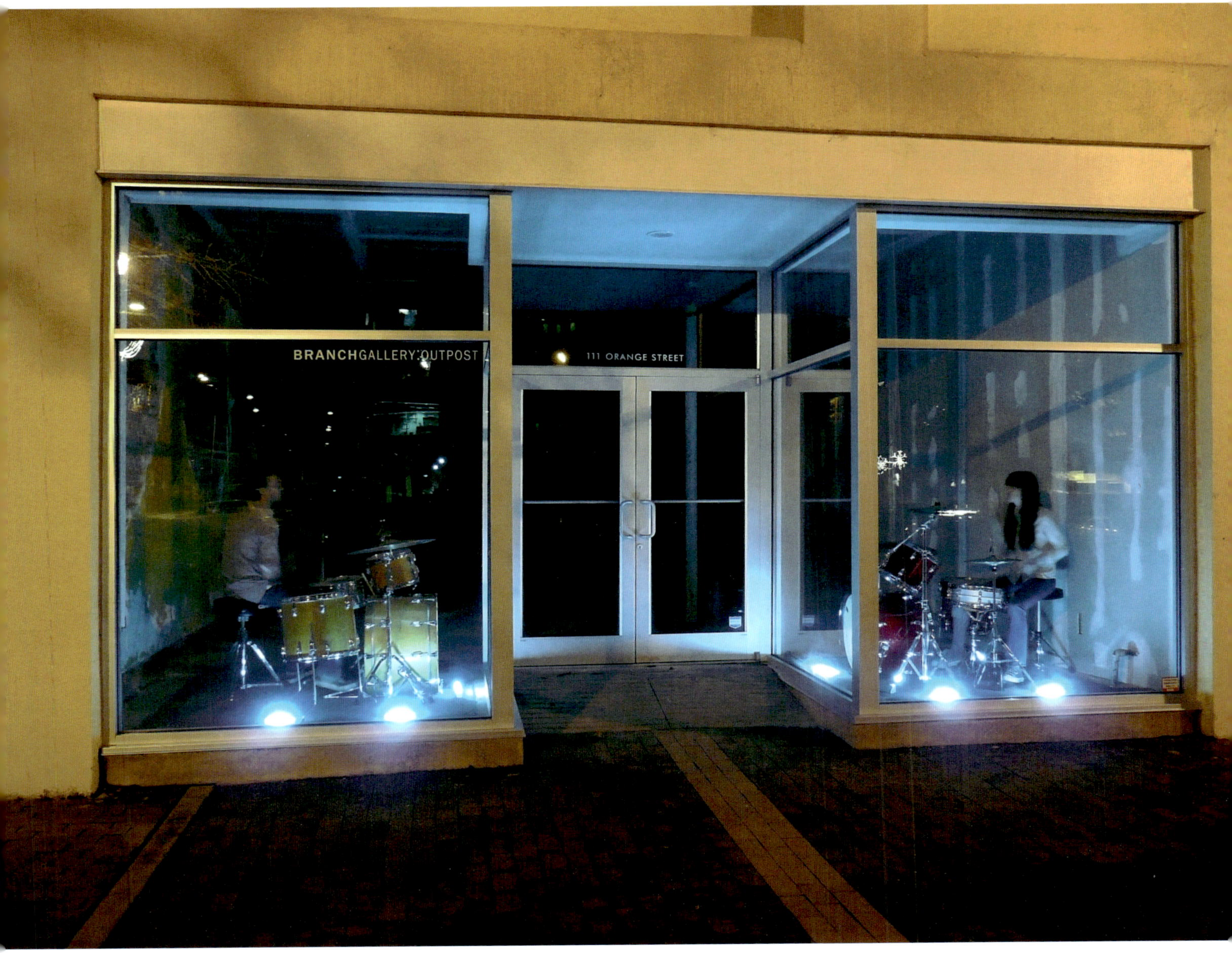

LRLL RLRR (with Casey Cook), 2008
Performance, Branch Outpost, Durham, NC
Dimensions variable
Photo by Katy Clove

SCOTT HOCKING

Born 1975, Detroit, Michigan
Lives in Detroit, Michigan

I am interested in forgotten places, and things kept out of sight. I don't know if this is because I am from Detroit, a city that has been known for forgotten neighborhoods and structures for most of my life; but I try to work the same way no matter where I am. I pay attention to my surroundings, exploring and gathering images and materials to create installations and photography projects. My installations often use objects found on site, and their lifespan is left up to chance.

Detroit is a fitting city for this kind of practice, and living here over three decades, I know my surroundings well. I've got a perpetual long-list of ideas—maybe a testament to the complexities of Detroit, or any place where you decide to hunker down and dig deeper. When I was a teenager, I wanted to leave; I tried (and failed) a couple of times. At 21, I had a car accident, days before moving away. It was surreal. I took it as a sign—maybe we're born in a place for a reason? I decided to try my hand at art, and within months, I was in school.

15 years later, I'm still here, and still inspired. I've experienced the Motor City on foot, found solace within the empty factories and overgrown lots, and discovered beauty in the decay and transformations. This is my home base. It has taken time, but I love the clarity that comes with that time. And I don't plan on leaving anytime soon.

Native Detroiter Scott Hocking uses the material ruins of the city to create site-specific installations. He explores derelict buildings and collects the abandoned objects and materials that he finds. The artist also extracts materials during his explorations. These specimens are catalogued and carefully stored until there is enough of a single phylum to be made into a gallery installation. The artifacts on display for ***here.*** are mineral deposits, stalagmites created as water invaded derelict structures. Hocking's installations in abandoned factories are often epic in scale with titles that invite mythological associations: *Zeus Whirlwind* (2010) or *Sisyphus and the Voice of Space* (2010). For *Garden of the Gods* (2009 – 10), he collected televisions left behind when the Packard Assembly Plant was deserted and placed them atop exposed martini glass shaped columns that stand among the ruins of the collapsed roof. He then documented the installation over a period of a year, noting seasonal changes in light, weather, and disintegration. Some of Hocking's favorite locations for interventions, like the Packard Plant, are abandoned Albert Kahn industrial buildings. Noteworthy for vast expanses of clear space, light, and geometric repetition, these ruins still reflect the order and logic of their design. The rhythms of architectural elements syncopate the artist's interventions, highlighting the tension between order and disorder. In these apocalyptic urban sites, Hocking's installations are American Arcadias: his interactions yoke the remnants of the built environment to ancient sagas, imbuing their entropic spaces with an energy that suggests the possibility of emergent new life.

Opposite top:
Hephaestus and the Garden of the Gods, Snow – exhibition print from the series: Garden of the Gods, 2009 – 2010, 2010
Archival pigment print/
Mixed media installation
Print: 33" x 49.5"/Installation:
Dimensions variable
Photo courtesy of the artist and
Susanne Hilberry Gallery

Opposite bottom:
Ziggurat, East, Summer II – exhibition print from the series: Ziggurat and FB21, 2007 – 2009, 2008
Archival pigment print/
Mixed media installation
Print: 33" x 49.5"/Installation:
Dimensions variable
Photo courtesy of the artist and
Susanne Hilberry Gallery

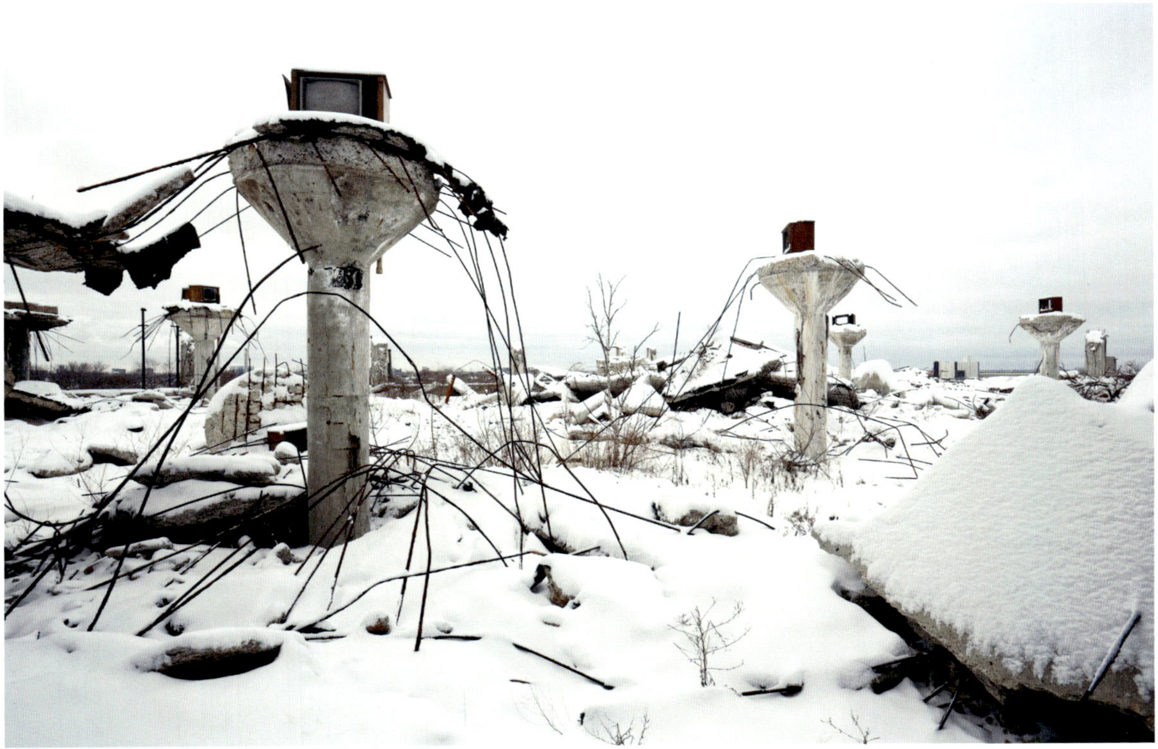

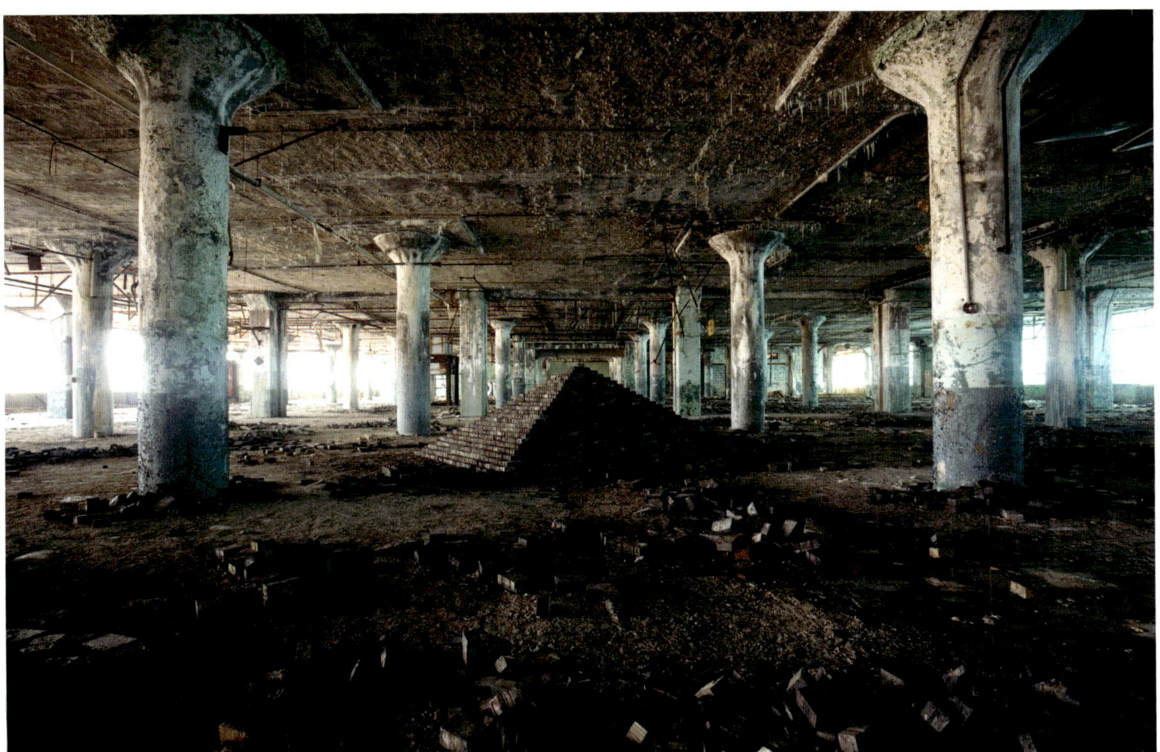

CHIDO JOHNSON

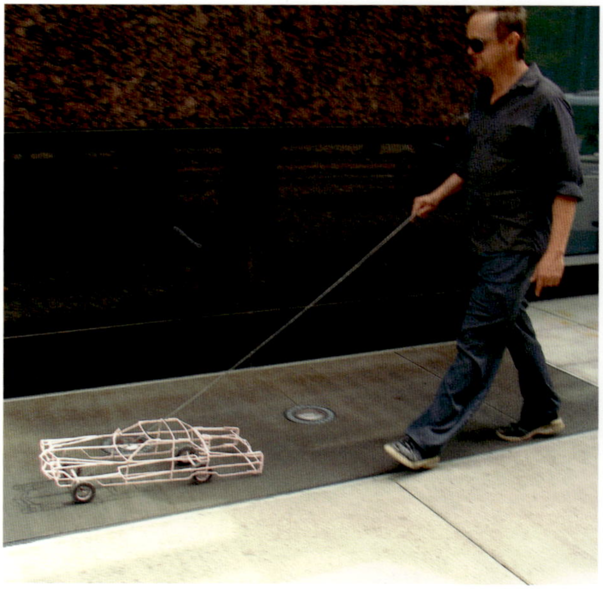

Born 1969, Nyadiri Mission, Mutoko (Zimbabwe)
Lives in Detroit, Michigan

Detroit has been my home for the past nine years, the longest I have lived in any city. I was born and raised in Zimbabwe and Zambia, then came to the USA to study fine art when I was seventeen. Since then, the longest I would stay in any place would be three years, until I moved to Detroit. There was something about the city that was so familiar in its difference, or "otherness." Having lived being affiliated to "other" places, Detroit's narrative felt so familiar. It is a city full of "others," relating to familiar stories of landscapes recovering and healing from wounds inflicted by previous oppressive regimes, yet surviving soulfully with such hope and passion. Detroit is very real and defies the heavily imposed hierarchy of a dominant European American culture's claim as the national character. It feels very different from any city in the USA; it is a border city, on the edge of the country, "other-ed" in its denied hegemony. Living between two ethos, the United States and Zimbabwe, has led my work to persistently locate cultural spaces—identified as other and different—in an attempt to find physical or narrativeperformances to transform and negotiate a new sense of self, place, and belonging.

Chido Johnson explores contradictions and divides between African and American culture. Because he was born in Zimbabwe, a child of white American missionaries, he experienced boyhood as a racially marked outsider. His physician mother delivered much-needed services in the town of Mutate. Johnson expresses this experience not in words but by displaying family photographs, snapshots of happy times that show a fair-headed child with dark skinned African playmates. Accordingly, Johnson bases his sculptures and performances on the dialectics of looking and otherness. The artist chooses images and forms that have valence in both African and American culture opting for miscegenation of sources that point to identity's constructed nature. Using American consumer culture and African sculptural traditions as a foundation, he mixes conflicting values and aesthetics to pronounce unnerving and sometimes humorous frictions.

His project *Jack's Vision* was triggered by a narrative related to a now-displaced sculpture that depicts the white colonialist Kingsley Fairbridge and his black manservant, Jack. This traditional bronze sculpture was installed during British colonization and later removed after the founding of Zimbabwe. Johnson and others from Mutare perform *Jack's Vision* by walking from Hartzell High School, where the artist was a student, to the top of nearby Mount Chiremba. Each performer wears a chair strapped to their back, backpack style, and a miner's helmet equipped with video cameras that record the journey. The chair is surmounted by a carved head made from Mupani wood, which was cut from a tree in a "taken" farm and has a traditional use in sorcery. Ever true to his African roots, the artist shows this journey from two views based on the orientation of the cameras. Two narratives, two viewpoints, are created with each journey. Johnson's work shape-shifts between African tradition and contemporary theory, negotiating the tough spaces created by the legacy of colonial occupation and racist practice.

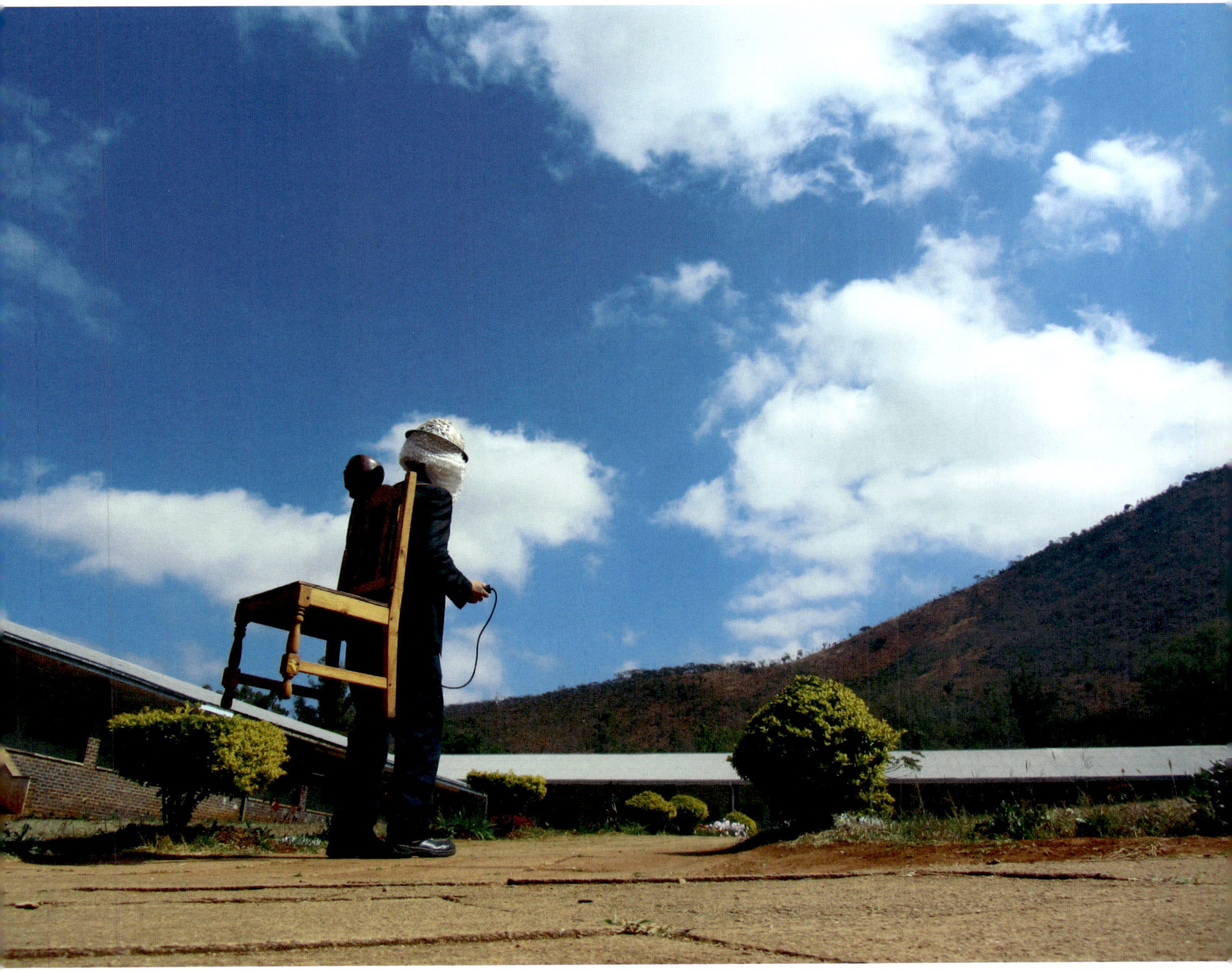

Opposite:
my pink caddi, 2009
Video installation
Dimensions variable
Photo by Kurt Greene

Above:
Begin climb
Chido Johnson, collaborator Naomie Nyanungo
Jack's Vision, 2010 – present
Mixed media
Dimensions variable
Chair: 42" x 18" x 18"
Photo by Calvin Dondo

MICHAEL KRUEGER

Born 1967, Kenosha, Wisconsin
Lives in Lawrence, Kansas

As far as the eye can see, the land stretches. The immense open spaces feel good, like a great embrace, and help me feel just the right size on the planet. There is humility in people from the Midwest that comes from the awe and understanding that we are diminutive in comparison to the land. In contrast, the infinite details of nature continually challenge one's curiosity, not just in relationship to the landscape but to everything.

My creative work has been impacted by my location in clear, as well as unperceivable, ways. The history of the West and the Great Plains has beguiled me since my childhood years in South Dakota. The lore, the reality, the wounds, the triumphs and grueling human perseverance, the conflict and contestation have all contributed to my understanding of the human pathos. These subjects, as well as the character traits that permeate the Midwest, reveal themselves in my process in abstract and literal ways. In particular, the notion that hard work in itself is a meaningful and fulfilling experience. Also, I believe the solitude of my locale fosters a freedom to be intensely idiosyncratic. There is motivation to go deeply inward and reveal inner truths and *high strangeness*.

These few rudiments that begin to describe my *HERE* no doubt play an important role in my greater investigation. In some ways, once I enter the studio I am liberated from my place and get to make work about here, nowhere, and everywhere.

History's ghosts haunt the curiously ambiguous narratives of Michael Krueger's prints and colored pencil drawings. Born in Wisconsin, Krueger spent most of his childhood exploring the flatlands of South Dakota and now makes Kansas his home. In his work, he couples this personal experience of the Midwest with a fierce appetite for the region's history and mythology.

Since accepting a teaching post at the University of Kansas, Lawrence, in 1995, Krueger has investigated the key socio-political events, figures, and cultural values that make this small town stand out as the state's liberal bastion. Past contestations over land rights, slavery, and the forced assimilation of Native Americans still simmer in its collective consciousness. Such events plague almost every community in the United States, but in Krueger's art, these histories provide the framework for posing productive questions about both the present and the future.

In *Kanopolis* (2009), Krueger pairs archetypes from the 17th century colonization of America and the 1960s hippy movement on top of Mushroom Rock, an iconic geological landmark in Central Kansas. The gross paradoxes embedded in our cultural history are illuminated by the juxtaposition of these historically disparate moments. However, the artist's purposeful quality of line and bright, techno-colored palette also suggest their shared utopian ideals. Perched on an alien rock in the middle of Kansas, these figures seem additionally to address the realities of being an artist in the Midwest: isolated as "other," yet well-poised to use history's lessons to better understand today and perhaps forecast the zeitgeist of tomorrow.

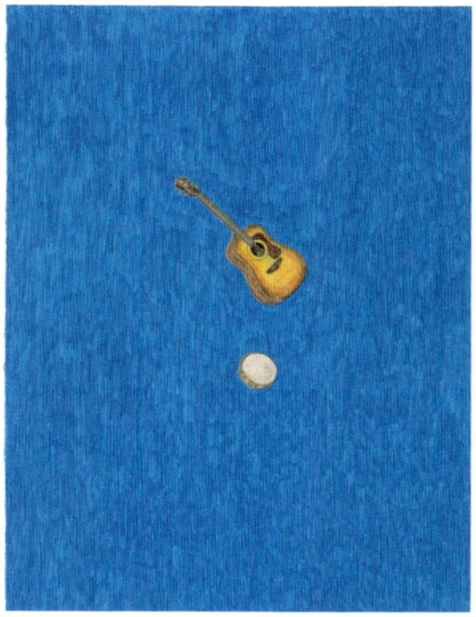

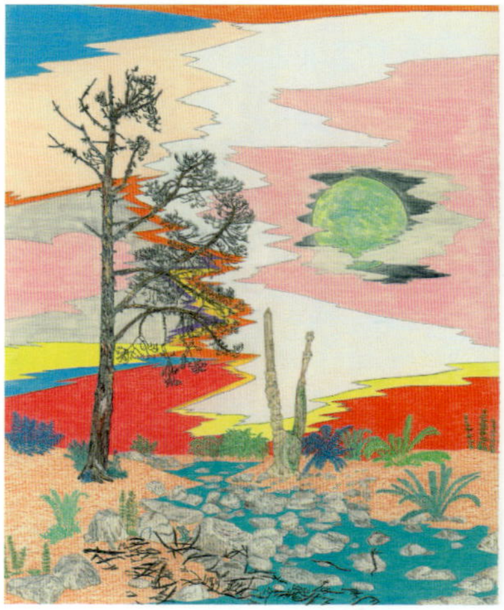

Left:
Guitar, 2011
Colored pencil on paper
30" x 22" (sheet)
Image courtesy of the artist

Right:
Green Moon, 2010
Colored pencil on paper
25" x 20" (sheet)
Image courtesy of the artist

Opposite:
Night Falls, 2011
Colored pencil on paper
40" x 30"
Image courtesy of the artist

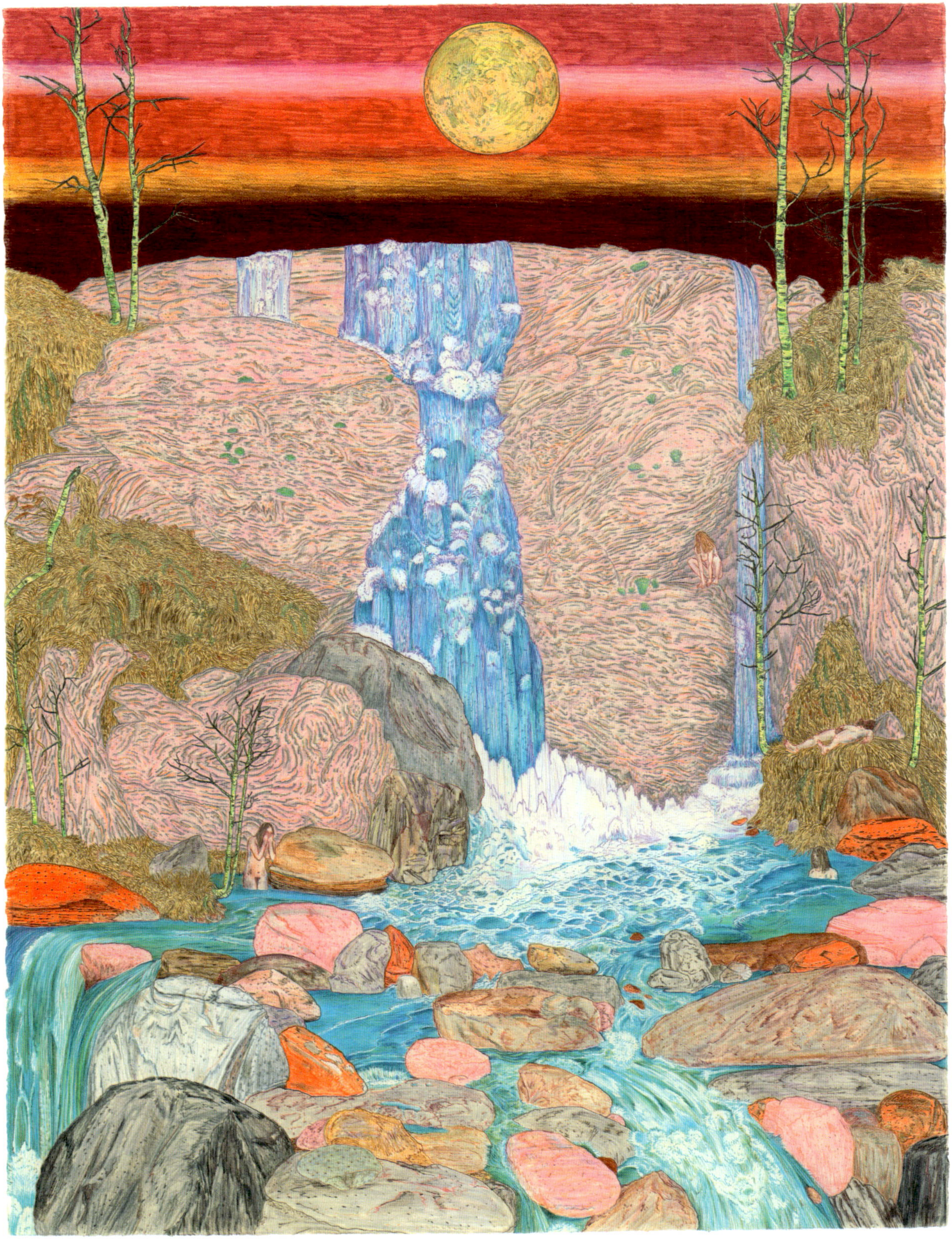

JENNIFER LEVONIAN

Born 1977, Martinsburg, West Virginia
Lives in Philadelphia, Pennsylvania

My cutout animations are intensely autobiographical. Most of the settings are based on my surroundings at home in Philadelphia. The interior of my Kensington row house and the upscale supermarket across town became the backdrops for my animation *Buffalo Milk Yogurt*, a collaboration with artist Corey Fogel. The climax of the animation's narrative—a man suffers a nervous breakdown and knocks a huge wheel of cheese into bottles of gourmet olive oil—was lifted from life. While goofing around in the same store years before, my sister accidentally sent a massive Parmesan wheel careening down an aisle. It was such a cartoonish event that I knew I had to include it in my animation that satirized contemporary food culture.

Philadelphia is famous for its filthy streets and spirited residents. I think it is the friction caused by the city's imperfections that makes it an appealing place to make works. From the class tension in my neighborhood that is undergoing gentrification to the gritty landscape, there is plentiful subject matter. After the Phillies won the 2008 World Series, some seriously overexcited fans celebrated by hurling pumpkins through store windows and flipping cars. The next morning, I saw pigeons pecking at smashed pumpkins in the streets, and I later included the scene in *Buffalo Milk Yogurt*. The moment captured my sense of the city and its competing qualities—its aggressive energy and the peaceful aftermath, the absurdity in the mundane, and a longing for something beyond what is in front of us.

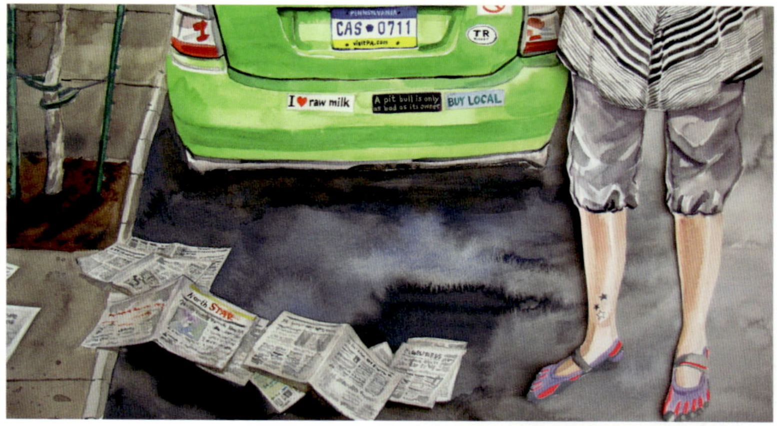

Jennifer Levonian describes her animated video films as "very low tech." In a process that begins with watercolor painting, she creates dozens of props and backdrops that are moved around and recorded as hundreds of digital photographs. Employing computer technology, she then organizes these images into narratives which, together with their accompanying soundtracks, transform the everyday into a series of bizarre and witty events. Including herself in many of her films, Levonian's stories are partly autobiographical, featuring people and places that are familiar to her.

In Levonian's new video, called *The Oven Sky* (2011), her story opens in a Philadelphia neighborhood undergoing gentrification. In the film, new arrivals to the neighborhood put pressure on a longtime resident, wanting to turn her lawn-ornament-filled yard into a dog park. She refuses but then receives a notice from the city that forces her to comply with their wishes. In the closing scene, an artist, who belongs to the pro-dog park camp, takes all of the woman's discarded lawn ornaments and redeploys them in an art gallery exhibition. Struggling with the changes wrought by gentrification, the main protagonist seems both to lament and transcend her lot as she sings Rachel Mason's ballad *The Oven Sky*.

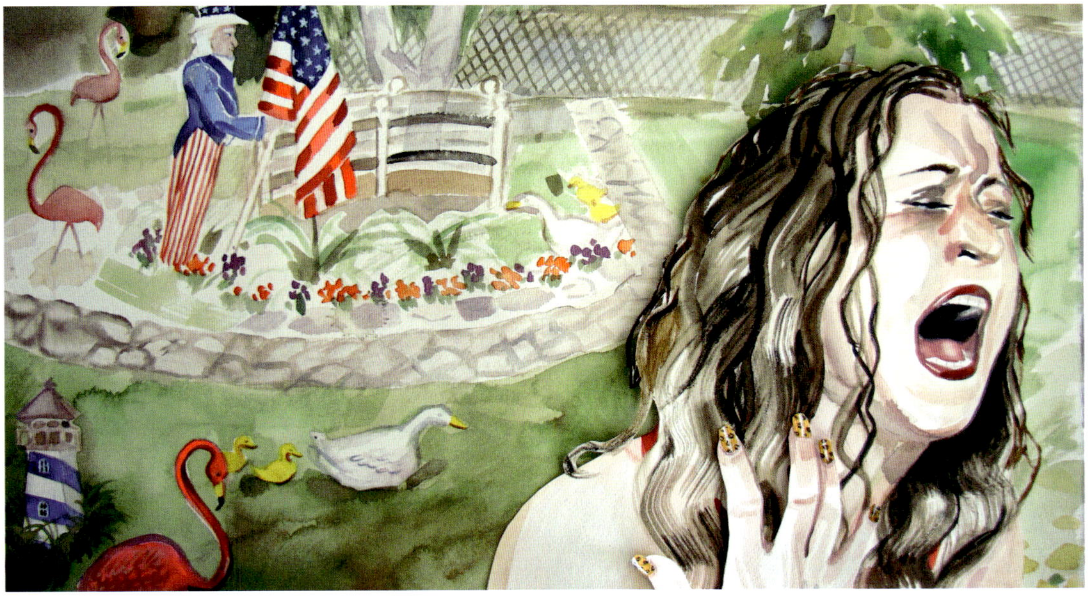

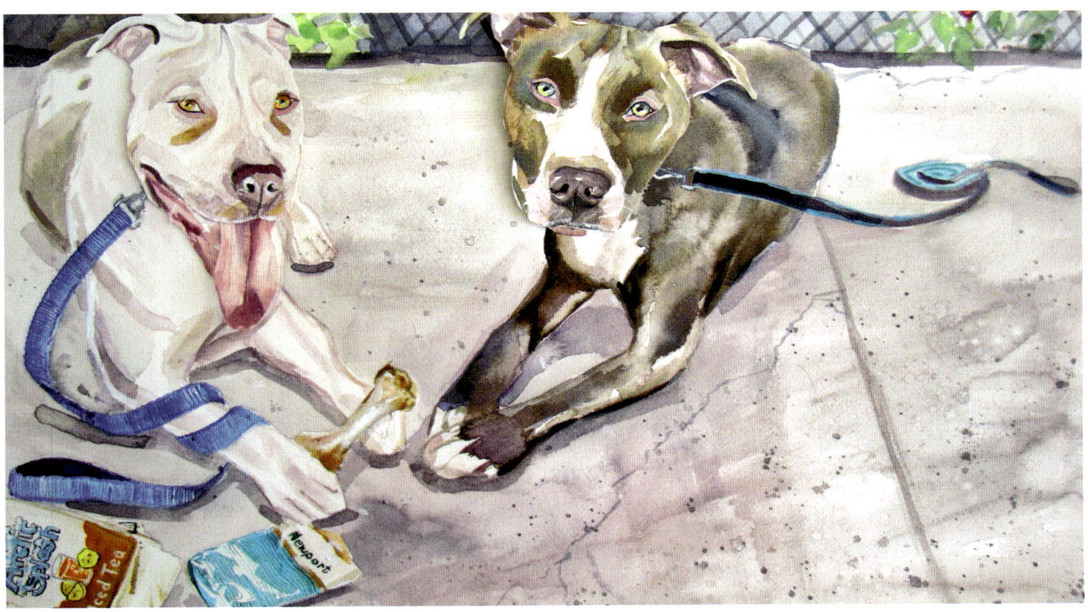

The Oven Sky, 2011
Cut-out animation using watercolor and collage, with music by Rachel Mason
Video stills courtesy of the artist and Fleisher/Ollman Gallery, Philadelphia

MEGAWORDS

Founded October 2005
Dan Murphy: born 1976,
Philadelphia, Pennsylvania
Lives in Philadelphia, Pennsylvania
Anthony Smyrski: born 1980,
Philadelphia, Pennsylvania
Lives in Philadelphia, Pennsylvania

For us, the idea of "here" is a flexible one. We draw a lot of energy and inspiration from the people around us and the diverse, interesting communities they create. These communities include the urban neighborhoods we grew up in, the subcultures of our youth, and the art, music, and professional worlds we live and work in here in Philadelphia and abroad.

Through Megawords, we search for the common links between people and places. We use these connections to generate new discussions and ideas. We are very interested in the patterns and idiosyncrasies that exist in one place, especially when those patterns and ideas can be useful and relevant in another different, distant, or seemingly foreign place. With this in mind, our experience and practice focuses less on a physical "here" and more on a temporary "here" that allows us to say something new.

Started in 2005, Megawords is an ongoing project conceived by Philadelphia artists Anthony Smyrski and Dan Murphy. Drawing inspiration from the urban neighborhoods they grew up in, the subcultures of their youth, and the art, music, and professional worlds they live and work in, they say their intention is to "document our surroundings and experience in a manner that is free from commercial interests, opening up a dialogue between Megawords and the community at large." In a practice that openly reaches out to a broad range of communities, Megawords has self-published fifteen issues of *Megawords* magazine, which is distributed free, not only in Philadelphia but also in New York, Los Angeles, Houston, Berlin, Stockholm, and other cities across the globe. Megawords has a website, a blog, a Twitter feed, and a Tumblr page and while the main focus of Smyrski and Murphy's project is the printed magazine, they are also interested in installation, the use of public space, radio, video, music, readings, and public events. Created with collaboration in mind, their site-specific, often temporary, installations in public spaces aim to foster communication and understanding and encourage new ways of thinking. Megawords' special installation at the entrance to ***here.*** creates a place to connect with the museum's audiences and a distribution point for a new issue of *Megawords* magazine.

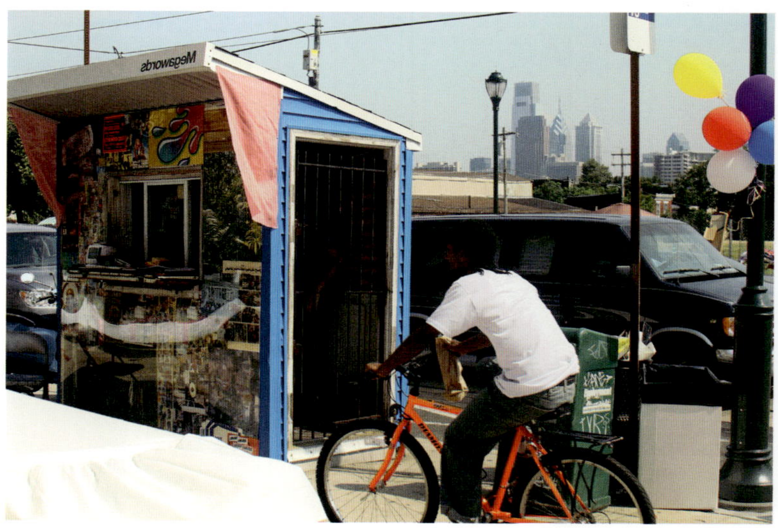

Exterior of Megawords Newsstand,
28th Street and Girard Avenue, 2010

Occupation of an abandoned newsstand that provided us with a chance to create a street level installation that could be used as a distribution point for the magazine. It also was an excellent opportunity to revitalize an abandoned structure, and return it to some of its former utility as a newsstand, if only for a weekend.

All images: Courtesy of the artists

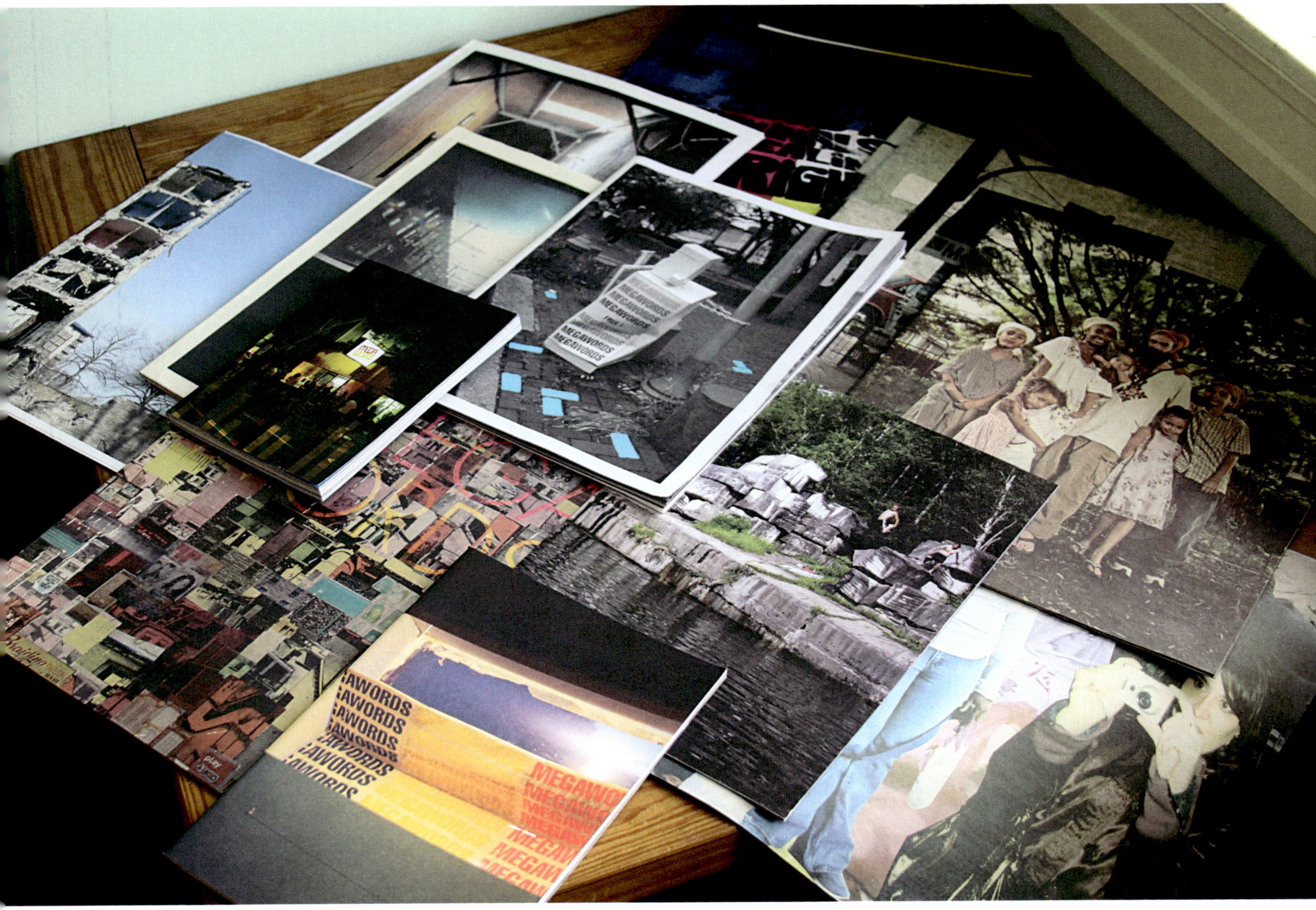

Various covers of *Megawords* magazine
produced between 2005 and 2010

ERIKA NELSON

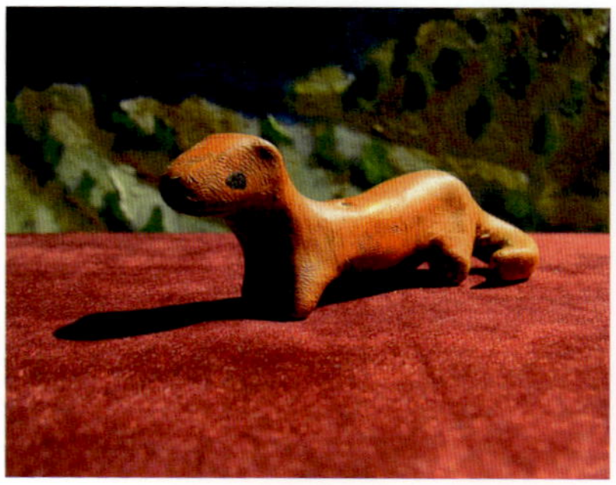

Born 1973, San Angelo, Texas
Lives in Lucas, Kansas

Here

Home

Location

My own practice embraces a seemingly oxymoronic duality of transience and permanence, which directly reflects my early history. Our family had a permanent home during the school year, in a small town with a deeply rooted family history. Daughters of the American Revolution, the Order of the Eastern Star, and extended family picnics brought in relations from the surrounding Ozark hills. Summers, holidays, and extended weekends would see our family on the road, covering miles and miles of highways and byways, criss-crossing the U.S. to our home (another Here) of the week or month or year. "Here" is where you are at any given point, both dependent upon and independent of geography. Traveling now, still leading a permanent-yet-nomadic lifestyle, from event to event, residency to residency, public art project to project, roadside attraction to attraction, Here is still a dual identity.

The roadside vernacular architecture (roadside attractions billed as "World's Largest Things") making up the bulk of my explorations has a dual identity, dual purpose, dual viewpoint. The towns and communities erecting these identity markers are creating cultural icons, symbols, and representations of who they are. Visitors and explorers coming to these monuments see these iconic structures as items built for them, tourist attractions designed to entice the traveler and make them stop for a moment. Visitors may or may not consider place, location, or the home they are visiting, the Here-ness, from the builders' points of view. Instead, they bring their own complementary experience to a common geographic place. My practice examines these perspectives, exploring the transient yet rooted stories that intersect at points on the atlas.

Under the enormity of the Kansas sky live some of the world's biggest roadside attractions: the largest ball of twine in Cawker City, the biggest steam shovel in Pittsburg, and the largest hand-dug well in Greensburg. Before the likes of discount malls and super-sized box stores, "the biggest" whatevers were definitive stops on any road trip.

Lucas, Kansas-based artist Erika Nelson knows this car-culture phenomenon intimately. In her nomadic childhood, Nelson spent many hours cruising the highways of the United States with her family, often patronizing these human-made oddities. Today, she bases her ongoing project *The World's Largest Collection of the World's Smallest Versions of the World's Largest Things* (2001 – present) on these iconic vernacular structures. To unpack the who, why, and how behind these monuments, Nelson travels the country in search of the next biggest thing. Having found the world's largest catsup bottle or the world's largest tire, she snaps a photo and, when back in the studio, creates a miniature replica. She then displays the picture and sculpture together in an old bus, her Mobile Museum. This project has toured the country, visiting festivals, museums, and TBS's *Conan* show, and although the bus now remains a permanent display in Lucas, Nelson continues to tour her collection as a full-on Sideshow Extravaganza with a Freak Show table, promotional banners, and her Art Car "Scout."

Nelson investigates each "biggest" structure's *raison d'etre*—what propels an individual or community to create such a monstrosity. These roadside attractions often serve small towns as engines for economic development or rallying points for civic camaraderie. More importantly perhaps, they illustrate a collective desire to assert a unique identity in an increasingly homogenized landscape. These towering landmarks differentiate one place from another: a here from a there.

Above:
World's Smallest Version of the World's Largest Otter, Fergus Falls, MN, 2004
Polymer clay and acrylic
1" x 0.75" x 2.75"
Photo courtesy of the artist

Opposite:
World's Largest Collection of the World's Smallest Versions of the World's Largest Things: Sideshow Extravaganza Banner #1, 2009
Oil and sign enamel on canvas
75" x 54"
Photo courtesy of the artist

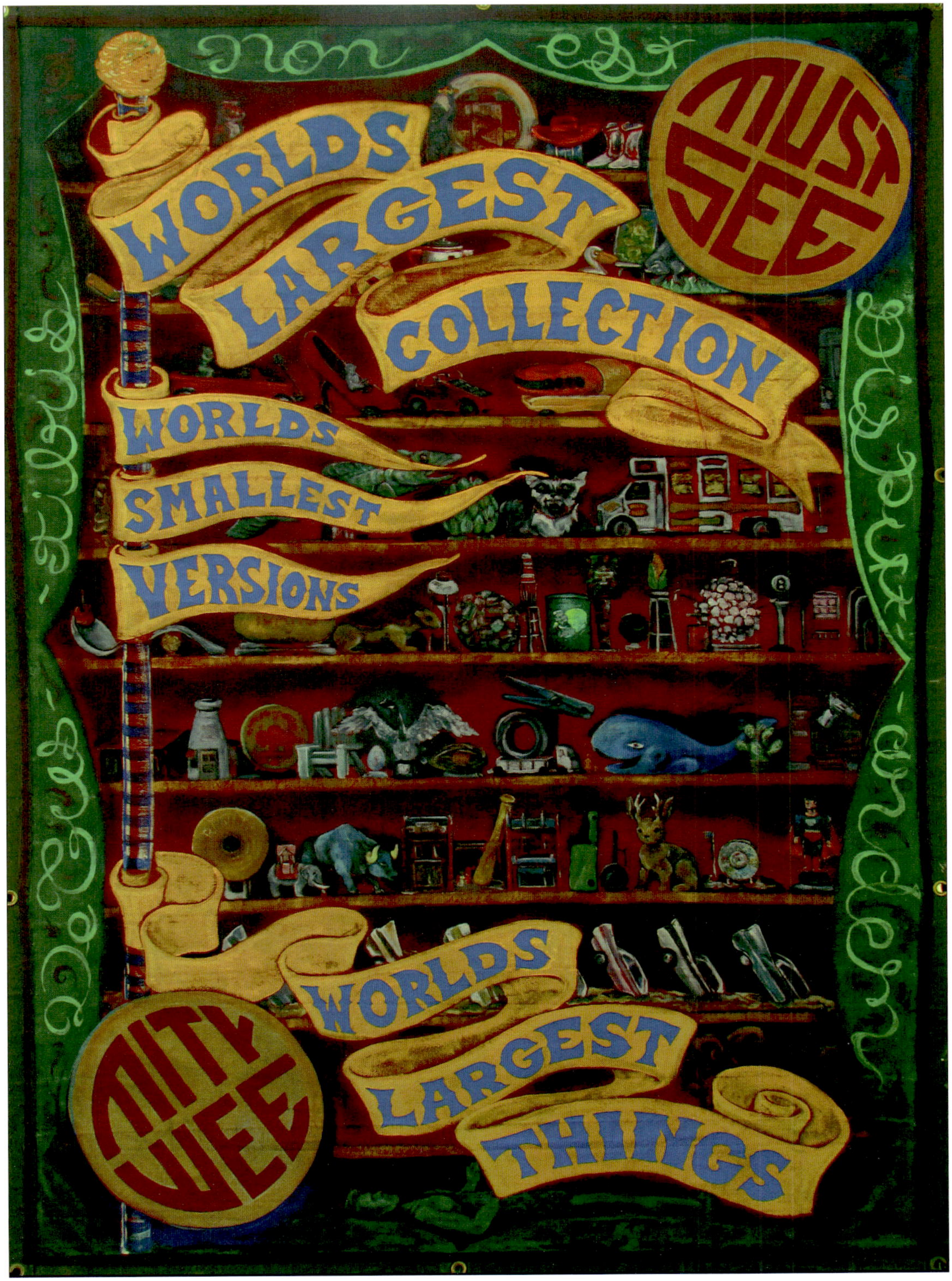
non est
MUST SEE
WORLDS LARGEST COLLECTION
WORLDS SMALLEST VERSIONS
WORLDS LARGEST THINGS

ABIGAIL ANNE NEWBOLD

Born 1976, Boston, Massachusetts
Lives in Cambridge, Massachusetts
(lived in Detroit, Michigan, for eight years until recently)

In my practice, *Here* is less a point fixed by time or place, rather it connotes a concept, inherently reliant on the transience of the perpetually unseen protagonist in my work. *Here*, always in the present tense, is a description of my current location in the moment, as well as defining placement in the larger context of my surroundings. Often in my installations, the protagonist is in the process of getting *there*—and not yet *here*. In defining that locus, I take ownership of it, even if temporarily, drawing you to my *here*.

The concept of *here* and the concept of *home* are closely related, as they both define an exclusive space. To be from *here* is to belong: to know a place and to be known by it. And in the process of being known, I am learning to make myself at home anywhere.

Detroit, a series of micro-communities strung together over a relatively vast space, often feels like a series of small, related towns, between which lie common resources of land and goods. Consequently, greater amounts of travel are required to get from point A to point B, with copious tracts of land available in-between, inspiring in me a sense of pioneering wanderlust. This peculiar set of conditions interests me in two ways: the process of perpetual travel—its means, style and process of preparation—as well as the potential that exists in the empty spaces in between points.

Being *here* means being home, whether I'm in the place of my current residence or traveling between points. My interest is in making wherever I am enough of a place that I can call "*here*" "*home*."

Reflecting on her lifestyle as a young adult, Abigail Anne Newbold realized that the choices she made have led to a peripatetic lifestyle of never staying in a single place very long, of creating *home* wherever she was. Although she didn't realize it at the time, a succession of moves taught her that locality (here) is always subject to revision, to the momentary. There was a second lesson also: that for her, living implied change in which—although it could lead to rootlessness—one need not be unrooted but could find *home* in self-sufficiency, in creating identity associated with temporary locations that offered the potential for shelter, order (occasionally comfort), and (sometimes) enduring memories.

It is small wonder that Newbold founded a studio practice about *making home*, about selecting, ordering, making specific, and ritually consecrating material objects that define who she is and the essential nature of a homestead or personal stake. Her installations include found and reimagined objects that display a sense of adventure or the pioneering spirit. Kits for both urban habitat and rustic life, they invite the possibility of one-off living, of DIY culture, of making shelter that is unique to an individual, thereby also constructing a physical counterpart to self.

Detroit is remarkable for its empty spaces, metaphoric open fields that spark an artist's imagination. With her *home maker* kits, Newbold invites us to make settlement with her, to establish a relationship contingent on the conditions of locality and the individual. In this practice, Newbold poses new solutions for living systems, domestic relationships, and personal identity.

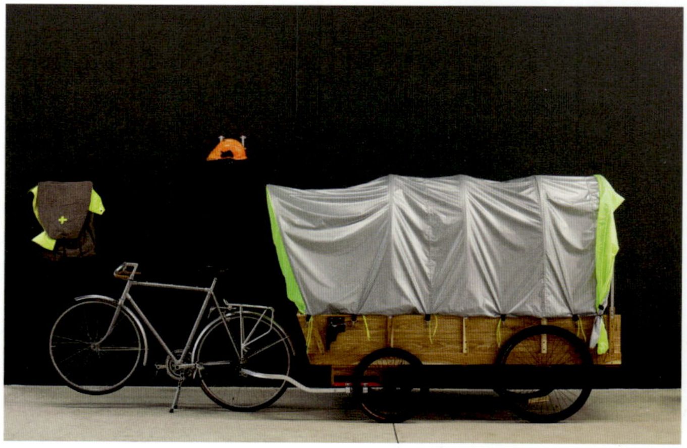

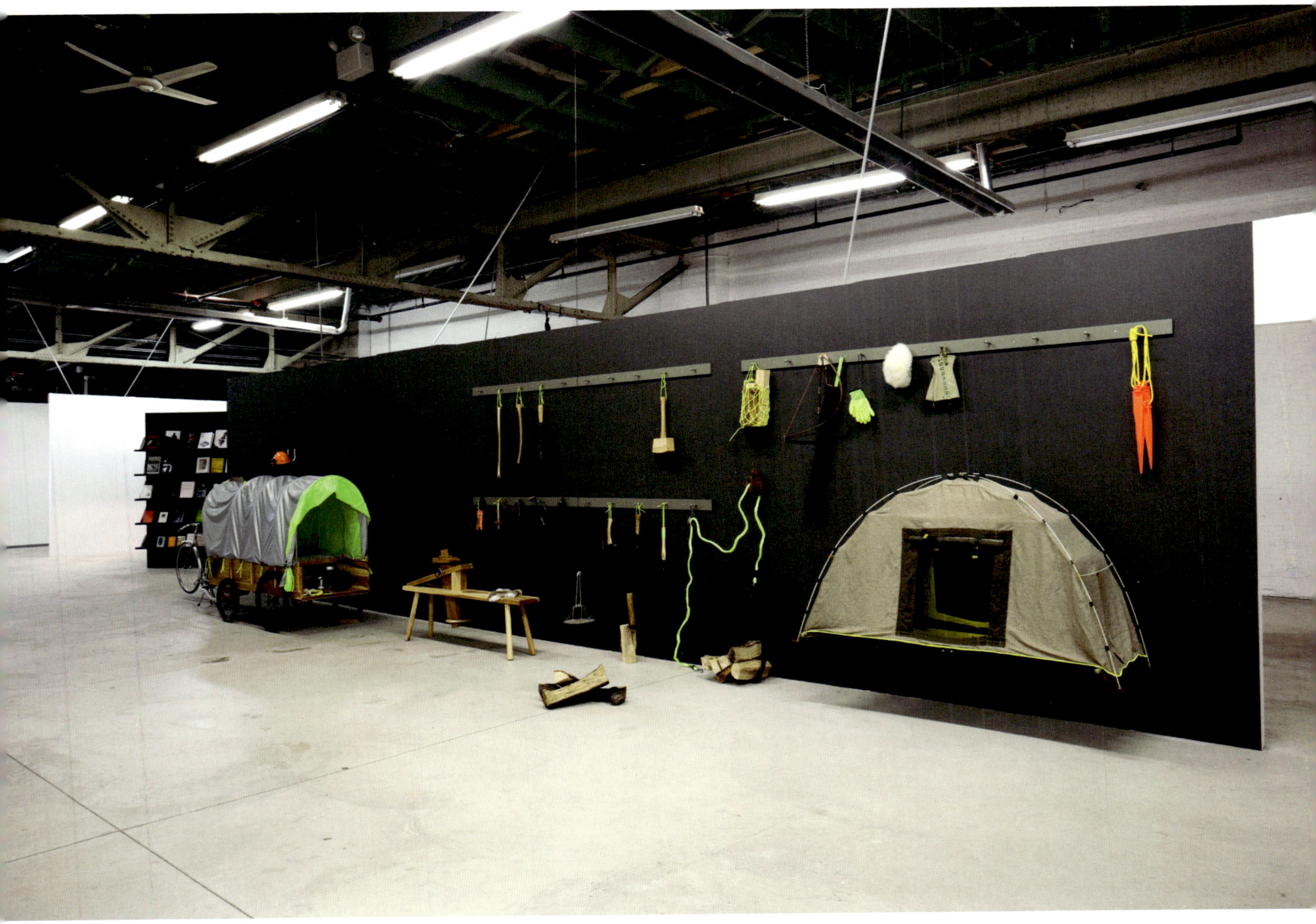

Homemaker series, 2010 – 2011
(installation view and detail)
Found and custom fabricated objects
Dimensions variable
Photos by Corine Vermeulen

TIM PORTLOCK

Born 1969, Chicago, Illinois
Lives in Philadelphia, Pennsylvania

Philadelphia is a significant place in the history of American Democracy, which is visible in a good deal of its older architecture and museum art collections. When I first moved to the city, I was struck by its large number of abandoned and dilapidated buildings. While other American cities, such as Detroit, Baltimore, or Stockton, also face such hardships, this seemed especially poignant for the foundling nation's original capital city. That initial shock in part came from the stark contrast between the ideals of the historical Philadelphia and the scale of the grossly deteriorated material condition of the present post-industrial city. Over time, the day-to-day mundane realities of my life, work, leisure time, and personal relationships have settled around these declining structures. While always visible, the visceral impact these decaying buildings initially made have become less immediate. Having now lived in Philadelphia for a number of years, I have grown to greatly appreciate some of the city's aspects that can only be known after living here for some time. However, to a certain extent, the work I make is a reconnection to the view of Philadelphia I first held in my early days of living in the city, and one that is refreshed each time I return from a trip.

Tim Portlock hails from Chicago and is an artist who has worked as a community based muralist as well as a studio painter. He moved to Philadelphia just over five years ago and is now a member of Vox Populi, one of the most established art collectives in the city. Since the late 90s, Portlock has increasingly employed new media in the production of his work and has expertise with a variety of tools—from gaming software to 3-D animation—that he uses to generate his imagery. Investigating the social and economic impact of America's rapid de-industrialization in visually unsettling images, he creates haunting, post-apocalyptic urban landscapes that are often viewed from an aerial perspective, that depict worlds where industrial culture has come and gone, leaving blight in its wake. Portlock says that, "In preparation for much of my work, I speak with experts in economics, urban planning, and sociology," and points to his lifelong artistic interest in "the dialogue between place, cultural vocabularies, and the formation of identity."

The works in ***here.*** further develop themes in Portlock's *Ghost Cities* series. These half-fictionalized portraits of Philadelphia, which he realizes as large scale inkjet prints, show familiar aspects of the city through a defamilarizing lens. Images that variously depict city buildings or run down neighborhoods with murals, they remain starkly empty. In them the only activity seems to be feral and undomesticated, suggesting not only the desertion of industrial cities by urban populations but also the encroachment of nature that follows.

Opposite top:
Municipal Services Building, 2011
Ink jet print
54" x 72"
Image courtesy of the artist

Opposite bottom:
Farm, 2011
Ink jet print
54" x 72"
Image courtesy of the artist

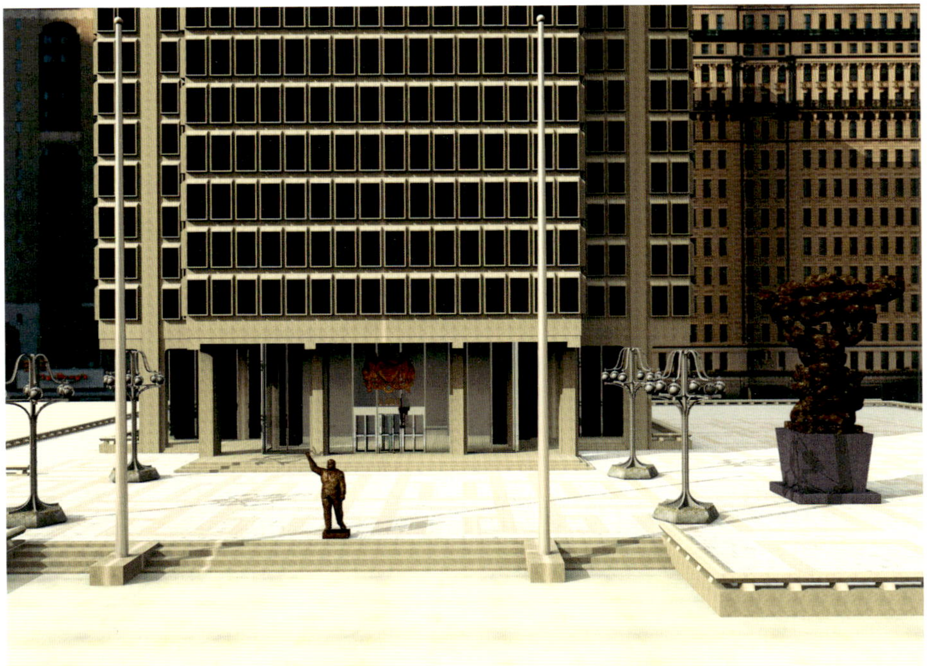

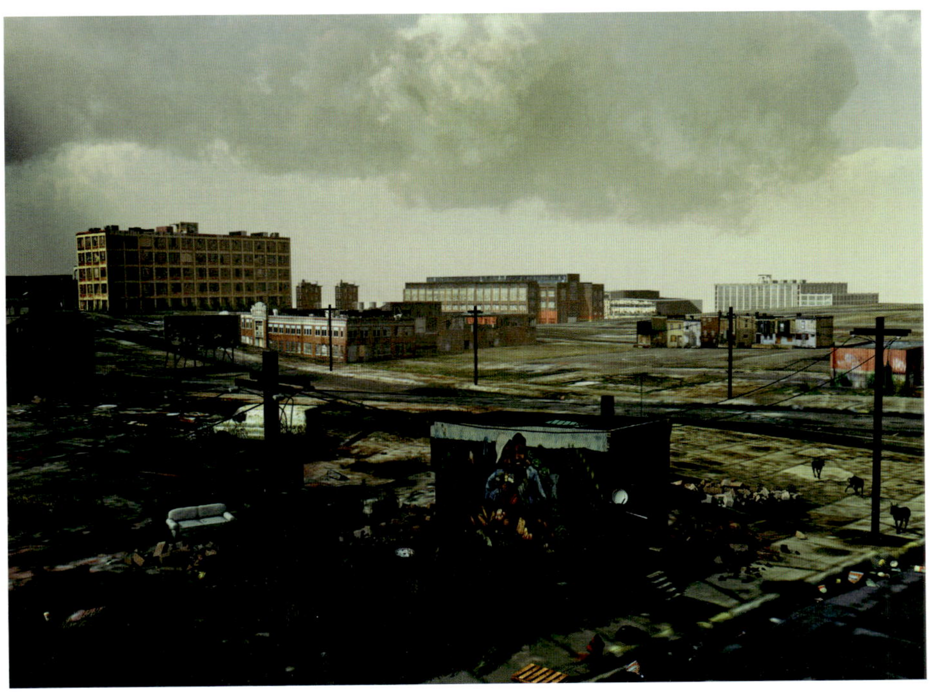

POSTCOMMODITY

Founded 2007
Raven Chacon: born 1977, Chinle, Arizona,
lives in Albuquerque, New Mexico
Cristóbal Martínez: born 1974, Santa Fe, New Mexico,
lives in Phoenix, Arizona
Kade L. Twist: born 1971, Bakersfield, California,
lives in Phoenix, Arizona
Nathan Young: born 1975, Tahlequah, Oklahoma,
lives in Albuquerque, New Mexico

Everything that defines us, as Indigenous people, and our relationships—worldview, culture, spirituality, memory, context, meaning, etc.—goes back to the land. Locality is not just a particular place that relates to a particular art practice; it is the source from which all things emerge, are experienced, accounted for, and remembered. Originating from, and working in, the Southwest (California, Arizona, New Mexico, and Oklahoma), Postcommodity occupies the traditional homelands of numerous tribes simultaneously, as well as the vastness of the region. Therefore, we seek respectful, cross-cultural dialogues as a means of performing reciprocity when engaging our work on our, or other Indigenous people's, historical lands. Through our art practice, we seek to advance a discourse about self-determination that is accountable to our locality—in terms of the interconnectedness of land, culture, and community—while engaging and responding to the assaultive manifestations of the global market and its ever-expanding, multinational, multiracial, and multiethnic colonizing force that is defining the 21st century.

A "red city," Phoenix is the most important place for indigenous intellectuals to come together in America, and it is here that the members of Postcommodity connected with each other, pooling their skills as composers and musicians, visual artists, engineers, writers, and filmmakers. An indigenous collective, Postcommodity creates intense multi-media installations that address the brutal transformation that has been effected upon the land and time-space of America by Western values. In so doing, they sustain and augment the revolutionary spirit of Native American leaders who have been coming to Phoenix for over sixty years to advocate for social justice, self-determination, and tribal sovereignty.

In *Na'nízhoozhí da' nijahigi na' a'ahi (Gallup Motel Butchering)* (2010), the slaughter of a sheep in a hotel bathroom might appear to outsiders as an excessively violent event. But, to those who share a cultural, social, and psychological connection to the land that spans multiple centuries, the work's imagery depicts a time-honored ritual that has been driven, out of necessity, into a non-place; a space whose generic conformity could be anywhere in America and that many say epitomizes new land-development in Arizona especially. Addressing the displacement and marginalization that result from cultural homogenization, in this new video installation made for ***here.***, Postcommodity challenges the notions of progress, individualism, speed, and knowledge that dominate and sustain our contemporary worldview. Yet, while the work can be understood to critique the imposition of modern values on time honored traditions, it also reveals that these rituals—whose rules and customs nurture respect, well-being, and continuity—remain alive, no matter where they must occur.

Opposite:
Gallup Motel Butchering, 2011
Four channel video installation with sound
Dimensions variable
Video stills courtesy of Postcommodity

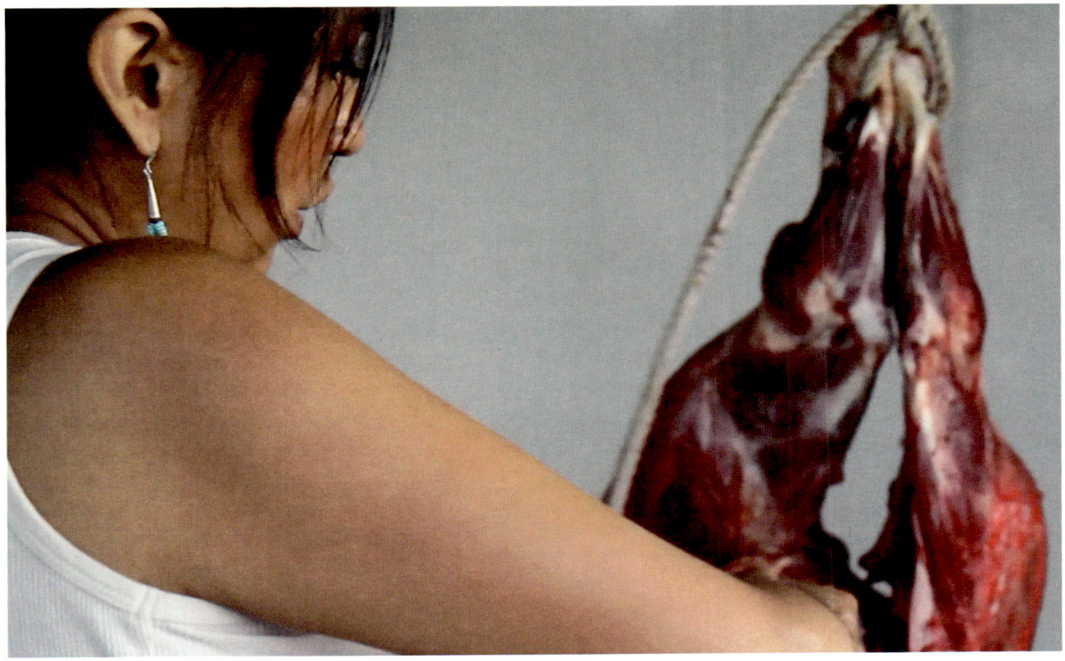

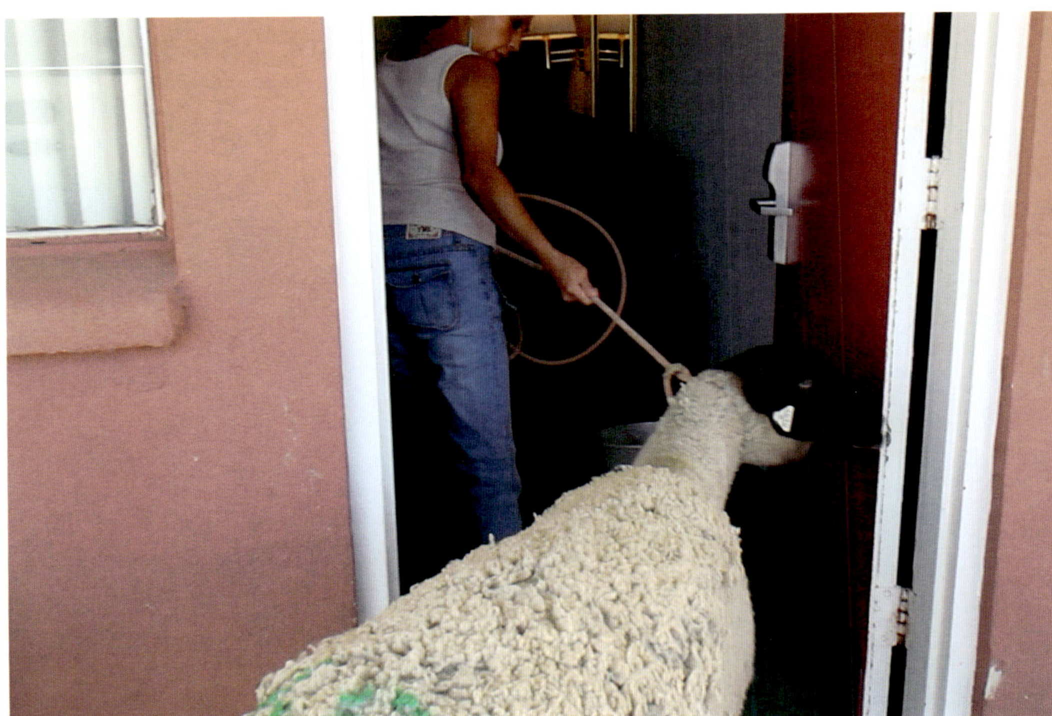

AARON ROTHMAN

Born 1974, Mountain View, California
Lives Phoenix, Arizona

I am still a bit surprised that I have ended up calling Phoenix my home. Like the desert that it occupies, Phoenix doesn't seem like much at first glance. Both city and landscape appear vastly monotonous, but variation, richness, and complexity are revealed with time and looking. The desert is a place that exists on the edge of conscious understanding. The vast scale of the space precludes a totalizing view; understanding is reached through the accumulation of piecemeal experience. Likewise, moving through the expansive grid of the city provides moments when pieces of the undifferentiated mass snap into focus, creating a fleeting sense of place and a strangely acute awareness of one's position on the surface of the earth.

The fragmentary nature of perception is, from time to time, overtaken by the apprehension of a vastness beyond comprehension. This tension is an essential part of my experience of this place in which I live and has become a core element in my work. I use photography as a transformational tool that activates an expanded awareness and points to the limits and possibilities of perception. The "here" of the place photographed mixes with the "here" of the process of making—the photo/digital process, my sensibilities, the caprice of the studio—to create a new "here" embedded in the experience of the work itself.

With a large format camera, years as a maker of prints and drawings, and immeasurable time spent in the desert, Aaron Rothman investigates how we know and comprehend the world through the act of looking. Focused on light, space, and awareness of their subtly ever-changing relationship over time, he affords us an opportunity to slow down and notice ourselves noticing where we are. He explores the complex relationship between nature, the built environment, and photography by creating images and installations that are self-aware; they heighten, extend, delay, or abstract an experience.

For ***here.***, Rothman has left the space of the site-specific installation where he previously recontextualized the very environment of the gallery itself—including altered images, videos, and sounds of the room at different seasons and times of day. He has also stepped away from the larger context of Phoenix, which he has been pursuing in a long-term project where he is documenting the grid from every minor axis looking east at Third Street during the extreme heat of summer, so as to illustrate the complexity found in uniformity. Instead, in the *Idle Speculation* (2011) series he has focused his lens on a small detail—a patch of flowering weeds near the airport. Multiple images of this detail are layered over each other—some with their tones reversed—to create finished works, where up to six "photographs" can be fused together, so that the individual images cancel each other out and the picture becomes a sea of gray. Yet, color explodes unpredictably from this abstracted sameness much the way it does, physically and culturally, in the city's desert mosaic.

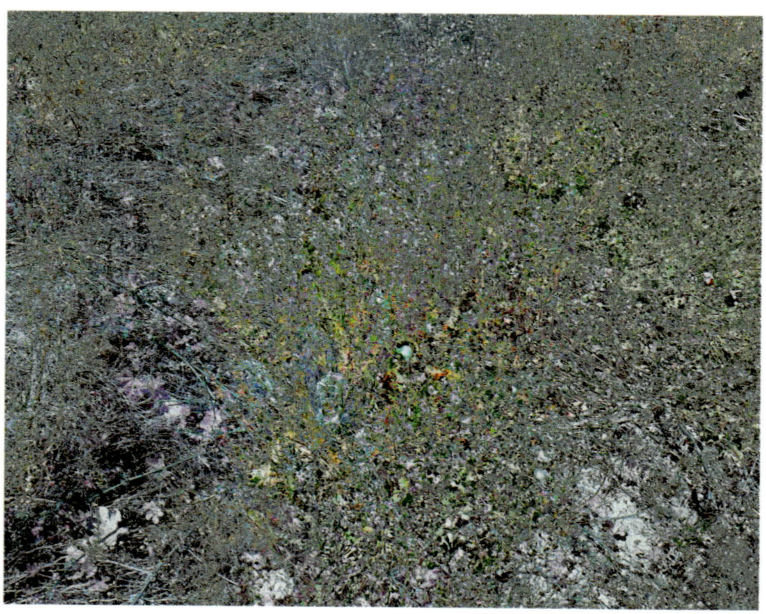

Idle Speculation 7, 2011
Archival inkjet print
40" x 50" (image)
Image courtesy of the artist

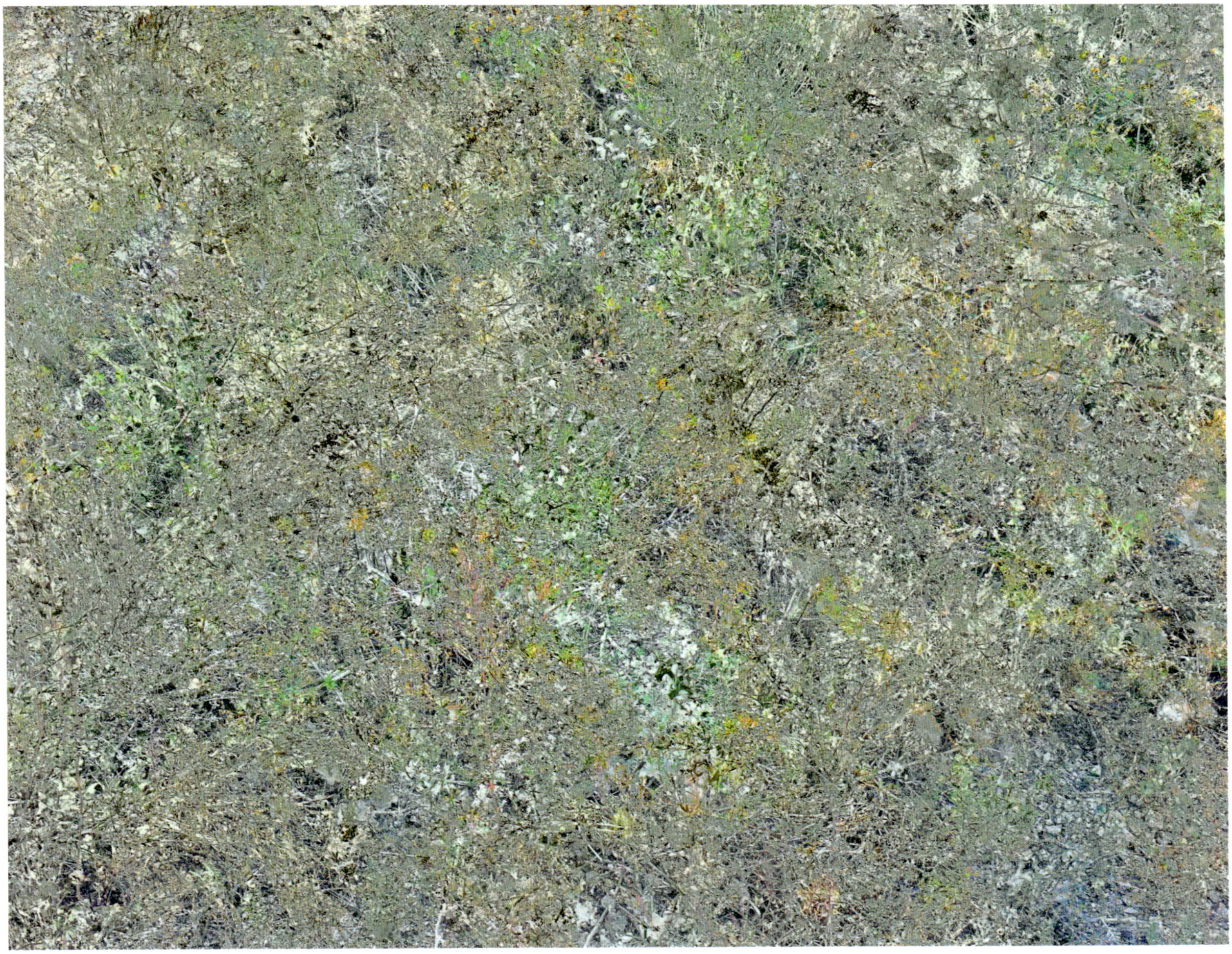

Idle Speculation 2, 2011
Archival inkjet print
40" x 50" (image)
Image courtesy of the artist

GREGORY SALE

Born 1961, Richmond, Virginia
Lives in Phoenix, Arizona

My current work germinates from dynamics in my community and a deep commitment to the southwestern region of the United States. It involves hundreds of people: some as active collaborators, others as participants, observers, or one-time visitors.

This work explores and exposes the many often-conflicting viewpoints, perspectives, and values that emerge from thoughtful considerations of justice and public safety. It gives voice to inmates and former convicts; those who jailed them, those who guard them, and those who stay in contact after they complete their sentence; their families and those they offended; those who draft new laws and those who apply those laws; those who advocate; and those who research or interpret. These individuals are both the makers and subject of this work.

Those of us in Arizona share common associations, codes, even verbal and visual languages that emerge from a local culture of imprisonment. With the complicity of the news media, a set of signs and signals, now in everyday parlance, has been championed by Sheriff Joe Arpaio of Maricopa County. Black-and-white-striped uniforms, pink underwear for male inmates, chain gangs for men, women and juveniles, and a Tent City jail in the desert have become commonplace. This local vernacular weaves its way throughout the artwork's multiple dialogues that serve as jumping off points for questions of how a country that prioritizes freedom and democracy could be the world leader in incarceration and how this could be the first generation to spend more on incarceration than education.

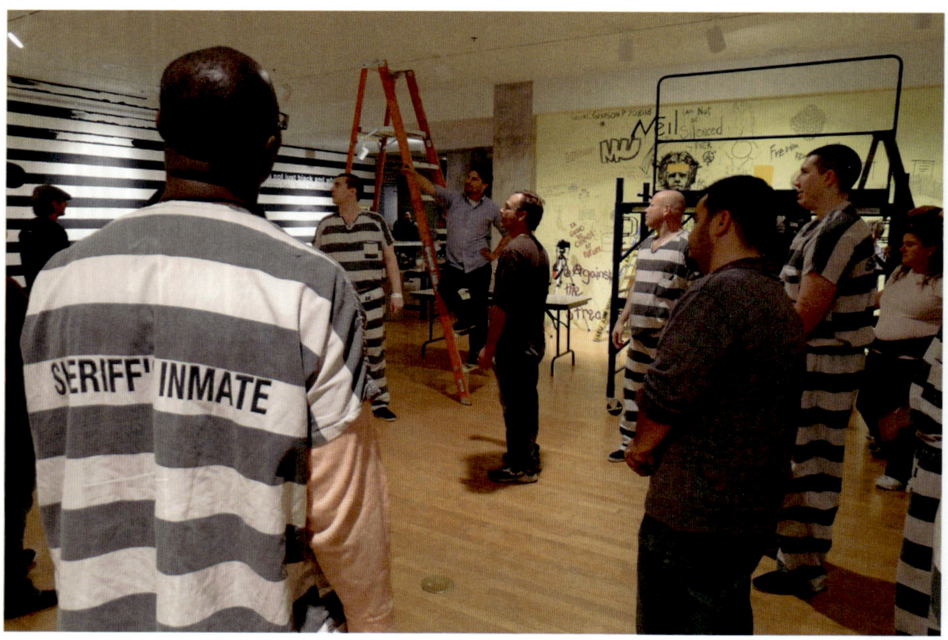

Gregory Sale in collaboration with Michael Bean, Joshua Adams, Ryan Landers, William Paskell, Brandon Reiswig, Michael Koveikis, Bryon Frank, Winston Arnold, De'Marko Pace, SR., Neil Rodgers, James Atwater, Louis Wilford, Nick Fletcher, Grayson Grumke, Officer Stephen Brown, Officer Thaddeus Cramer, Officer Timothy Medina, Officer Angel Alvarado, Officer Petia Strashilova, Sergeant Larry Irby, John Spiak, Brett Thomas, Cory Berquist, Stephen Gittins, Matt Garcia, Jason Dillon, Kara Roschi, Jane Lindsey, Jeffery Kirk

It's not just black and white, 2011
Photo by Stephen Gittins

Supported by grants from The Andy Warhol Foundation for the Visual Arts and Friends of ASU Art Museum and in partnership with ASU Art Museum Social Studies Series (Artist Residency) and the Maricopa County Sheriff's Office, Arizona.

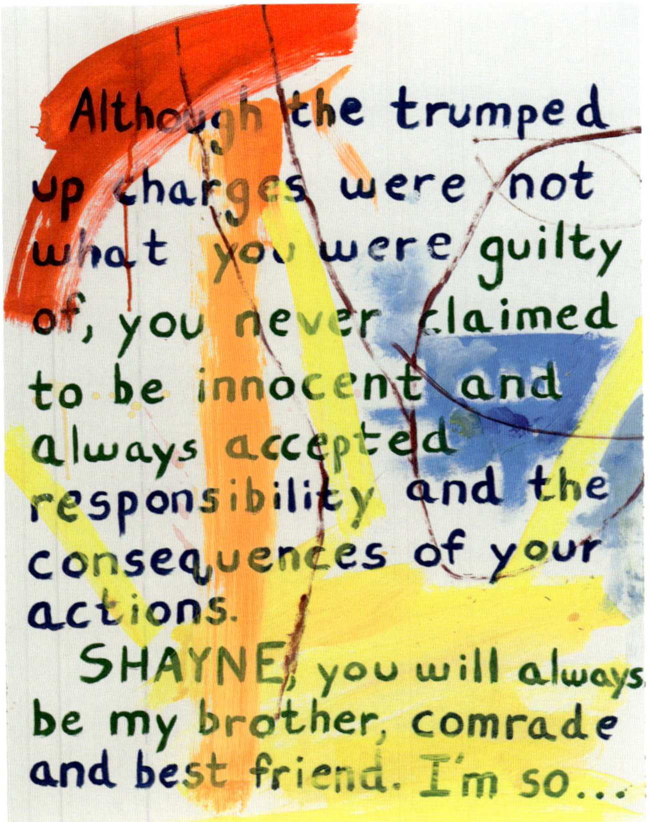

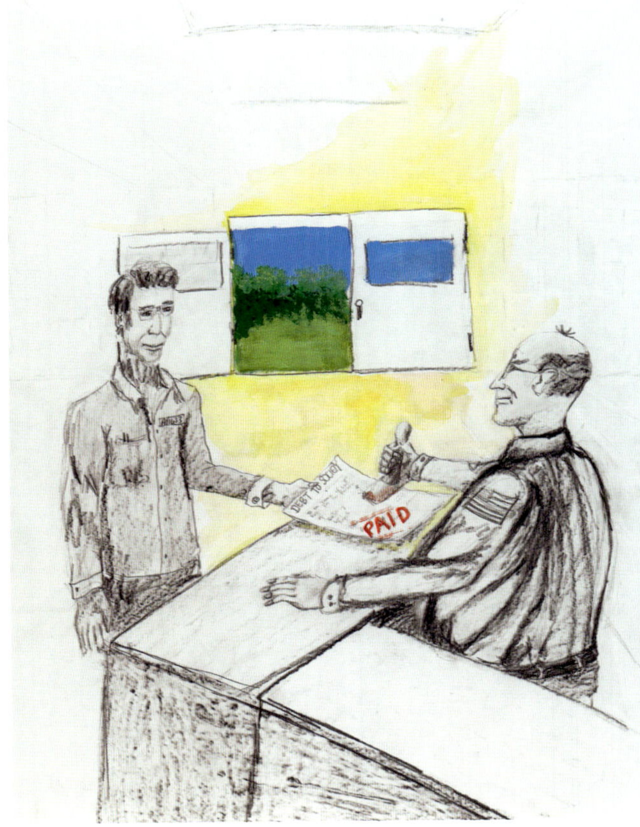

Gregory Sale brings people together. His multi-disciplinary, social art practice draws on his talents as an artist, educator, super-connector, diplomat, public arts administrator, and provocateur. Sale's investigations range widely, from Arizona's criminal justice system and a Mexican-American neighborhood, during a period of growing political animosity, to inner-human relations of love and death. Key elements remain constant—a desire to facilitate direct experience, a willingness to face difficult or uncomfortable issues, and an impulse to bridge private and public discourse. Through all of the social interactions Sale initiates run optimism, complexity, and an intense honesty. He has the ability to critique whatever system or ideology he confronts while highlighting the humanity of all involved.

In Phoenix this past spring, Sale created *It's not just black and white* (2011), a three-month residency where the public could explore the impact of the modern criminal justice system through artistic gestures, fact-based tours, dialogues, and programs—all within a process-oriented context. For ***here.***, Sale brings his "experiments in communication" to Philadelphia. He continues his multi-authored and collaborative methodology with Mural Arts Restorative Justice program and inmates serving life-without-parole sentences at the State Correctional Institution at Graterford. Text-based artwork produced with the inmates will open communication and engender discussion between the incarcerated and the larger world.

Gregory Sale in collaboration with Van, Stan, Tom, Roy, John, Zafir, Spel, Chuck, Toan, Felix, Eric

Life is life, 2011
Two from a suite of ten works on paper
Each 22" x 30"
Photos by Barbara Katus

Supported by grants from The Ford Foundation through the City of Philadelphia Mural Arts Program's Restorative Justice program (Teaching Artist Program) and the State Correctional Institution at Graterford, Pennsylvania.

AARON STORCK

Born 1978, (Manhattan)
New York City, New York
Lives in Lawrence, Kansas

I actually grew up on the Upper West Side of Manhattan and went to high school in the Bronx, but I love to live and work in Lawrence, Kansas. I have relatives in Kansas, that's how I came to know how cool it is. I love to see farms, open country, and big sky when I drive. Here in Lawrence, there are plenty of hip Liberals, also hard-core Conservatives. I drive to *Wal-mart* and *Home Depot* and I feel connected to the enigma that this country *is*. I drive to *Cabela's Outfitters* to buy guns and gear. I complete my sublimation of *Heartland Pride* when I charge the purchases to my *Cabela's Visa*. I love to look at the new subdivisions, strip malls, and *Tru-Green Chem Lawns*. When politicians talk about *Main Street USA*, I feel the vibe.

There is another reason why I'm here. I'm intrigued by the question, *who is a Kansas Artist*? If there were to be *Brilliant* new work to come out of Kansas, what would that even be like? There are few precedents. I live in the *id* of the nation, and the territory surrounding this question is inherently feral and undefined.

***Here* is risky. There are disadvantages in working apart from major Art hives, but for me the separation is a source of strength: the mythos of the west, the rugged individual. Here I claim the status of *Different* and *Artist As Wizard*. Nobody in NYC is doing anything close to what I'm doing.**

"Take a chip! Take a soda! Together we can do this, together we can make it through nuclear war, genetic engineering... feudal systems!" So rants the talking head in Aaron Storck's 2009 video *New Ministries*. The humorously absurd and staggeringly schizophrenic character plays dominant roles in Storck's artwork, consistently causing viewers to ask: Who is this person and what the hell is he preaching?

Adorned with a conical, star-studded hat and shiny robe, the wizard-like character often delivers rambling, almost non-sensical speeches with mundane props—trash, brand-name drinks and snacks—to an off-screen audience. In other scenarios, he hunkers down in the woods shooting guns and proselytizing. While the meaning is vague, the message is clear. With sharp wit, Storck's magical showman spoofs on the notion of the artist as shaman or mythological genius. The clichés of mystery, power, and eccentricity often associated with artists—and with such popular Kansas lore as the lone cowboy or Dorothy's wizard—are undermined by this unbalanced personality.

More broadly, Storck challenges anyone in a self-proclaimed position of power. Spouting passionately and fearlessly, the wizard astutely parodies anyone—politician, religious fundamentalist, or liberal extremist—claiming to speak the truth. This, of course, begs the question: How does one discern between artifice and authenticity in our contemporary culture? As a New Yorker now living in Lawrence, Kansas, Storck employs the mystery of a wild wizard to address and revel in the contradictions he finds in his new place and in the broader human condition.

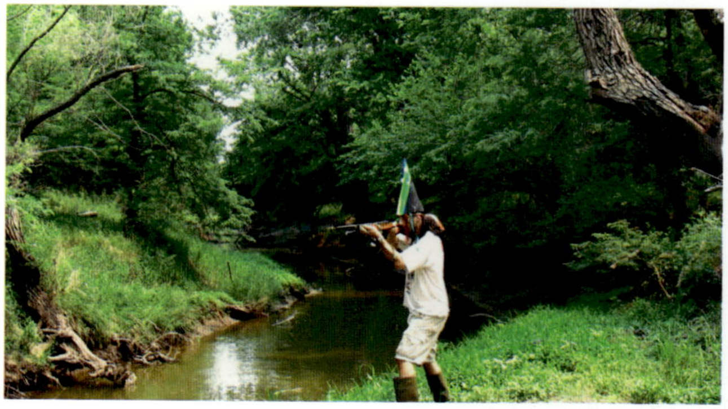

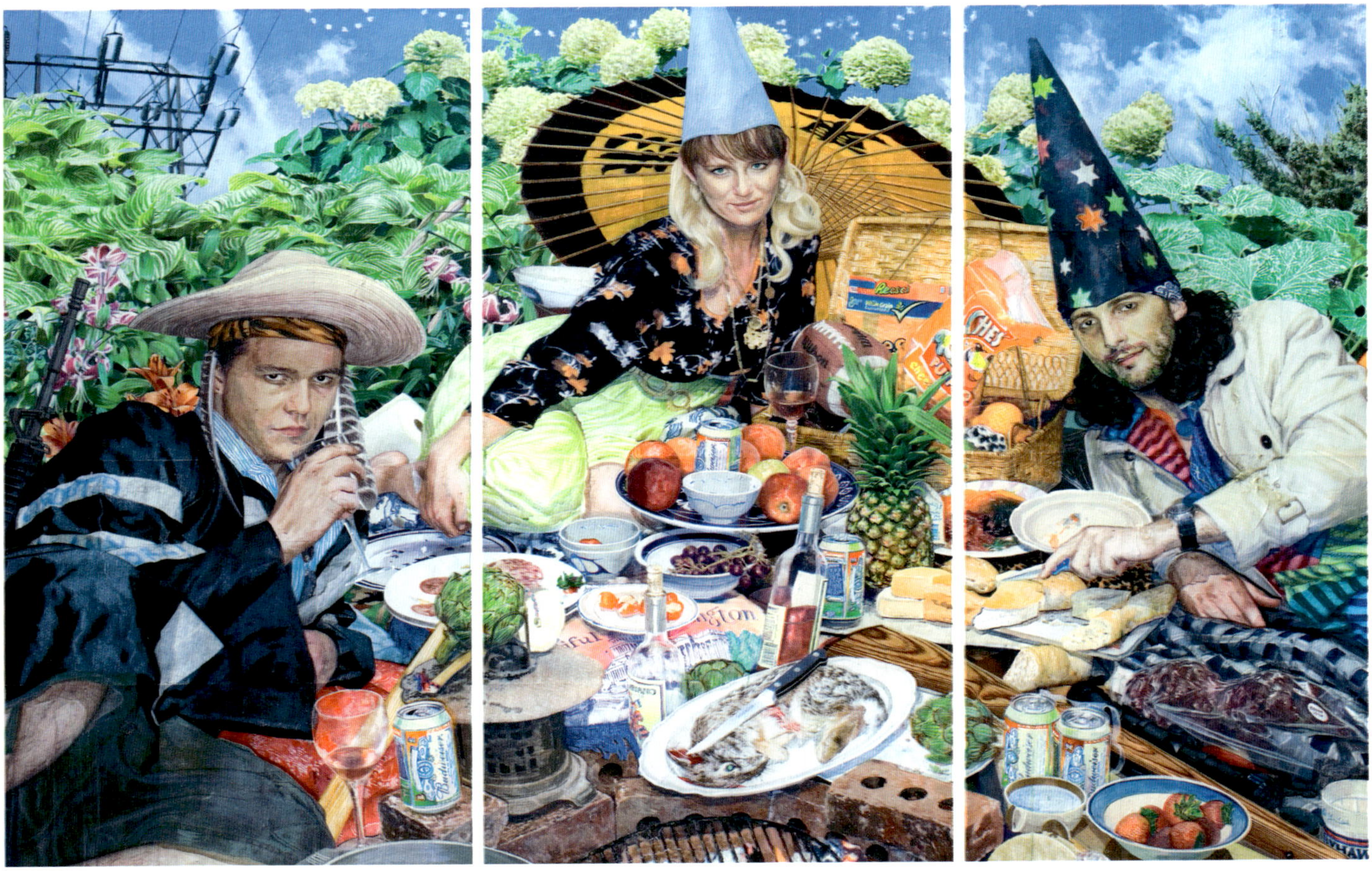

Above:
Wizard/Exclusive Picnickers on a Hill, 2010
Acrylic and inkjet print collage on canvas
60" x 90"
Collection of Jim and Ellen Hubbel
Photo courtesy of the artist

Opposite:
Poetry and Music in Kansas Bush, 2011
Video still courtesy of the artist

STACY LYNN WADDELL

Born 1966, Washington, DC
Lives in Chapel Hill, North Carolina

It is in vain to dream of a wilderness
distant from ourselves.
There is none such.
It is the bog in our brains and bowels,
the primitive vigor of Nature in us,
that inspires that dream.

HENRY DAVID THOREAU
JOURNAL, AUGUST 30, 1856

The American panorama is saturated in strangeness and dark folly. No region reflects these attributes more distinctly than the South. Here, the properties of light, shadow, and space are clarified in such ways that leave me bound.

From this vantage point, I am able to appropriate the power invested in linguistics, portraiture, cultural leitmotifs, and the American vista with a particular sensibility that both engages and disables. Each provides a fitting context for me to critique the contradictions and misunderstandings of American culture and history that have remained relevant since its beginnings.

Although the account of the American South is by and large dense, it exists in many respects as an apparition or a series of imaginings, whose form is revealed gradually. Like many artists from this region, I have a commitment to the past and arguably a predisposition to myth and romance. As such, I destroy, transform, and reconstruct materials in search of a mythology that best exemplifies the beauty, melancholy, and vagaries of a collective experience that is born of the South, yet uniquely American.

Stacy Lynn Waddell creates large-scale works and installations that reflect the deep complexities of culture and history. Working with media including printmaking, collage, and sculpture, Waddell employs fire and blacksmithing tools to destroy, transform, and reconstruct both traditional materials and familiar cultural leitmotifs of the North American landscape. Images, text, and symbols populate the ethereally scarred surfaces of her works as apparitions and graphic imaginings that, removed from their familiar contexts, take on a lyrical quality. Purposefully and poetically ambiguous, her work searches for a visual language that exemplifies the mythological beauty, melancholy, and vagaries of collective American experience.

Waddell's new, site-specific installation *Aarkaydea* (2011) takes as its starting point a pivotal moment in Philadelphia—and North American—history: the opening of the nation's first zoo in 1874 and World's Fair in 1876. Through this lens, *Aarkaydea* considers America's collective interest in the oddities and eccentricities of spectacle, particularly as it relates to the powerlessness of the bodies on display. Interpreting the zeitgeist around the events of the 19th century, Waddell builds a stage of her own. As viewers populate the space with their presence, they become part of the consumption of "otherness," both physically present and socially invisible. Like a visual mash-up of Ralph Ellison's and H.G. Well's novels of the same name, *The Invisible Man, Aarkaydea* is part fantasy, part social critique—revealing the contradictions and misunderstandings of culture, religion, science, and history that have remained relevant in the United States since its beginnings.

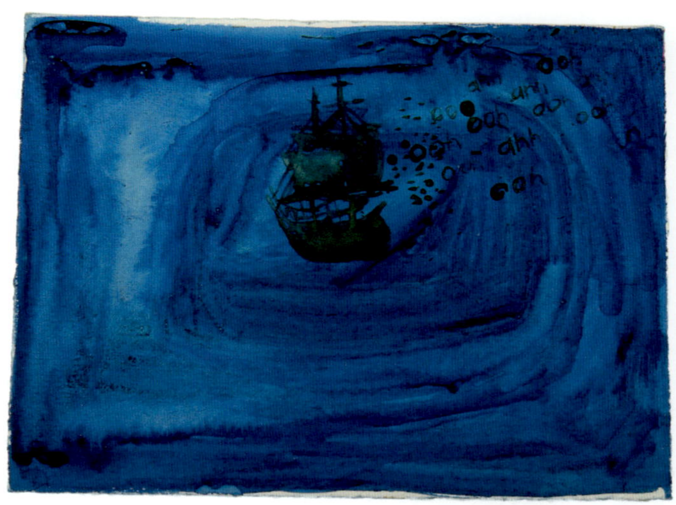

Untitled (ooh-ahh), 2007
Singed paper with watercolor and pigment
6" x 8"
Photo by Christopher Ciccone Photography

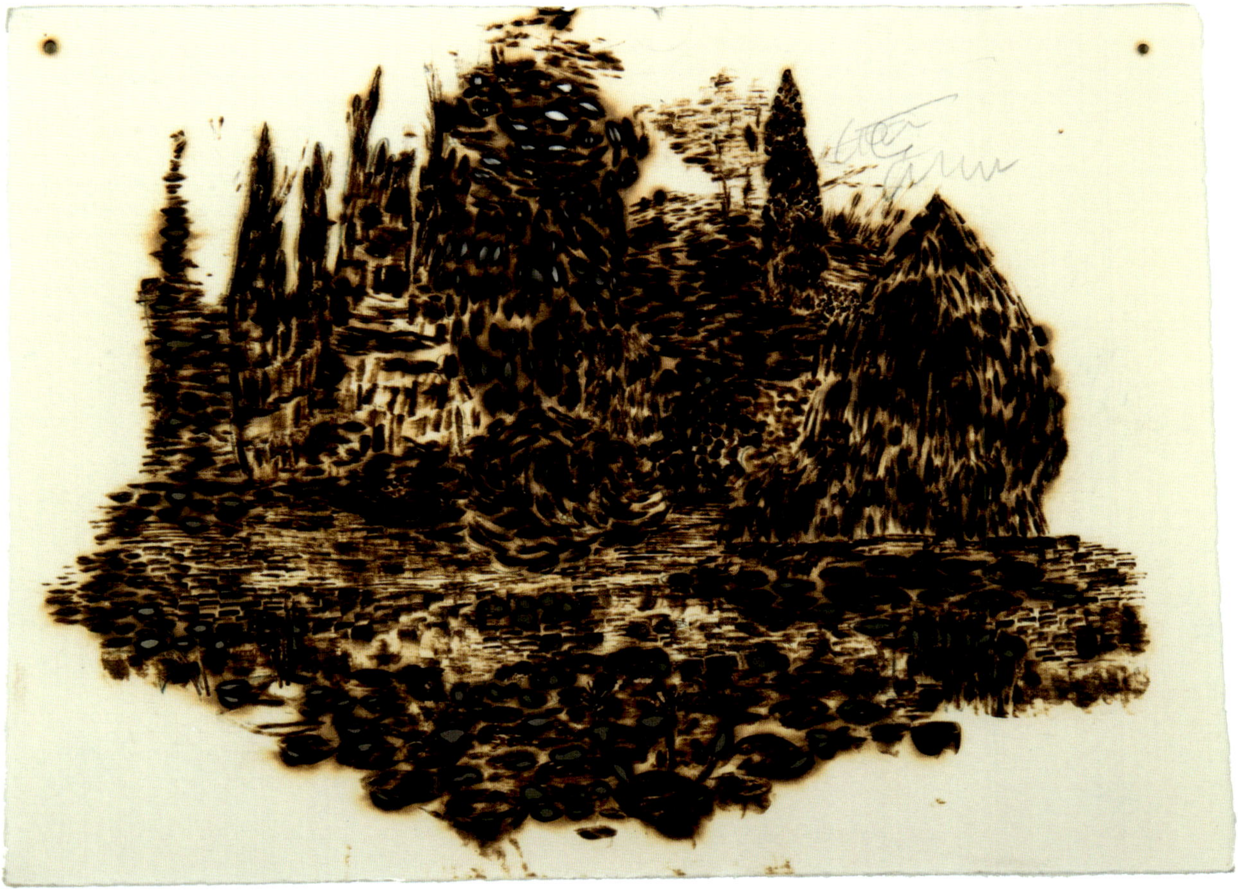

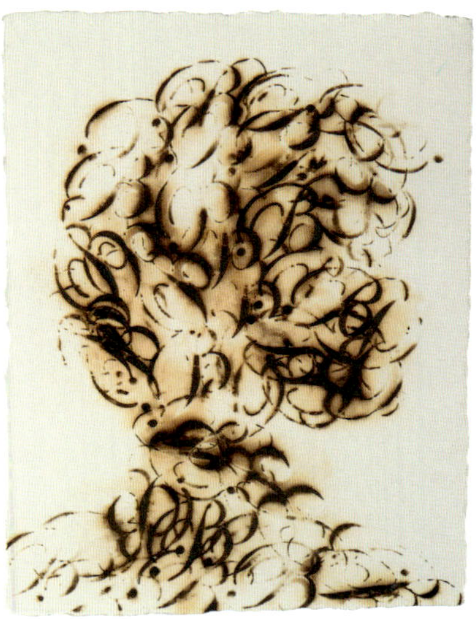

Top:
Untitled (English View), 2010
Burned paper
6" x 8"
Photo by Christopher Ciccone Photography

Bottom:
Untitled (Head), 2010
Branded paper
12" x 9"
Photo by Christopher Ciccone Photography

GLENDA WHARTON

Born 1954, Winston-Salem, North Carolina
Lives in Winston-Salem, North Carolina

Home

A child runs through a shadowy house. She opens door after door and a huge faceless form rises up out of the darkness.

I knew I was the child in that nightmare when I woke up. But it was years later when I knew that the nightmare house was a dream house of my subconscious. It was not until I came home to North Carolina that I realized that the walls and windows of my film were rearranging windows of my childhood.

I came home to visit and stayed years. I had not meant to come home, but life stopped me and put me where I needed to be. When I came home, the middle part of the film expanded and memory and time dissolved and reformed.

I do not believe this dark alchemy could have occurred anywhere else. It needed time. It needed distance. It needed the smell of honeysuckle and the faint glow of lightning bugs, so many green stars in twilight.

That twilight and the twilight of dreams are indistinguishable now. 5,000 sheets of transparent paper recreated the dream house of my childhood in the paper dream of *The Zo*. *The Zo* is not the recreation of the dream, it is the dream you cannot awake from. A child holds a moth. The moth flutters away. An old movie projector runs shadows of running horses. An unopened door.

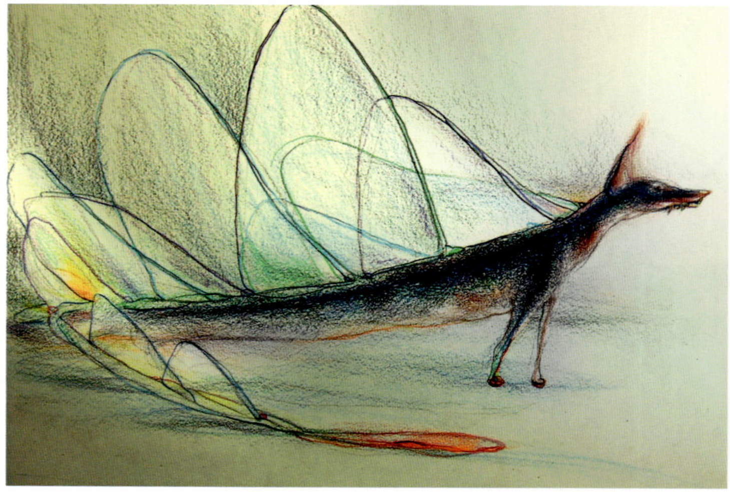

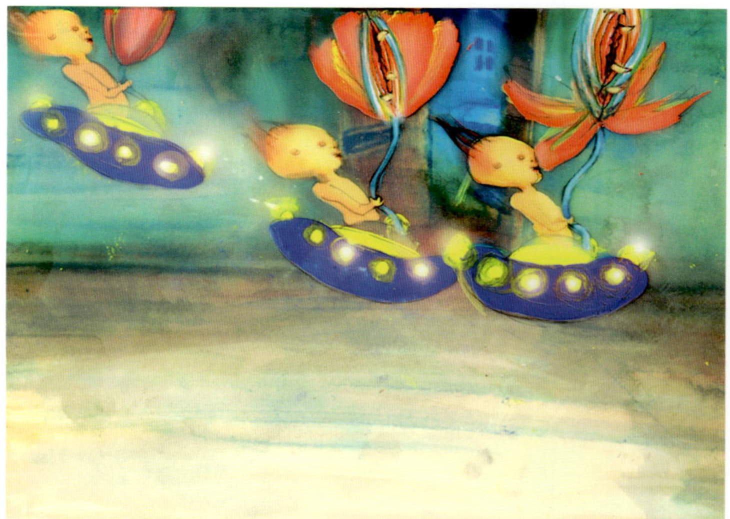

Top:
Dog Dragon, 2011
Still from the hand-drawn animated film, "The Zo"
Colored pencil on animation cel
Image courtesy of the artist

Bottom:
Flower Chopper, 2011
Still from the hand-drawn animated film, "The Zo"
Hand-painted animation cel
Image courtesy of the artist

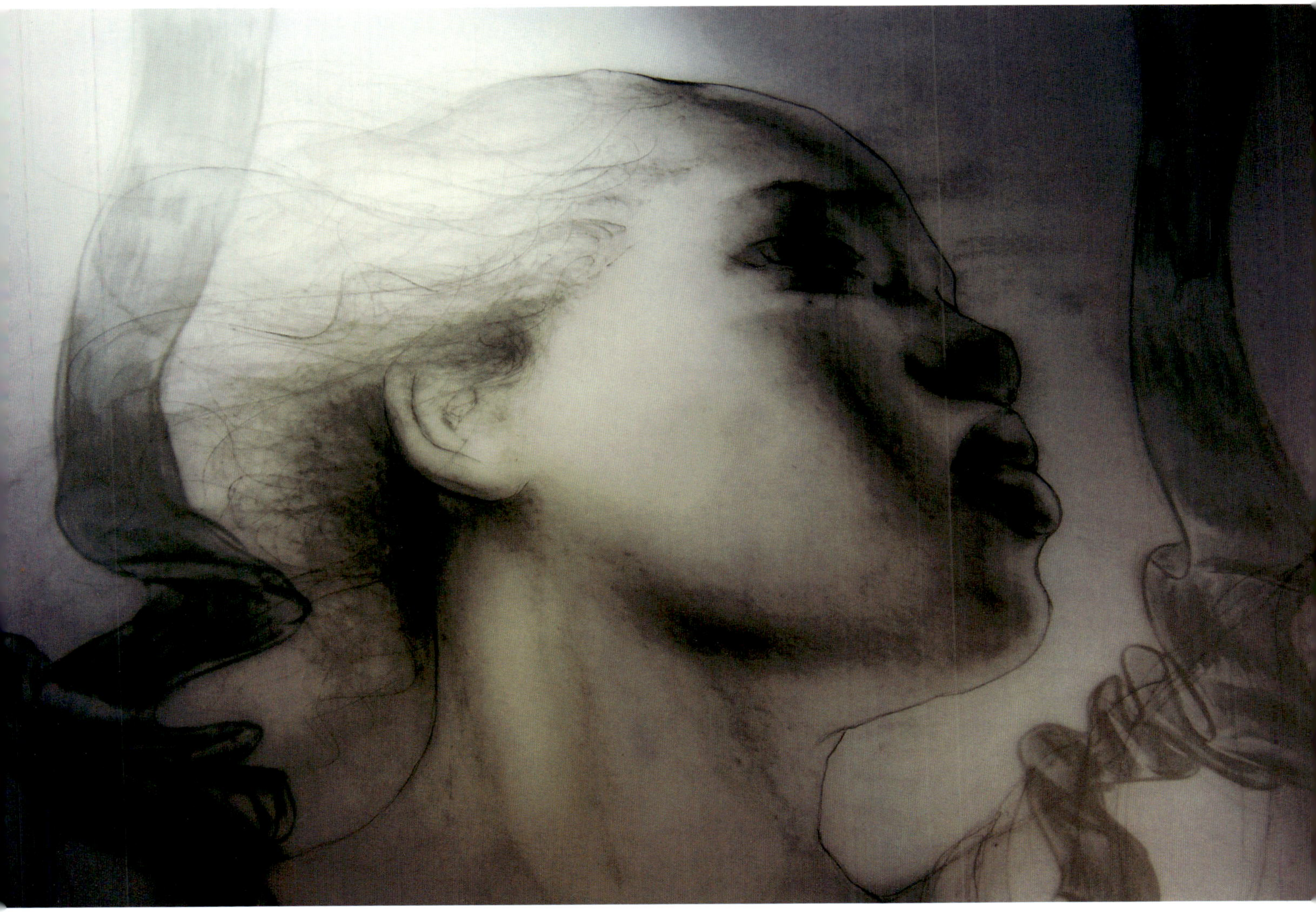

Glenda Wharton works in the increasingly rare medium of hand-drawn animation, creating strikingly beautiful compositions marked by the artist's remarkable attention to line and detail. Originally trained in costume and production design, her natural understanding of how comportment reflects character and context builds ambiance is evident in her film works. Wharton, who studied with experimental animators Vibeke Sorensen and Christine Panushka, infuses her works with qualities that move it beyond the realm of traditional storytelling and into the space of immersive, transporting experience in what she describes as "walking hallucinations."

The Zo (2010) centers around the adventures of a young girl in her journey through the harsh realities of abuse and the reverie she creates to escape it. Like a nightmare that hovers on the edge of a dream, the hulking, anthropomorphic figure of the Zo constantly threatens the young heroine, even as she struggles towards her escape and eventual freedom. Made up of over five thousand drawings created over the course of five years, Wharton employs a multi-plane approach to animation, where each frame is composed of several exquisitely rendered, layered images. The work pulses and vibrates, subtle shifts in the weight and quality of line building a complex landscape with extraordinary depth. An atmospheric soundtrack by Ian Melchinger adds another layer of complexity. The resulting work is phantasmagorical—an amalgamation of brutal reality and magical illusion that is utterly transporting, even as it reveals the ravages of physical abuse.

Ribbons fall on Child, 2011
Still from hand-drawn animated film, "The Zo"
Pencil on animation cel
Image courtesy of the artist

WHOOP DEE DOO

Founded 2006
Based in Kansas City, Missouri, and is produced by over 20 Kansas City artists and performers.

Whoop Dee Doo is based in Kansas City, MO.

Kansas City proper has a population of around 480,000 people. That means that roughly 1 in 10,000 Kansas City residents have been involved in Whoop Dee Doo at some point. It's hard to find information on Kansas City animal populations, but one can assume a similar figure for pet/stray involvement. Whoop Dee Doo is a group of artists and non-artists who work together to create large-scale projects.

Producing work as a large collaborative body has immeasurable rewards—mainly, being a part of a community/second family that stimulates both personal growth and telekinesis. Telekinesis can be used to move heavy objects blocking access to treasure (rubies, diamonds, whatever). However, a sizable group of collaborators can be slow to relocate, travel constantly, etc., so, some of the opportunities open to individual artists are closed to Whoop Dee Doo.

No matter.

The determination and extra-sensory powers that come with group work has driven Whoop Dee Doo to seek out less traditional means of creative progression. Whoop Dee Doo likes where it's at and likes what it does. Call Whoop Dee Doo if you're in town. Whoop Dee Doo has air mattresses for visitors.

UGGGGHHHH.....

"Let's dance!!!" The call shoots out of Whoop Dee Doo co-host Jaimie Warren's mouth like confetti from a shotgun. Loud and infectious, this is a regular invitation extended by her jubilant character, who is often costumed as a walking, family-sized bag of junk food—fun, familiar, and oh-so delicious. Her cohort, Matt Roche, plays a dour, simply unimpressed werewolf that is ready for anything but excited about nothing. These two lovable stage personas provide structure and guidance to an otherwise frenetically-paced, wildly eclectic variety show performed live to diverse audiences around the globe.

Based in Kansas City, Missouri, Whoop Dee Doo is the brain-child of Warren and Roche but designed as a non-profit organization and facilitated by a legion of artists throughout the United States. These intelligent, energetic, young collaborators function as curators, stage-designers, volunteer organizers, crowd-controllers, and a band of out-right magic makers to present family-friendly talent shows loosely inspired by the popular television programs *Pee Wee's Playhouse, Soul Train,* and *Hee Haw*. The local talent of the community in which each show is based drives its content. For instance, Whoop Dee Doo's recent performance in Omaha, Nebraska, mashed-up a black-metal band, body builders, beauty-pageant youngsters, and a dance-squad from a school in an underserved neighborhood in the city. The power of these chaotic free-for-alls is their inclusive nature, the way in which they always highlight and celebrate the unique talents, interests, and cultures of a specific place. And, in between the outrageous skits, there is always time to dance.

Opposite top:
Feed the Snake, Walnut Space, Kansas City, MO, 2010
Performance still
Photo by Megan Mantia

Opposite bottom:
Candyman and the Renaissance Brass Band, Walnut Space, Kansas City, MO, 2010
Performance still
Photo by Megan Mantia

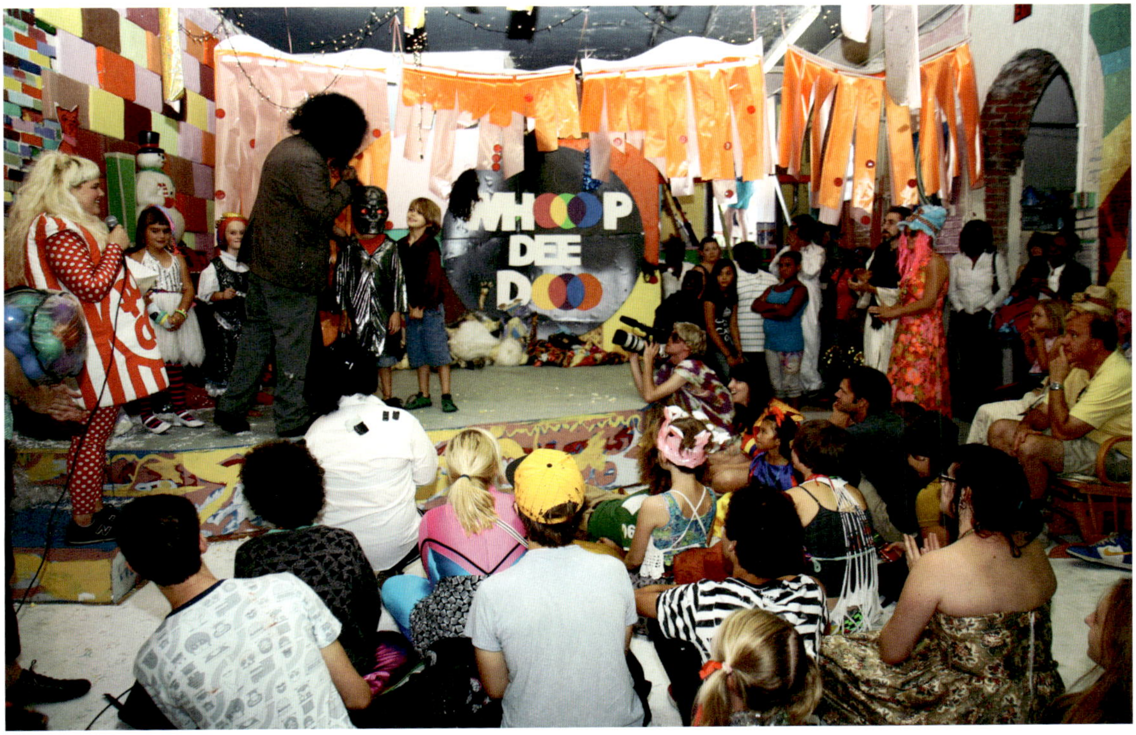
WHOOP
DEE
DOO

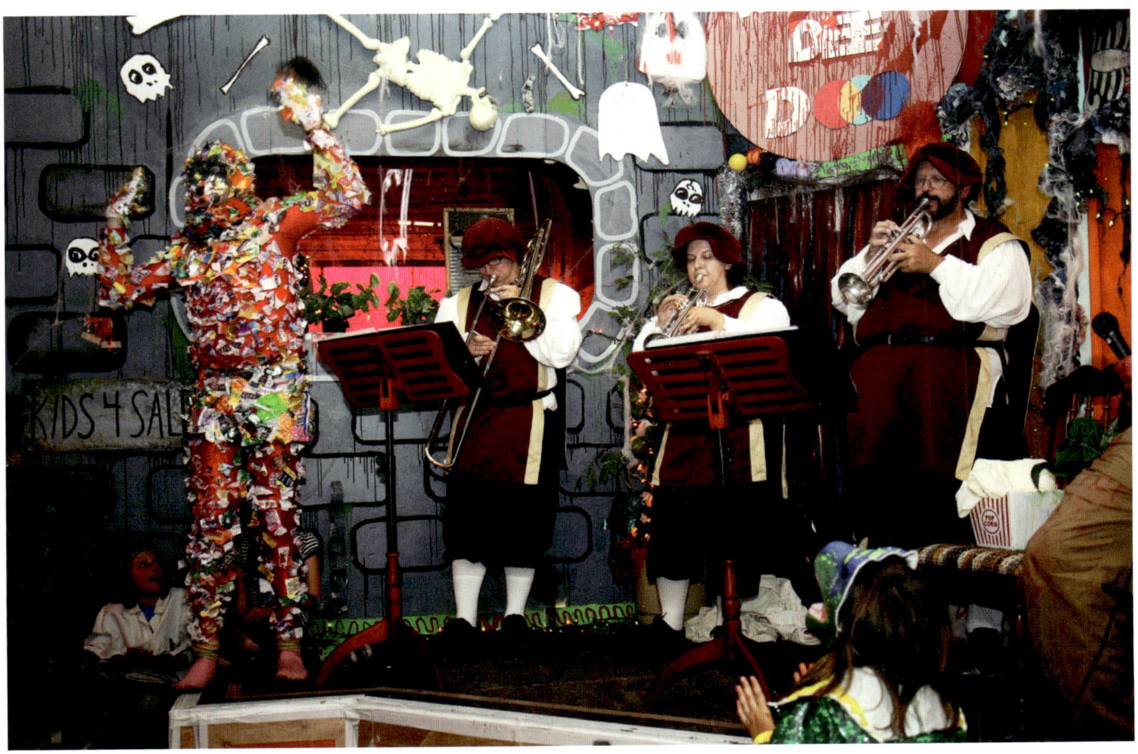

checklist of the exhibition

BUNK NEWS ARTS COLLECTIVE
Tao Twin Blue, 2011
Acrylic and india ink on wood
141" x 72" x .5"
Courtesy of the artists

Tao Twin Red, 2011
Acrylic and india ink on wood
141" x 72" x .5"
Courtesy of the artists

Bunk Box #1, 2011
Acrylic on wood, found objects
96" x 48" x 20"
Courtesy of the artists

Bunk Box #2, 2011
Acrylic on wood, found objects
96" x 48" x 20"
Courtesy of the artists

Mandala, 2011
Acrylic, india ink on wood
90" x 90" x .5"
Courtesy of the artists

Skull Collaboration, 2011
Xerox Enlargement on wood
30" x 45" x .5"
Courtesy of the artists

Monumental Now, 2009
Xerox
Courtesy of the artists

Colin Murray
All is One, 2009
Xerox
Courtesy of the artist

Jim Swill
Baby Resuscitation, 2009
Xerox
Courtesy of the artist

Colin Murray, Bunk News
Entertainment for the Psychic Youth, 2009
Xerox
Courtesy of the artists

Jim Swill
Da Last Suppa, 2009
Xerox
Courtesy of the artist

Jim Swill
"Da Last Suppa" Alternate, 2009
Xerox
Courtesy of the artist

Jim Swill
Evolve Album Release #1, 2009
Xerox
Courtesy of the artist

Jim Swill
Evolve Album Release #2, 2009
Xerox
Courtesy of the artist

John Caldwell/Solace Media
Bunk Cinco De Mayo, 2009
Xerox
Courtesy of the artist

Colin Murray
Something Other Than TV, 2009
Xerox
Courtesy of the artist

Robert Inhuman
Anarchist, 2009
Xerox
Courtesy of the artist

SUE CHENOWETH
To Climb the Highest Peak, 2011
Gouache, acrylic, ink, graphite, Letraset, and Pantone paper on paper
80" x 80"
Courtesy of the artist

Wouldn't He Remember his First Home? What Passed for Wisdom There?, 2011
Gouache, acrylic, ink, graphite, Letraset, and Flocked paper on paper
80" x 80"
Courtesy of the artist

Pulled Out in an Iron Bucket, 2011
Gouache, acrylic, ink, graphite, Letraset, Flocked paper, copper, and Pantone paper on paper
80" x 80"
Courtesy of the artist

LIZ COHEN
Zwickau Routine: Black Execution, 2010
C print
16" x 20"
Courtesy of the artist and David Klein Gallery

Zwickau Routine: Yellow Inward Turn, 2010
C print
16" x 20"
Courtesy of the artist and David Klein Gallery

Zwickau Routine: Red Cossack, 2010
C print
16" x 20"
Courtesy of the artist and David Klein Gallery

Zwickau Routine: Yellow Push-Up Arch, 2010
C print
16" x 20"
Courtesy of the artist and David Klein Gallery

Zwickau Routine: White Optionals, 2010
C print
16" x 20"
Courtesy of the artist and David Klein Gallery

Bikini Carwash, 2002
Video
Courtesy of the artist and David Klein Gallery

Hydro Force, 2011
HD video
Courtesy of the artist and David Klein Gallery

LEWIS COLBURN
Untitled (Set for a Homestead) 2011
Plywood, steel, acrylic, found objects, and mixed media
180" x 148" x 180"
Courtesy of the artist

PAUL COORS
Oz & Them, 2010 - 2011
Offset print on paper, edition of 100
27" x 39"
Courtesy of the artist

1 Day, 2010 - 2011
Offset print on paper, edition of 100
27" x 39"
Courtesy of the artist

Spiderman Uncivilized, 2010 - 2011
Offset print on paper, edition of 100
27" x 39"
Courtesy of the artist

Space Money
2010 - 2011
Offset print on paper, edition of 100
27" x 39"
Courtesy of the artist

Back To The Future, 2010 - 2011
Offset print on paper, edition of 100
27" x 39"
Courtesy of the artist

Stonehenge, 2011
Yard sign installation
Dimensions variable
Courtesy of the artist

GUY MICHAEL DAVIS AND KATIE PARKER
Hy-que Monkey in Captivity, 2011
Porcelain, china paint, hand printed wallpaper
5 monkeys on sconces
Each 48" x 24" x 7"
Courtesy of the artists

Still[ed] Life, 2011
Porcelain and china paint
3 busts on sconces
Each 24" x 7" x 6"
Courtesy of the artists

ELSEWHERE
Cabinet of Wonder, 2010
Mixed media sculpture
Approximately 3' x 5' x 6'
Courtesy of the artists

TERENCE HAMMONDS
Stand Up! Organize!, 2010
21 screen prints on paper
Each 24" x 24"
Courtesy of the artist

Cincinnati Goddamn, 2011
21 screen prints on paper
Each 24" x 24"
Courtesy of the artist

HARRISON HAYNES
LRLL RLRR, 2011
Video installation
Dimensions variable
Courtesy of the artist

SCOTT HOCKING
Ziggurat, East, Summer II – exhibition print from the series: Ziggurat and FB21, 2007 – 2009
2008
Archival pigment print / Mixed media installation
Print: 33" x 49.5" / Installation: Dimensions variable
Courtesy of the artist and Susanne Hilberry Gallery

Zeus Whirlwind – exhibition print from the series: Garden of the Gods, 2009 – 2010, 2010
Archival pigment print / Mixed media installation
Print: 33" x 49.5" / Installation: Dimensions variable
Courtesy of the artist and Susanne Hilberry Gallery

Hephaestus and the Garden of the Gods, Snow – exhibition print from the series: Garden of the Gods, 2009 – 2010, 2010
Archival pigment print / Mixed media installation
Print: 33" x 49.5" / Installation: Dimensions variable
Courtesy of the artist and Susanne Hilberry Gallery

Ziggurat, West, Summer – exhibition print from the series: Ziggurat and FB21, 2007 – 2009
2008
Archival pigment print / Mixed media installation
Print: 33" x 49.5" / Installation: Dimensions variable
Courtesy of the artist and Susanne Hilberry Gallery

Garden of the Gods, West, Winter – exhibition print from the series: Garden of the Gods, 2009 – 2010, 2009
Archival pigment print / Mixed media installation
Print: 33" x 49.5" / Installation: Dimensions variable
Courtesy of the artist and Susanne Hilberry Gallery

Garden of the Gods, South, Winter – exhibition print from the series: Garden of the Gods, 2009 – 2010, 2010
Archival pigment print / Mixed media installation
Print: 33" x 49.5" / Installation: Dimensions variable
Courtesy of the artist and Susanne Hilberry Gallery

Metropolis Hole, Winter – exhibition print from the series: Garden of the Gods, 2009 – 2010
2010
Archival pigment print
33" x 49.5"
Courtesy of the artist and Susanne Hilberry Gallery

Nike's Tower – exhibition print from the series Nike and Ajax, 2010 – 2011, 2010
Archival pigment print
33" x 49.5"
Courtesy of the artist and Susanne Hilberry Gallery

The Cauldron and Roosevelt Warehouse – exhibition print from the series: The Cauldron and Roosevelt Warehouse, 2007 – 2011
2011
Archival pigment print / Mixed media installation
Print: 33" x 49.5" / Installation: Dimensions variable
Courtesy of the artist and Susanne Hilberry Gallery

The Egg and MCTS – exhibition print from the series: The Egg and MCTS, 2007 – 2011, 2011
Archival pigment print / Mixed media installation
Print: 33" x 49.5" / Installation: Dimensions variable
Courtesy of the artist and Susanne Hilberry Gallery

The Egg and MCTS, 2 – exhibition print from the series: The Egg and MCTS, 2007 – 2011, 2011
Archival pigment print
33" x 49.5"
Courtesy of the artist and Susanne Hilberry Gallery

The Egg and MCTS, 3 – exhibition print from the series: The Egg and MCTS, 2007 – 2011, 2011
Archival pigment print
33" x 49.5"
Courtesy of the artist and Susanne Hilberry Gallery

Artifacts and Specimens, 2011
Mixed media installation – including various stalagmites – collected from the sites: FB21, MCTS, Packard, and Roosevelt Warehouse.
Installed upon three tables.
Dimensions variable
Courtesy of the artist and Susanne Hilberry Gallery

CHIDO JOHNSON
Jack's Vision, 2010 – present
Mixed media
Dimensions variable
Courtesy of the artist

me me me, 2008
Carved from an existing tourist artifact
11" x 2" x 1.7"
Courtesy of the artist

my pink caddi, 2009
Video installation
Dimensions variable
Courtesy of the artist

MICHAEL KRUEGER
Green River, 2007
Colored pencil on paper
16" x 28" (sheet)
Courtesy of the artist

What Is Here is the Same as What is There, 2007
Colored pencil on paper
13" x 22" (sheet)
Courtesy of the artist

Kanopolis, 2009
Colored pencil on paper
44" x 27" (sheet)
Courtesy of the artist

High Life, 2009
Color lithograph on paper
16" x 10" (sheet)
Courtesy of the artist

Oh Yeah, 2009
Color lithograph on paper
16" x 10" (sheet)
Courtesy of the artist

Gone, 2009
Color lithograph on paper
16" x 10" (sheet)
Courtesy of the artist

Drop It, 2009
Color lithograph on paper
16" x 10" (sheet)
Courtesy of the artist

Green Moon, 2010
Colored pencil on paper
25" x 20" (sheet)
Courtesy of the artist

Blue Guitar, 2011
Colored pencil on paper
30" x 22" (sheet)
Courtesy of the artist

Arts & Crafts Stack, 2011
Colored pencil on paper
30" x 22" (sheet)
Courtesy of the artist

Highboy, 2011
Colored pencil on paper
30" x 22" (sheet)
Courtesy of the artist

Night Falls, 2011
Colored pencil on paper
40" x 30" (sheet)
Courtesy of the artist

JENNIFER LEVONIAN
The Oven Sky, 2011
Cut-out animation using watercolor and collage, with music by Rachel Mason
Video
Running time: 4 min. 45 sec.
Courtesy of the artist and Fleisher/Ollman Gallery, Philadelphia

MEGAWORDS
Untitled Installation, 2011
Mixed media
Dimensions variable
Courtesy of the artists

ERIKA NELSON
World's Largest Collection of the World's Smallest Versions of the World's Largest Things Sideshow Extravaganza
2001 – present
Mixed media
Dimensions variable
Courtesy of the artist

"SCOUT" Daily Driver Art Car
2003 – present
Mixed media on 1995 Toyota Pickup
Courtesy of the artist

ABIGAIL ANNE NEWBOLD
Homemaker series, 2010 – 2011
A collection of found and custom fabricated objects. Linen, cotton, hickory, sheepskin, and leather were used to fabricate with.
Dimensions variable
Courtesy of the artist

TIM PORTLOCK
Municipal Services Building, 2011
Ink jet print
54" x 72"
Courtesy of the artist

Farm, 2011
Ink jet print
54" x 72"
Courtesy of the artist

Sunrise, 2011
Ink jet print
54" x 72"
Courtesy of the artist

Sundown, 2011
Ink jet print
54" x 72"
Courtesy of the artist

Night, 2011
Ink jet print
54" x 72"
Courtesy of the artist

Salon, 2011
Ink jet print
54" x 72"
Courtesy of the artist

POSTCOMMODITY
Gallup Motel Butchering, 2011
Four channel video installation with sound
Dimensions variable
Courtesy of Postcommodity

AARON ROTHMAN
Idle Speculation 1, 2011
Archival inkjet print
40" x 50" (image)
Courtesy of the artist

Idle Speculation 2, 2011
Archival inkjet print
40" x 50" (image)
Courtesy of the artist

Idle Speculation 6, 2011
Archival inkjet print
40" x 50" (image)
Courtesy of the artist

Idle Speculation 7, 2011
Archival inkjet print
40" x 50" (image)
Courtesy of the artist

Idle Speculation 9, 2011
Archival inkjet print
40" x 50" (image)
Courtesy of the artist

Idle Speculation 10, 2011
Archival inkjet print
40" x 50" (image)
Courtesy of the artist

Field, 2011
Archival inkjet print
19.25" x 24" (image)
Courtesy of the artist

GREGORY SALE
Gregory Sale in collaboration with Michael Bean, Joshua Adams, Ryan Landers, William Paskell, Brandon Reiswig, Michael Koveikis, Bryon Frank, Winston Arnold, De'Marko Pace, SR., Neil Rodgers, James Atwater, Louis Wilford, Nick Fletcher, Grayson Grumke, Officer Stephen Brown, Officer Thaddeus Cramer, Officer Timothy Medina, Officer Angel Alvarado, Officer Petia Strashilova, Sergeant Larry Irby, John Spiak, Brett Thomas, Cory Berquist, Stephen Gittins, Matt Garcia, Jason Dillon, Kara Roschi, Jane Lindsey, Jeffery Kirk

It's not just black and white: an artifact, 2011
Artifact from social art experiment.
Latex paint on canvas
96" x 128" x 2"
Courtesy of the artist

Supported by grants from The Andy Warhol Foundation for the Visual Arts and Friends of ASU Art Museum. The social art experiment *It's not just black and white* was a component of ASU Art Museum Social Studies Series and was created with the support of community partners including the Maricopa County Sheriff's Office, Arizona.

Jason Dillon with Gregory Sale
It's not just black and white: a framing, 2011
Video document
Courtesy of the artist

Supported by grants from The Andy Warhol Foundation for the Visual Arts and Friends of ASU Art Museum. The social art experiment *It's not just black and white* was a component of ASU Art Museum Social Studies Series and was created with the support of community partners including the Maricopa County Sheriff's Office, Arizona.

Gregory Sale in collaboration with Van, Stan, Tom, Roy, John, Zafir, Spel, Chuck, Toan, Felix, Eric

Life is life, 2011
Suite of 10 works on paper
Each 22" x 30"
Courtesy of the artist

Supported by grants from The Ford Foundation through the City of Philadelphia Mural Arts Program's Restorative Justice program (Teaching Artist Program). The project was realized in conjunction with Mural Arts and the Pennsylvania State Correctional Institution at Graterford.

AARON STORCK
STROM PEM, STIM-PONERO, 2011
Diptych
Acrylic and inkjet print collage on canvas
Each 78" x 64"
Courtesy of the artist

Poetry and Music in Kansas Bush
2011
Video
Running time: Approximately 12 minutes
Courtesy of the artist

New Ministries, 2009
Video
Running time: Approximately 12 minutes
Courtesy of the artist

STACY LYNN WADDELL
Aarkaydea, 2011
Mixed media installation consisting of framed works, photo-lithographic, wall-sized paper panels, and miscellaneous items like string and fabric.
100" x 498"
Courtesy of the artist

GLENDA WHARTON
The Zo, 2010
Hand-drawn animated film
Running time: Approximately 26 minutes
Courtesy of the artist

WHOOP DEE DOO
Untitleed, 2011
Mixed media site-specific installation
Dimensions variable
Courtesy of the artists

contributor biographies

CHRISTOPHER COOK In July 2009, Christopher Cook joined the Salina Art Center in Salina, Kansas, as the Executive Director and Curator. In this leadership role, Cook continues the institution's mission and distinguished track record of supporting contemporary art and artists through experimental programs. Previously, he was Curator of the Kemper Museum of Contemporary Art, Kansas City, Missouri, and Curator of the Sioux City Art Center, Sioux City, Iowa. Since 2002, Cook has organized over forty exhibitions and commissioned projects with artists Dan Attoe, Johanna Billing, Chakaia Booker, Anne Collier, Julian Dashper, Patrick Dougherty, Sharon Engelstein, Keltie Ferris, Nancy Hwang, Anthony Lepore, Julia Oschatz, Adam Pendleton, Fred Sandback, Melanie Schiff, and Stephen Vitiello, among others. He has contributed critical essays and artist interviews to numerous publications and actively lectures on contemporary art practices. Cook received his MA in Art History, Theory, and Criticism from the School of the Art Institute of Chicago and his BA in Art History from the University of Florida, Gainesville.

ERIKA DOSS is professor and chair in the Department of American Studies at the University of Notre Dame, where she teaches courses in American, modern, and contemporary art and cultural studies. She is the author of *Benton, Pollock, and the Politics of Modernism: From Regionalism to Abstract Expressionism* (1991), *Spirit Poles and Flying Pigs: Public Art and Cultural Democracy in American Communities* (1995), *Elvis Culture: Fans, Faith, and Image* (1999), *Looking at Life Magazine* (editor, 2001), *Twentieth-Century American Art* (2002), and *Memorial Mania: Public Feeling in America* (2010). Doss is also the editor of the "Culture America" series at the University Press of Kansas, and is on the editorial boards of *Memory Studies, Public Art Dialogue*, and *Material Religion: The Journal of Objects, Art, and Belief*. Her current research project, "Picturing Faith: American Modernism and Religion," considers what religion meant to certain mid-century American modern artists.

MARK HARRIS Currently Director of the School of Art at the University of Cincinnati, Mark Harris has an MA in Painting from The Royal College of Art, London, an MA in Continental Philosophy from Warwick University, Coventry, and a PhD in Philosophy from Goldsmiths College, London.

In 2005, he received an Arts Council England Fellowship with the Long March Project, Beijing. Recent exhibitions of his work include *State Fare* (Wexner Center, Columbus, 2007); *Utopian-Bands* (2 kolegas, Beijing, 2006, and Weston Art Gallery, Cincinnati, 2008); and *Morning Star* (Country Club Gallery, Cincinnati, 2010). In 2011, his video work has been shown in *High Times* at the Wellcome Collection, London, and at the Baltimore Contemporary Museum.

In 2009, he received a Warhol Foundation/Creative Capital Art Writers Grant. Published essays include "Pipilotti Rist's Music" (Contemporary Arts Museum, Houston), "Chelsea Hotel, March 14, 2008" (on Marcia Farquhar), and "The City Sings" (on Heather Phillipson). He has contributed an essay to *The Countercultural Experiment: Consciousness and Encounters at the Edge of Art* to be published in 2011 by University of Minnesota Press.

REBECCA RUTH HART is the associate curator of contemporary art for the Detroit Institute of Arts. Most recently she facilitated Matthew Barney's Detroit-based performance *Khu*. At the DIA she was the organizing co-curator for *Julie Mehretu: City Sitings* and *Artists Take on Detroit: projects for the tricentennial* and curator for *Action Reaction*. She was project manager and curator for the reinstallation of the DIA contemporary collection and specializes in public art and large-scale sculpture. Hart graduated with a Bachelor of Arts degree in Art History from Williams College and a Bachelors of Fine Arts, Fiber, from Kansas City Art Institute. She earned a Master of Fine Arts degree from the Cranbrook Academy of Arts, Fiber (1995), and a Master of Arts in Art History from Wayne State University (2005), where she received the Mary Kirk Haggerty Award for art historical research. Her work has been recognized by the Warhol Foundation for the Visual Arts, the Association of Art Museum Curators, and the Joyce Foundation.

JULIEN ROBSON Curator of Contemporary Art, Julien Robson joined the staff at PAFA in 2008 after eight years in Louisville, Kentucky, where he was Curator of Contemporary Art at the Speed Art Museum and Adjunct Professor at the University of Louisville. At PAFA, Robson has overseen the Morris Gallery program, featuring solo exhibitions by Malcolm McLaren, Roxana Perez-Mendez, Tom LaDuke, Hiro Sakaguchi, and Jayson Musson. In 2009 he curated *Man in the Mirror*, an important exhibition of works on paper by Sidney Goodman, and in 2010, he co-curated *Philagrafika: The Graphic Unconscious*, a five-venue exhibition concerned with the expanded field of print in contemporary art. He has also presented exhibitions of gifts to PAFA's collections, the *Dorothy and Herbert Vogel Collection*, and *Warhol Polaroids and B&W prints*. Robson initially trained as an artist at Bath Academy of Art, and the Slade School of Fine Art in London, before taking up curatorial positions at the University of Sussex and, subsequently, the University of Southampton, England. During the 1990s, he lived in Austria, working in the commercial gallery sector in Vienna, and in 1998, he spent six months as Guest Professor at the University of California, Santa Barbara.

CLAIRE SCHNEIDER is an art historian and independent curator who has worked on projects in numerous American cities. She previously held the position of Senior Curator at the Scottsdale Museum of Contemporary Art. Prior to that, Schneider spent ten years at the Albright-Knox Art Gallery in Buffalo, New York, which culminated in the exhibition *Extreme Abstraction* (2005), a monumental site-specific international survey of abstraction in modern and contemporary art practice. Recent exhibitions include developing the series *Architecture + Art* in Scottsdale, Arizona, which was inaugurated with the installation *90 Days Over 100°*, a *Military Day* with Mel Ziegler in Nashville, Tennessee, and a design survey of everyday music objects, *Rewind Remix Replay*. She is known for her creative vision and energetic commitment to both artists and museum audiences through exhibitions such as *Seriously Funny* (2009), *Remix: Color and Light* (2007), and projects with Janine Antoni, John Armleder, Nick Cave, Paul Noble, Franz West, and Andrea Zittel, among others. In 2007, she was the director of the biennial *Beyond/In Western New York*. Schneider received an MA in Art History from Williams College.

TEKA SELMAN is Assistant Director of the MFA in Experimental and Documentary Arts at Duke University, an interdisciplinary program that couples experimental visual practice with the documentary arts in both analog and digital media. She was previously Partner at Branch Gallery in Durham, North Carolina, which received national attention for its focus on the work of emerging artists. Prior to relocating to the southeast in 2006, Selman was Director at Sikkema Jenkins & Co. Gallery in New York, having previously held positions at Gagosian Gallery in London and New York. She holds an MA in Art History and Visual Culture from Goldsmith's, University of London, and a BA in Art History and Anthropology from the University of Michigan, Ann Arbor. Her writing on artists such as Mark Bradford, Coco Fusco, and Kara Walker has been featured in publications including *The Black Moving Cube* (The Green BoxKunstedition, 2006), *Freestyle* (Studio Museum in Harlem, 2001), and *OneWorld Magazine*.

PENNSYLVANIA ACADEMY
OF THE FINE ARTS

MUSEUM STAFF

Page 160:
Gregory Sale
It's not just black and white, 2011
Photo by Stephen Gittins

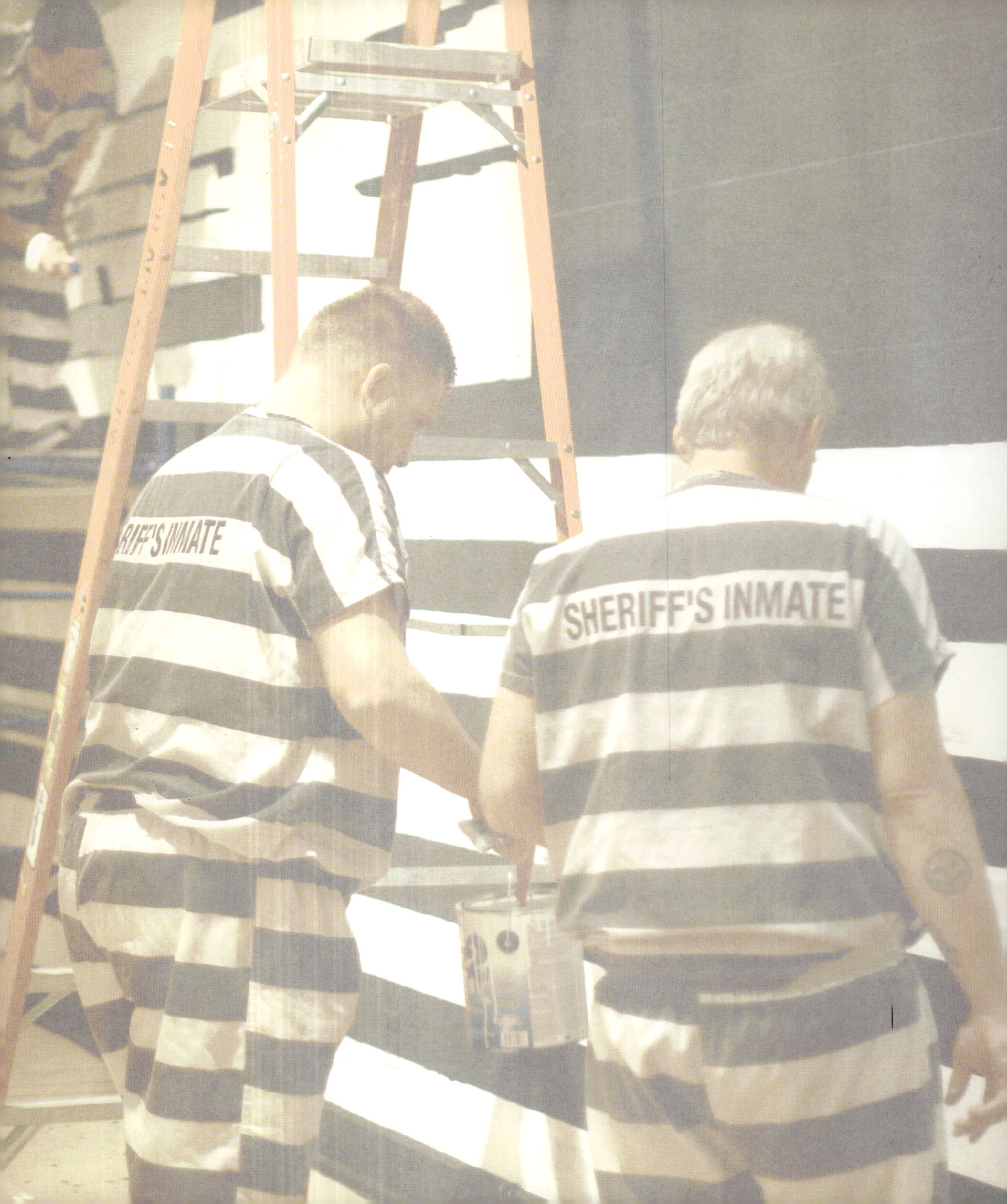
HERIFF'S INMATE
SHERIFF'S INMATE